An Outline of Occult Science

An Outline of Occult Science

By
Rudolf Steiner, Ph.D.

CONTENTS

PREFACE TO THE FOURTH EDITION.

One who undertakes to represent certain results of scientific spiritual research of the kind recorded in this book,must above all things be prepared to find that this kind of investigation is at the present time almost universally regarded as impossible. For things are related in the following pages about which those who are today esteemed exact thinkers, assert that they will probably remain altogether indeterminable by human intelligence. One who knows and can respect the reasons which prompt many a serious person to assert this impossibility,would fain make the attempt again and again to show what misunderstandings are really at the bottom of the belief that it is not given to human knowledge to penetrate into the superphysical worlds.

For two things present themselves for consideration. First,no human being will,on deeper reflection,be able in the long run to shut his eyes to the fact that his most important questions as to the meaning and significance of life must remain unanswered,if there be no access to higher worlds. Theoretically we may delude ourselves concerning this fact and so get away from it; the depths of our soul-life,however,will not tolerate such self-delusion. The person who will not listen to what comes from these depths of the soul will naturally reject any account of supersensible worlds. There are however people--and their number is not small--who find it impossible to remain deaf to the demands coming from the depths of the soul. They must always be knocking at the gates which,in the opinion of others,bar the way to what is "incomprehensible."

Secondly,the statements of "exact thinkers" are on no account to be despised. Where they have to be taken seriously,one who occupies himself with them will thoroughly feel and appreciate this seriousness. The writer of this book would not like to be taken for one who lightly disregards the enormous thought-labour which has been expended in determining the limits of the human intellect. This thought-labour cannot be put aside with a few phrases about "academic wisdom" and the like. In many cases it has its source in true striving after knowledge and in genuine discernment. Indeed,even more than this must be admitted; reasons have been brought forward to show that that knowledge which is to-day regarded as scientific cannot penetrate into supersensible worlds,and these reasons _are in a certain sense irrefutable_.

Now it may appear strange to many people that the writer of this book admits this freely,and yet undertakes to make statements about supersensible worlds. It seems indeed almost impossible that a person should admit _in a certain sense_ the reasons why knowledge of superphysical worlds is unattainable,and should yet speak about those worlds.

Yet it is possible to take this attitude,and at the same time to understand that it impresses others as being inconsistent. It is not given to every one to enter into the experiences we pass through when we approach supersensible realms with the human intellect. Then it turns out that intellectual proofs may certainly be irrefutable,and that _notwithstanding this_,they need not be decisive with regard to reality. Instead of all sorts of theoretical explanations,let us now try to make this comprehensible by a comparison. That comparisons are not in themselves proofs is readily admitted,but this does not prevent their often making intelligible what has to be expressed.

Human understanding,as it works in everyday life and in ordinary science, is actually so constituted that it cannot penetrate into superphysical worlds. This may be proven beyond the possibility of denial. But this proof can have no more value for a certain kind of soul-life than the proof one would use in showing that man's natural eye cannot,with its visual faculty,penetrate to the smallest cells of a living being,or to the constitution of far-off celestial bodies.

Just as the assertion is true and demonstrable that the ordinary power of seeing does not penetrate as far as the cells,so also is the other assertion which maintains that ordinary knowledge cannot penetrate into supersensible worlds. And yet the proof that the ordinary power of vision has to stop short of the cells in no way excludes the investigation of cells. Why should the proof that the ordinary power of cognition has to stop short of supersensible worlds,decide anything against the possibility of investigating those worlds?

One can well sense the feeling which this comparison may evoke in many people. One can even understand that he who doubts and holds the above comparison against this labor of thought,does not even faintly sense the whole seriousness of that mental effort. And yet the present writer is not only fully convinced of that seriousness,but is of opinion that that work of thought may be numbered among the noblest achievements of humanity. To
show that the human power of vision cannot perceive the cellular structure
without the help of instruments,would surely be a useless undertaking; but in exact thinking,to become conscious of the nature of that thought is a necessary work of the mind. It is only natural that one who devotes himself to such work,should not notice that reality may refute him. The preface to this book can be no place for entering into many "refutations" of former editions,put forth by those who are entirely devoid of appreciation of that for which it strives,or who direct their unfounded attacks against the personality of the author; but it must,none the less, be emphasized that belittling of serious scientific thought in this book can only be imputed to the author by one who wishes to shut himself off from the _spirit_ of what is expressed in it.

Man's power of cognition may be augmented and made more powerful,just as
the eye's power of vision may be augmented. Only the means for strengthening the capacity of cognition are entirely of a spiritual nature; they are inner processes,belonging purely to the soul. They consist of what is described in this book as meditation and concentration (contemplation). Ordinary soul-life is bound up with the bodily instrument; the strengthened soul-life liberates itself from it. There are schools of thought at the present time to which this assertion must appear
quite senseless,to which it must seem based only upon self-delusion. Those who think in this way will find it easy,from their point of view, to prove that "all soul-life" is bound up with the nervous system. One who holds the standpoint from which this book has been written,can thoroughly understand such proofs. He understands people who say that only superficiality can assert that there may be some kind of soul-life independent of the body,and who are quite convinced that in such experiences of the soul there exists a connection with the life of the nervous system,which the "dilettantism of occult science" merely fails to detect.

Here certain quite comprehensible habits of thought are in such sharp contradiction to what has been described in this book,that there is as yet no prospect of coming to an understanding with many people. It is here
that we come to the point where the desire must arise that it should no

longer be a characteristic of our present day culture to at once decry as fanciful or visionary a method of research which differs from its own. But on the other hand it is also a fact at the present time that a number of people can appreciate the supersensible method of research,as it is presented in this book,people who understand that the meaning of life is not revealed in general phrases about the soul,self,and so on,but can only result from really entering into the facts of superphysical research.

Not from lack of modesty,but with a sense of joyful satisfaction,does the author of this book feel profoundly the necessity for this fourth edition after a comparatively short time. The author is not prompted to this statement by lack of modesty,for he is entirely too conscious of how little even this new edition approaches that "outline of a supersensuous world concept" which it is meant to be. The whole book has once more been
revised for the new edition,much supplementary matter has been inserted at important points,and elucidations have been attempted. But in numerous
passages the author has realized how poor the means of presentation accessible to him prove to be in comparison with what superphysical research discovers. Thus it was scarcely possible to do more than point out the way in which to reach conceptions of the events described in this book as the Saturn,Sun,and Moon evolutions. An important aspect of this subject has been briefly remodelled in this edition. But experiences in relation to such things diverge so widely from all experiences in the realm of the senses,that their presentation necessitates a continual striving after expressions which may be,at least in some measure, adequate. One who is willing to enter into the attempted presentation which has here been made,will perhaps notice that in the case of many things which cannot possibly be expressed by mere words,the endeavour has
been made to convey them by the _manner_ of the description. This manner
is,for instance,different in the account of the Saturn evolution from that used for the Sun evolution,and so on.

Much complementary and additional matter has been inserted in this edition
in the part dealing with "Perception of the Higher Worlds." The endeavour has been made to represent in a graphic way the kind of inner soul-processes by which the power of cognition liberates itself from the limits which confine it in the world of sense and thereby becomes qualified for experiencing the supersensible world. The attempt has been made to show that these experiences,even though gained by entirely inner ways and methods,still do not have a merely subjective significance for the particular individual who gains them. The description attempts to show
that _within_ the soul stripped of its individuality and personal peculiarities,an experience takes place which _every_ human being may have in the same way,if he will only work at his development from out his subjective experiences. It is only when "knowledge of supersensible worlds" is thought of as bearing this character that it may be differentiated from old experiences of merely subjective mysticism. Of this mysticism it may be said that it is after all more or less a subjective concern of the mystic. The scientific spiritual training of the soul,however,as it is described here,strives for objective experiences, the truth of which,although recognized in an entirely inner way,may yet, for that very reason,be found to be universally valid. This again is a point on which it is very difficult to come to an understanding concerning many of the habits of thought of our time.

In conclusion,the author would like to observe that it would be well if even the sympathetic reader of the book would take its statements exactly

as they stand. At the present time there is a very prevalent tendency to give this or that spiritual movement an historical name,and to many it is only such a name that seems to make it valuable. But,it may be asked, what would the statements in this book gain by being designated "Rosicrucian," or anything else of the kind? What is of importance is that in this book a glimpse into supersensible worlds is attempted with the means which in our present period of evolution are possible and suitable for the human soul; and that from this point of view the problems of human
destiny and human existence are considered beyond the limits of birth and death. It is not a question of an endeavor which shall bear this or that old name,but of a striving after truth.

On the other hand,expressions have also been used,with hostile intention,for the conception of the universe presented in this book. Leaving out of account that those which were intended to strike and discredit the author most heavily are absurd and objectively untrue,these expressions are stamped as unworthy by the fact that they disparage a fully _independent_ search for truth; because the aggressors do not judge it on its own merits,but try to impose on others,as a judgment of these investigations,erroneous ideas about their dependence upon this or that tradition,--ideas which they have invented,or adopted from others without reason. However necessary these words are in face of the many attacks on
the author,it is yet repugnant to him in this place to enter further into the matter.

RUDOLF STEINER
June,1913.

AUTHOR'S REMARKS TO FIRST EDITION

In placing a book such as this in the hands of the public,the writer must calmly anticipate every kind of criticism regarding his work which is likely to arise in the present day. A reader,for instance,whose opinions are based upon the results of scientific research,after noting certain statements made here touching these things,may pronounce the following judgment: "It is astounding that such statements should be possible in our time. The most elementary conceptions of natural science are distorted in such a manner as to denote positively inconceivable ignorance of even the rudiments of science. The author uses such terms,for instance,as 'heat' in a way that would lead one to infer that he had let the entire wave of modern thought on the subject of physics sweep past him unperceived. Any
one familiar with the mere elements of this science would show him that not even the merest dilettante could have made these statements,and they
can only be dismissed as the outcome of rank ignorance."

This and many a similar verdict might be pronounced,and we can picture our reader,after the perusal of a page or two,laying the book aside,--smiling or indignant,according to his temperament,--and reflecting on the singular growths which a perverse tendency of thought may put forth
in our time. So thinking,he will lay this volume aside,with his collection of similar freaks of the brain. What,however,would the author say should such opinions come to his knowledge? Would he not,from his point of view,also set the critic down as incapable of judgment or,at least,as one who has not chosen to bring his good will to bear in forming

an intelligent opinion? To this the answer is most emphatically--No! In no sense whatever does the author feel this,for he can easily conceive of his critic as being not only a highly intelligent man,but also a trained scientist,and one whose opinions are the result of conscientious thought. The author of this book is able to enter into the feelings of such a person and to understand the reasons which have led him to form these conclusions.

Now,in order to comprehend what the author really means,it is necessary to do here what generally seems to him to be out of place,but for which there is urgent cause in the case of this book,namely,to introduce certain personal data. Of course,nothing will be said in this connection but what bears upon the author's decision to write this book. What is said in it could not be justified if it bore merely a personal character. A book of this kind is bound to proffer views to which any person may attain,and these views must be presented in such a way as to suggest no shade of the personal element,that is,as far as such a thing is possible.

It is therefore not in this sense that the personal note is sounded. It is only intended to explain how it was possible for the author to understand the above characterized opinions concerning his presentations,and yet was able to write this book.

It is true there is one method which would have made the introduction of the personal element unnecessary--this would have been to specify in detail all those particulars which would show that the statements here made are in agreement with the progress of modern science. This course would, however,have necessitated the writing of many volumes,and as such a task is at present out of the question,the writer feels it necessary to state the personal reasons which he believes justify him in thinking such an agreement thoroughly possible and satisfactory. Were he not in a position to make the following explanations,he would most certainly never have gone so far as to publish such statements as those referring to heat processes.

Some thirty years ago the author had the opportunity of studying physics in its various branches. At that time the central point of interest in the sphere of heat phenomena was the promulgation of the so-called "Mechanical Theory of Heat," and it happened that this theory so particularly engrossed his attention that the historical development of the various interpretations associated with the names of Julius Robert Mayer, Helmholtz,Joule,Clausius,and others,formed the subject of his continuous study. During that period of concentrated work he laid those foundations which have enabled him to follow all the actual advances since made with regard to the theory of physical heat,without experiencing any difficulty in penetrating into what science is achieving in this department. Had he been obliged to confess himself unable to do this,the writer would have had good reason for leaving unsaid and unwritten much that has been brought forward in this book.

He has made it a matter of conscience,when writing or speaking on occult science,to deal only with matters on which he could also report,in what seemed an adequate manner,the views held by modern science. With this, however,he does not wish in the least to give the impression that this is always a necessary prerequisite. Any one may feel a call to communicate or to publish whatever his judgment,his sense of truth,and his feelings may prompt him to,even if he is ignorant of the attitude taken by contemporary science in the matter. The writer wishes to indicate merely

that he holds to the pronouncements he has made. For instance,he would never have written those few sentences on the human glandular system, nor
those regarding man's nervous system,contained in this volume,were he not in a position to discuss both subjects in the terms used by the modern
scientist,when speaking of the glandular and nervous systems from the standpoint of science.

In spite of the fact that it may be said that he who speaks concerning "heat," as is done here,knows nothing of the elements of modern physics, yet the author feels himself quite justified,because he believes that he knows present day research along those lines,and because if it were unknown to him,he would have left the subject alone. He knows that such utterances may be ascribed to lack of modesty,but it is necessary to declare his true motives,lest they should be confounded with others of a very different nature,a result infinitely worse than a verdict of mere vanity.

He who reads this book as a philosopher,may well ask himself,"Has this author been asleep to present day research in the field of the theory of cognition? Had he never heard of the existence of a man called Kant?" this philosopher might ask,"and did he not know that according to this man it was simply inadmissible,from a philosophic point of view,to put forward such statements?" and so on,while in conclusion he might remark that stuff of so uncritical,childish,and unprofessional a nature should not be tolerated among philosophers,and that any further investigation would be waste of time. However,here again,for reasons already advanced and at the risk of being again misinterpreted,the writer would fain introduce certain personal experiences.

His studies of Kant date from his sixteenth year,and he really believes he is now capable of criticizing quite objectively,from the Kantian point of view,everything that has been put forward in this book. On this account,too,he might have left this book unwritten were he not fully aware of what moves a philosopher to pass the verdict of "childishness" whenever the critical standard of the day is applied. Yet one may actually know that in the Kantian sense the limits of possible knowledge are here exceeded: one may know in what way Herbart (who never arrived at an "arrangement of ideas") would discover his "naive realism." One may even know the degree to which the modern pragmatism of James and Schiller and
others would find the bounds of "true presentments" transgressed--those presentments which we are able to make our own,to vindicate,enforce,and to verify.

We may know all these things and yet,for this very reason,feel justified in holding the views here presented. The writer has dealt with the tendencies of philosophic thought in his works: "The Theory of Cognition of Goethe's World-Concept"; "Truth and Science"; "Philosophy of Freedom"; "Goethe's World Concept" and "Views of the World and Life in the Nineteenth Century."

Many other criticisms might be suggested. Any one who had read some of the
writer's earlier works: "Views of the World and Life in the Nineteenth Century," for instance,or a smaller work on _Haeckel and his Opponents_, might think it incredible that one and the same man could have written those books as well as the present work and also his already published "Theosophy." "How," he might ask,"can a man throw himself into the breach for Haeckel,and then,turn around and discredit every sound theory concerning monism that is the outcome of Haeckel's researches?" He might
understand the author of this book attacking Haeckel "with fire and

sword"; but it passes the limits of comprehension that,besides defending him,he should actually have dedicated "Views of the World and Life in the Nineteenth Century" to him. Haeckel,it might be thought,would have emphatically declined the dedication had he known that the author was shortly to produce such stuff as _An Outline of Occult Science_,with all its unwieldy dualism.

The writer of this book is of the opinion that one may very well understand Haeckel without being bound to consider everything else as nonsense which does not flow directly from Haeckel's own presentments and premises. The author is further of the opinion that Haeckel cannot be understood by attacking him with "fire and sword," but by trying to grasp what he has done for science. Least of all does he hold those opponents of Haeckel to be in the right,against whom he has in his book,_Haeckel and his Opponents_,sought to defend the great naturalist; for surely,the fact of his having gone beyond Haeckel's premises by placing the spiritual conception of the world side by side with the merely natural one conceived by Haeckel,need be no reason for assuming that he was of one mind with the latter's opponents. Any one taking the trouble to look at the matter in the right light must see that the writer's recent books are in perfect accord with those of an earlier date.

But the author can also conceive of a critic who in general and offhand looks upon the presentations of this book as the out-pourings of a fantasy run wild or as dreamy thought-pictures. Yet all that can be said in this respect is contained in the book itself,and it is explicitly shown that sane and earnest thought not only can but _must_ be the touch-stone of all the facts presented. Only one who submits what is here advanced to logical and adequate examination,such as is applied to the facts of natural science,will be in a position to decide for himself how much reason has to say in the matter.

After saying this much about those who may at first be inclined to take exception to this work,we may perhaps be permitted to address a few words to those on whose sympathetic attention we can rely. These will find all broad essentials contained in the first chapter,"Concerning the Nature of Occult Science." A word,however,must here be added. Although this book deals with investigations carried beyond the confines of intellect limited to the world of the senses,yet nothing has been asserted except what can be grasped by any person possessed of unprejudiced reasoning powers backed by a healthy sense of truth,and who is at the same time willing to turn these gifts to the best account; and the writer emphatically wishes it to be understood that he hopes to appeal to readers who will not be content with merely accepting on "blind faith" the matters presented,but who will take the trouble to test them by the light of their own understanding and by the experiences of their own lives. Above all,he desires _cautious_ readers,who will allow themselves to be convinced only by what can be logically justified. The writer is well aware that his work would be worth nothing were its value to rest on blind belief; it is valuable only in the degree to which it can be justified by unbiased reason. It is an easy thing for "blind faith" to confound folly and superstition with truth,and doubtless many,who have been content to accept the supersensible on mere faith,will be inclined to think that this book makes too great demands upon their powers of thought. It is not a question of merely making certain communications,but rather of presenting them in a manner consistent with a conscientious view of the corresponding plane of life;

for this is the plane upon which the loftiest matters are often handled with unscrupulous charlatanism,and where knowledge and superstition come
into such close contact as to be liable to be confused one with the other.

Any one acquainted with supersensual research will,on reading this book, be able to see that the author has sought to define the boundary line sharply between what can be communicated now from the sphere of supersensible cognition,and that which will be given out,at a later time,or at least,in a different form.

RUDOLF STEINER
December,1909.

CHAPTER I. THE CHARACTER OF OCCULT SCIENCE

At the present time the words "occult science" are apt to arouse the most
varied feelings. Upon some people they work like a magic charm,like the announcement of something to which they feel attracted by the innermost
powers of their soul; to others there is in the words something repellent, calling forth contempt,derision,or a compassionate smile. By many, occult science is looked upon as a lofty goal of human effort,the crown of all other knowledge and cognition; others,who are devoting themselves with the greatest earnestness and noble love of truth to that which appears to them true science,deem occult science mere idle dreaming and fantasy,in the same category with what is called superstition. To some, occult science is like a light without which life would be valueless; to others,it represents a spiritual danger,calculated to lead astray immature minds and weak souls,while between these two extremes is to be
found every possible intermediate shade of opinion.

Strange feelings are awakened in one who has attained a certain impartiality of judgment in regard to occult science,its adherents and its opponents,when one sees how people,undoubtedly possessed of a genuine feeling for freedom in many matters,become intolerant when they meet with this particular line of thought. And an unprejudiced observer will scarcely fail in this case to admit that what attracts many adherents of occult science--or occultism--is nothing but the fatal craving for what is unknown and mysterious,or even vague. And he will also be ready to own
that there is much cogency in the reasons put forward against what is fantastic and visionary by serious opponents of the cause in question. In fact,one who studies occult science will do well not to lose sight of the fact that the impulse toward the mysterious leads many people on a vain chase after worthless and dangerous will-o'-the-wisps.

Even though the occult scientist keeps a watchful eye on all errors and vagaries on the part of adherents of his views,and on all justifiable antagonism,yet there are reasons which hold him back from the immediate
defence of his own efforts and aspirations. These reasons will become apparent to any one entering more deeply into occult science. It would therefore be superfluous to discuss them here. If they were cited before the threshold of this science had been crossed,they would not suffice to convince one who,held back by irresistible repugnance,refuses to cross that threshold. But to one who effects an entry,the reasons will soon

manifest themselves,with unmistakable clearness from within.

This much,however,implies that the reasons in question point to a certain attitude as the only right one for an occult scientist. He avoids, as much as he possibly can,any kind of outer defence or conflict,and lets the cause speak for itself. He simply puts forward occult science; and in what it has to say about various matters,he shows how his knowledge is related to other departments of life and science,what antagonism it may encounter,and in what way reality stands witness to the
truth of his cognitions. He knows that an attempted vindication would,--not
merely on account of current defective thinking but by virtue of a certain inner necessity,--lead into the domain of artful persuasion; and he desires nothing else than to let occult science work its own way quite independently.

The first point in occult science is by no means the advancing of assertions or opinions which are to be proven,but the communication,in a purely narrative form,of experiences which are to be met with in a world other than the one that is to be seen with physical eyes and touched with physical hands. And further,it is an important point that through this science the methods are described by which man may verify for himself the
truth of such communications. For one who makes a serious study of genuine
occult science will soon find that thereby much becomes changed in the conceptions and ideas which are formed--and rightly formed--in other spheres
of life. A wholly new conception necessarily arises also about what has hitherto been called a "proof." We come to see that in certain domains such a word loses its usual meaning,and that there are other grounds for insight and understanding than "proofs" of this kind.

All occult science is born from two thoughts,which may take root in any human being. To the occult scientist these thoughts express facts which may be experienced if the right methods for the purpose are used. But to many people these same thoughts represent highly disputable assertions, which may arouse fierce contention,even if they are not regarded as something which may be "proven" impossible.

These two thoughts are,first,that behind the visible world there is another,the world invisible,which is hidden from the senses and also from thought that is fettered by these senses; and secondly,that it is possible for man to penetrate into that unseen world by developing certain faculties dormant within him.

Some will say that there is no such hidden world. The world perceived by man through his senses is the only one. Its enigmas can be solved out of itself. Even if man is still very far from being able to answer all the questions of existence,the time will certainly come when sense-experience and the science based upon it will be able to give the answers to all such questions.

Others say that it cannot be asserted that there is no unseen world behind
the visible one,but that human powers of perception are not able to penetrate into that world. Those powers have bounds which they cannot pass. Faith,with its urgent cravings,may take refuge in such a world; but true science,based on ascertained facts,can have nothing to do with it.

A third class looks upon it as a kind of presumption for man to attempt to penetrate,by his own efforts of cognition,into a domain with regard to which he should give up all claim to knowledge and be content with faith. The adherents of this view feel it to be wrong for weak human beings to wish to force their way into a world which should belong to religious life.

It is also alleged that a common knowledge of the facts of the sense-world
is possible for mankind,but that in regard to supersensible things it can be merely a question of the individual's personal opinion,and that in these matters there can be no possibility of a certainty universally recognized. And many other assertions are made on the subject.

The occult scientist has convinced himself that a consideration of the visible world propounds enigmas to man which can never be solved out of the facts of that world itself. Their solution in this way will never be possible,however far advanced a knowledge of those facts may be. For visible facts plainly point,through their own inner nature,to the existence of a hidden world. One who does not see this closes his eyes to the problems which obviously spring up everywhere out of the facts of the sense-world. He refuses to recognize certain questions and problems,and therefore thinks that all questions can be answered through facts within reach of sense perception. The questions which he is willing to ask are all capable of being answered by the facts which he is convinced will be discovered in the course of time. Every genuine occultist admits this. But why should one,when he asks no questions,expect answers on certain subjects? The occult scientist says that to him such questioning is natural,and must be regarded as a wholly justifiable expression of the human soul. Science is surely not to be confined within limits which prohibit impartial inquiry.

The opinion that there are bounds to human knowledge which it is impossible to pass,compelling man to stop short of the invisible world, is thus met by the occult scientist: he says that there can exist no doubt concerning the impossibility of penetrating into the unseen world by means
of the kind of cognition here meant. One who considers it the only kind can come to no other opinion than that man is not permitted to penetrate into a possibly existing higher world. But the occult scientist goes on to say that it is possible to develop a different sort of cognition,and that this leads into the unseen world. If this kind of cognition is held to be impossible,we arrive at a point of view from which any mention of an invisible world appears as sheer nonsense. But to an unbiased judgment there can be no basis for such an opinion as this,except that its adherent is a stranger to that other kind of cognition. But how can a person form an opinion about a subject of which he declares himself ignorant? Occult science must in this case maintain the principle that people should speak only of what they know,and should not make assertions
about anything of which they are ignorant. It can only recognize every man's right to communicate his own experiences,not every man's right to declare the impossibility of what he does not,or will not,know. The occult scientist disputes no one's right to ignore the invisible world; but there can be no real reason why a person should declare himself an authority,not only on what he may know,but also on things considered unknowable.

To those who say that it is presumption to penetrate into unseen regions, the occult scientist would merely point out that this _can_ be done,and that it is sinning against the faculties with which man has been endowed if he allows them to waste instead of developing and using them.

But he who thinks that views about the unseen world are necessarily wholly dependent on personal opinion and feeling is denying the common essence of all human beings. Even though it is true that every one must find light on these things within himself,it is also a fact that all those,who go far enough,arrive at the same,not at different conclusions regarding them. Differences exist only as long as people will not approach the highest truths by the well-tested path of occult science,but attempt ways of their own choosing. Genuine occult science will certainly fully admit that only one who has followed,or at any rate has begun to follow the path of occult science,is in a position to recognize it as the right one. But all those who follow that path will recognize its genuineness,and have always done so.

The path to occult knowledge will be found,at the fitting moment,by every human being who discerns in what is visible the presence of something invisible,or who even but dimly surmises or divines it,and who,from his consciousness that powers of cognition are capable of development,is driven to the feeling that what is hidden may be unveiled to him. One who is drawn to occult science by such experiences of the soul will find opening up before him,not only the prospect of finding the answers to certain questions which press upon him,but the further prospect of overcoming everything which hampers and enfeebles his life. And in a certain higher sense it implies a weakening of life,in fact a death of the soul,when a person is compelled to turn away from,or to deny,the unseen. Indeed,under certain circumstances despair is the result of a man's losing all hope of having the invisible revealed to him. This death and despair,in their manifold forms,are at the same time inner spiritual foes of occult science. They make their appearance when a person's inner force is dwindling away. In that case,if he is to possess any vital force it must be supplied to him from without. He perceives the things,beings,and events which approach his organs of sense,and analyzes them with his intellect. They afford him pleasure and pain,and impel him to the actions of which he is capable. For a while he may go on in this way: but at length he must reach a point at which he inwardly dies. For that which may thus be extracted for man from the outer world, becomes exhausted. This is not a statement arising from the personal experience of one individual,but something resulting from an impartial survey of the whole of human life. That which secures life from exhaustion lies in the unseen world,deep at the roots of things. If a person loses the power of descending into those depths so that he cannot be perpetually drawing fresh vitality from them,then in the end the outer world of things also ceases to yield him anything of a vivifying nature.

It is by no means the case that only the individual and his personal weal and woe are concerned. Through occult science man gains the conviction that from a higher standpoint the weal and woe of the individual are intimately bound up with the weal and woe of the whole world. This is a means by which man comes to see that he is inflicting an injury on the entire world and every being within it,if he does not develop his own powers in the right way. If a man makes his life desolate by losing touch with the unseen,he not only destroys in his inner self something,the decay of which may eventually drive him to despair,but through his weakness he constitutes a hindrance to the evolution of the whole world in which he lives.

Now man may delude himself. He may yield to the belief that there is nothing invisible,and that that which is manifest to his senses and intellect contains everything which can possibly exist. But such an illusion is only possible on the surface of consciousness and not in its depths. Feeling and desire do not yield to this delusive belief. They will be perpetually craving,in one way or another,for that which is invisible. And if this is withheld,they drive man to doubt,to uncertainty about life,or even to despair. Occult science,by making manifest what is unseen,is calculated to overcome all hopelessness, uncertainty,and despair,--everything,in short,which weakens life and makes it unfit for its necessary service in the universe.

The beneficent effect of occult science is that it not only satisfies thirst for knowledge but gives strength and stability to life. The source whence the occult scientist draws his power for work and his confidence in
life is inexhaustible. Any one who has once had recourse to that fount will always,on revisiting it,go forth with renewed vigour.

There are people who will not hear anything about occult science,because they think they discern something unhealthy in what has just been said. These people are quite right as regards the surface and outer aspect of life. They do not desire that to be stunted,which life,in its so-called reality,offers. They see weakness in man's turning away from reality and seeking his welfare in an unseen world which to them is synonymous with what is chimerical and visionary. If as occult scientists we do not desire to fall into morbid dreaming and weakness,we must admit that such objections are partially justified. For they are founded upon sound judgment,which leads to a half truth instead of a whole truth merely because it does not penetrate to the roots of things,but remains on the surface. If occult science were calculated to weaken life and estrange man from true reality,such objections would certainly be strong enough to cut the ground from under the feet of those who follow this spiritual line of life. But even in regard to such opinions as these,occult science would not be taking the right course in defending itself in the ordinary sense of the word. Even in this case it can only speak by means of what it gives to those who really penetrate into its meaning,that is,by the real force and vitality which it bestows. It does not weaken life,but strengthens it,because it equips man not only with the forces of the manifest world but with those of the invisible world of which the manifest is the effect. Thus it does not imply an impoverishment,but an enrichment,of life. The true occult scientist does not stand aloof from the world,but is a lover of reality,because he does not desire to enjoy the unseen in a remote dream-world,but finds his happiness in bringing to the world ever fresh supplies of force from the invisible sources from whence this very world is derived,and from which it must be continually fructified.

Some people find many obstacles when they enter upon the path of occult science. One of these is expressed in the fact,that a person,attempting to take the first steps,is sometimes discouraged because at the outset he is introduced to the details of the supersensible world,in order that he may,with entire patience and devotion,become acquainted with them. A series of communications is made to him concerning the invisible nature of man,about certain definite occurrences in the kingdom of which death opens the portals,and regarding the evolutions of man,the earth,and the entire solar system. What he expected was to enter the supersensible world
easily,at a bound. Now he is heard to say: "Everything which I am told to study is food for my mind,but leaves my soul cold. I am seeking the deepening of my soul-life. I want to find myself within. I am seeking something that will lift my soul into the sphere of the divine,leading it to its true home; I do not want information about the human being and world-processes." People who talk in this way have no idea that by such feelings they are barring the door to what they are really seeking. For it is just when,and only when,with a free and open mind,in self-surrender and patience,they assimilate what they call "merely" food for the intellect,that they will find that for which their souls are athirst.
That road leads the soul to union with the divine,which brings to the soul knowledge of the works of the divine. The uplifting of the heart is the result of learning to know about the creations of the spirit.

On this account occult science must begin by imparting the information which throws light on the realms of the spiritual world. So too,in this book,we shall begin with what can be unveiled concerning unseen worlds through the methods of occult research. That which is mortal in man,and that which is immortal,will be described in their connection with the world,of which he is a member.

Then will follow a description of the methods by which man is able to develop those powers of cognition latent within him,which will lead him into that world. As much will be said about the methods as is at present possible in a work of this kind. It seems natural to think that these methods should be dealt with first. For it seems as though the main point would be to acquaint man with what may bring him,by means of his own powers,to the desired view of the higher world. Many may say,"Of what use is it for me that others tell me what they know about higher worlds? I wish to see them for myself."

The fact of the matter is that for really fruitful experience of the mysteries of the unseen world,previous knowledge of certain facts belonging to that world is absolutely necessary. Why this is so,will be sufficiently brought out from what follows.

It is a mistake to think that the truths of occult science which are imparted by those qualified to communicate them,before mention is made of the means of penetrating into the spiritual world itself,can be understood and grasped only by means of the higher vision which results from developing certain powers latent in man. This is not the case. For investigating and discovering the mysteries of a supersensible world,that higher sight is essential. No one is able to discover the facts of the unseen world without the clairvoyance which is synonymous with that higher vision. When however,the facts have been discovered and imparted,every one who applies to them the full range of his ordinary intellect and unprejudiced powers of judgment,will be able to understand them and to rise to a high degree of conviction concerning them. One who maintains that the mysteries are incomprehensible to him,does not do so because he is not yet clairvoyant,but because he has not yet succeeded in bringing into activity those powers of cognition which may be possessed by every one,even without clairvoyance.

A new method of putting forward these matters consists in so describing them,after they have been clairvoyantly investigated,that they are quite accessible to the faculty of judgment. If only people do not shut themselves off by prejudice,there is no obstacle to arriving at a conviction,even without higher vision. It is true that many will find that the new method of presentment,as given in this book,is far from corresponding to their customary ways of forming an opinion. But any objection due to this will soon disappear if one takes the trouble to follow out these customary methods to their final consequences.

When,by an extended application of ordinary thought,a certain number of the higher mysteries have been assimilated and found intelligible by any one,then the right moment has come for the methods of occult research to be applied to his individual personality:--these will give him access to the unseen world.

Nor will any genuine scientist be able to find contradiction,in spirit and in truth,between his science,which is built upon the facts of the sense-world,and the way in which occult science carries on its researches. The scientist uses certain instruments and methods. He

constructs his instruments by working upon what "nature" gives him. Occult
science also uses an instrument,but in this case the instrument is man himself. And that instrument too must first be prepared for that higher research. The faculties and powers given to man by nature at the outset without his co-operation,must be transformed into higher ones. In this way man is able to make himself into an instrument for the investigation of the unseen world.

CHAPTER II. THE NATURE OF MAN

With the consideration of man in the light of occult science,what this signifies in general,immediately becomes evident. It rests upon the recognition of something hidden behind that which is revealed to the outer senses and to the intellect acquired through perception. These senses and this intellect can apprehend only a part of all that which occult science unveils as the total human entity,and this part is the _physical body_.
In order to throw light upon its conception of this physical body,occult science at first directs attention to a phenomenon which confronts all observers of life like a great riddle,--the phenomenon of death,--and in connection with it,points to so-called inanimate nature,the mineral kingdom. We are thus referred to facts,which it devolves on occult science to explain,and to which an important part of this work must be devoted. But to begin with,only a few points will be touched upon,by way of orientation.

Within manifested nature the physical body,according to occult science, is that part of man which is of the same nature as the mineral kingdom. On
the other hand,that which distinguishes man from minerals is considered as not being part of the physical body. From the occult point of view, what is of supreme importance is the fact that death separates the human
being from that which,during life,is of like nature with the mineral world. Occult science points to the dead body as that part of man which is to be found existing in the same way in the mineral kingdom. It lays strong emphasis upon the fact that in this principle of the human being, which it looks upon as the physical body,and which death reduces to a corpse,the same materials and forces are at work as in the mineral realm; but no less emphasis is laid upon the fact that at death disintegration of the physical body sets in. Occult science therefore says: "It is true that the same materials and forces are at work in the physical body as in the mineral,but during life their activity is placed at the disposal of something higher. They are left to themselves only when death occurs. Then
they act,as they must in conformity with their own nature,as decomposers
of the physical body."

Thus a sharp distinction must be drawn between the manifested and the hidden elements in man. For during life,that which is hidden from view has to wage perpetual war on the materials and forces of the mineral world. This indicates the point at which occult science steps in. It has to characterize that which wages the war alluded to,as a principle which is hidden from sense-observation. Clairvoyant sight alone can reveal its workings. How man arrives at awareness of this hidden element,as plainly as his ordinary eyes see the phenomena of sense,will be described in a later part of this book. Results of clairvoyant observation will be given now for the reason already pointed out in the preceding pages,that is, that communications about the way in which the higher sight is obtained can only be of value to the student when he has first become acquainted, in the form of a narrative,with the results of clairvoyant research. For in this sphere it is quite possible to understand things which one is not yet able to observe. Indeed,the right path to higher vision starts with understanding.

Now,although the hidden something which wages war on the disintegration of the physical body can be observed only by the higher sight,it is plainly visible in its effects to the human faculty of judgment which is limited to the manifested world; and these effects are expressed in the form or shape in which mineral materials and forces are combined during life. When death has intervened,the form disappears little by little,and the physical body becomes part of the rest of the mineral world. But the clairvoyant is able to observe this hidden something as an independent member of the human organism,which during life prevents the physical materials and forces from taking their natural course,which would lead to the dissolution of the physical body. This independent principle is called the etheric or vital body.

If misunderstandings are not to arise at the outset,two things must be borne in mind in connection with this account of a second principle of human nature. The word "etheric" is used here in a different sense from that of modern physics,which designates as "ether" the medium by which light is transmitted. In occult science the use of the word is limited to the sense given above. It denotes that which is accessible to higher sight,and can be known to physical observation only by its effects,that is,by its power of giving a definite form or shape to the mineral materials and forces present in the physical body. Again,the use of the word "body" must not be misunderstood. It is necessary to use the words of
every day language in describing things on a higher plane of existence, and these terms,when applied to sense-observation,express only what is physical. The etheric body has,of course,nothing of a bodily nature in the physical sense,however ethereal we might imagine such a body to be. As soon as the occultist mentions this etheric or vital body,he reaches the point at which he is bound to encounter the opposition of many contemporary opinions. The development of the human mind has been such
that the mention of such a principle of human nature is necessarily looked upon as unscientific. The materialistic way of thinking has arrived at the conclusion that there is nothing to be seen in a living body but a combination of physical substances and forces such as are also found in the so-called inanimate body of the mineral,the only difference being that they are more complicated in the living than in the lifeless body. Yet it is not very long since other views were held,even by official science.

It is evident to any one who studies the works of many earnest men of science,produced during the first half of the nineteenth century,that at that time many a genuine investigator of nature was conscious of some factor acting within the living body other than in the lifeless mineral. It was termed "vital force." It is true this vital force is not represented as being what has been above characterized as the vital body, but underlying the conception was a dim idea of the existence of such a body. Vital force was generally regarded as something which in a living body was united with physical matter and forces in the same way that the force of a magnet unites itself with iron. Then came the time when vital force was banished from the domain of science. Mere physical and chemical
causes were accounted all sufficient.

At the present moment,however,there is a reaction in this respect in some scientific quarters. It is sometimes conceded that the hypothesis of

something of the nature of "vital force" is not pure nonsense. Yet even the scientist who concedes this much is not willing to make common cause
with the occultist with regard to the vital body. As a rule,it serves no useful purpose to enter upon a discussion of such views from the standpoint of occult science. It should be much more the concern of the occultist to recognize that the materialistic way of thinking is a necessary concomitant phenomenon of the great advance of natural science
in our day. This advance is due to the vast improvements in the instruments used in sense-observation. And it is in the very nature of man to bring some of his faculties to a certain degree of perfection at the expense of others. Exact sense-observation,which has been evolved to such
an important extent by natural science,was bound to leave in the background the cultivation of those human faculties which lead into the hidden worlds. But the time has come when this cultivation is once more necessary; and recognition of the invisible will not be won by combating opinions which are the logical outcome of a denial of its existence,but rather by setting the invisible in the right light. Then it will be recognized by those for whom the "time has come."

It was necessary to say this much,in order that it may not be imagined that occult science is ignorant of the standpoint of natural science when mention is made of an "etheric body," which,in many circles must necessarily be considered as purely imaginary.

Thus the etheric body is the second principle of the human being. For the clairvoyant,it possesses a higher degree of reality than the physical body. A description of how it is seen by the clairvoyant can be given only in later parts of this book,when the sense in which such descriptions are to be taken will become manifest. For the present it will be enough to say that the etheric body penetrates the physical body in all its parts,and is to be regarded as a kind of architect of the latter. All the physical organs are maintained in their form and shape by the currents and movements of the etheric body. The physical heart is based upon an etheric
heart,the physical brain,upon an etheric brain,and the physical,with this difference,that in the etheric body the parts flow into one another in active motion,whereas in the physical body they are separated from each other.

Man has this etheric body in common with all plants,just as he has the physical body in common with minerals. Everything living has its etheric body.

The study of occult science proceeds upwards from the etheric body to another principle of the human being. To aid in the formation of an idea of this principle,it draws attention to the phenomenon of sleep,just as in connection with the etheric body attention was drawn to death. All human work,so far as the manifested world is concerned,is dependent upon
activity during waking life. But that activity is possible only as long as man is able to recuperate his exhausted forces by sleep. Action and thought disappear,pain and pleasure fade away during sleep,and on re-awaking,man's conscious powers ascend from the unconsciousness of sleep as though from hidden mysterious sources of energy. It is the same consciousness which sinks down into dim depths on falling asleep and ascends from them again on re-awaking.

That which awakens life again out of this state of unconsciousness is, according to occult science,the third principle of the human being. It is called the astral body. Just as the physical body cannot keep its form by means of the mineral substances and forces it contains,but must,in order

to be kept together,be interpenetrated by the etheric body,so is it impossible for the forces of the etheric body to illuminate themselves with the light of consciousness. An etheric body left to its own resources would be in a permanent state of sleep.(1) An etheric body awake,is illuminated by an astral body. This astral body seems to sense-observation to disappear when man falls asleep; to clairvoyant observation it is still present,with the difference that it appears separated from or drawn out of the etheric body. Sense-observation has nothing to do with the astral body itself,but only with its effects in the manifested world,and these cease during sleep. In the same sense in which man possesses his physical
body in common with plants,he resembles animals as regards his astral body.

Plants are in a permanent state of sleep. One who does not judge accurately in these matters may easily make the mistake of attributing to plants the same kind of consciousness as that of animals and human beings
in the waking state; but this assumption can only be due to an inaccurate conception of consciousness. In that case it is said that,if an external stimulus is applied to a plant,it responds by certain movements,as would an animal. The _sensitiveness_ of some plants is spoken of,--for example, of those which contract their leaves when certain external things act upon
them. But the characteristic mark of consciousness is not that a being reacts in a certain way to an impression,but that it experiences something in its inner nature which adds a new element to mere reaction. Otherwise we should be able to speak of the consciousness of a piece of iron when it expands under the influence of heat. Consciousness is present
only when,through the effect of heat,the being feels pain or pleasure inwardly.

The fourth principle of being which occult science attributes to man is one which he does not share in common with the rest of the manifested world. It is that which differentiates him from his fellow creatures and makes him the crown of creation. Occult science helps in forming a conception of this further principle of human nature by pointing out the existence of an essential difference between the kinds of experience in waking life. On the one hand,man is constantly subjected to experiences which must of necessity come and go; on the other,he has experiences with
which this is not the case. This fact comes out with special force if human experiences are compared with those of animals. An animal experiences the influences of the outer world with great regularity; under the influence of heat and cold it becomes conscious of pain or pleasure, and during certain regularly recurring bodily processes it feels hunger and thirst. The sum total of man's life is not exhausted by such experiences; he is able to develop desires and wishes which go beyond these things. In the case of an animal it would always be possible,on going far enough into the matter,to ascertain the cause--either within or without its body--which impelled it to any given act or feeling. This is by no means the case with man. He may engender wishes and desires for which
no adequate cause exists either inside or outside of his body. A particular source must be found for everything in this domain; and according to occult science this source is to be found in the human "I" or "ego." Therefore the ego will be spoken of as the fourth principle of the human being.

Were the astral body left to its own resources,feelings of pleasure and pain,and sensations of hunger and thirst,would take place within it,but there would be lacking the consciousness of something lasting in all these feelings. It is not the permanent as such,which is here designated the "ego," but rather that which experiences this permanent element. In this domain,conceptions must be very exactly expressed if misunderstandings are not to arise. With the becoming aware of something permanent, lasting, within the changing inner experiences,begins the dawn of "ego consciousness."

The sensation of hunger,for instance,cannot give a creature the feeling of having an ego. Hunger sets in when the recurring causes make themselves felt in the being concerned,which then devours its food just because these recurring conditions are present. For the ego-consciousness to arise,there must not only be these recurring conditions,urging the being to take food,but there must have been pleasure derived from previous satisfaction of hunger,and the consciousness of the pleasure must have remained,so that not only the present experience of hunger but the past experience of pleasure urges the being to take nourishment.

Just as the physical body falls into decay if the etheric body does not keep it together,and as the etheric body sinks into unconsciousness if not illuminated by the astral body,so the astral body would necessarily allow the past to be lost in oblivion unless the ego rescued the past by carrying it over into the present. What death is to the physical body and sleep to the etheric,the power of forgetting is to the astral body. We may put this in another way,and say that life is the special characteristic of the etheric body,consciousness that of the astral body, and memory that of the ego.

It is still easier to make the mistake of attributing memory(2) to an animal than that of attributing consciousness to a plant. It is so natural to think of memory when a dog recognizes its master,whom perhaps it has not seen for some time; yet in reality the recognition is not due to memory at all,but to something quite different. The dog feels a certain attraction toward its master which proceeds from the personality of the latter. This gives the dog a sense of pleasure whenever its master is present,and every time this happens it is a cause of the repetition of the pleasure. But memory only exists in a being when he not only feels his present experiences,but retains those of the past. A person might admit this,and yet fall into the error of thinking the dog has memory. For it might be said that the dog pines when its master leaves it,and therefore it retains a remembrance of him. This too is an inaccurate opinion. Living with its master has made his presence a condition of well-being to the dog,and it feels his absence much in the same way in which it feels hunger. One who does not make these distinctions will not arrive at a clear understanding of the true conditions of life.

Memory and forgetfulness have for the ego much the same significance that waking and sleeping have for the astral body. Just as sleep banishes into nothingness the cares and troubles of the day,so does forgetfulness draw a veil over the sad experiences of life and efface part of the past. And just as sleep is necessary for the recuperation of the exhausted vital forces,so must a man blot out from his memory certain portions of his past life if he is to face his new experiences freely and without prejudice. It is out of this very forgetfulness that strength arises for the perception of new facts. Let us take the case of learning to write. All the details which a child has to go through in this process are forgotten. What remains is the ability to write. How would a person ever be able to write if each time he took up his pen all his experiences in learning to write rose up before his mind?

Now there are many different degrees of memory. Its simplest form is manifest when a person perceives an object and,after turning away from it,retains its image in his mind. He formed the image while looking at the object.A process was then carried out between his astral body and his ego. The astral body lifted into consciousness the outward impression of the object,but knowledge of the object would last only as long as the thing itself was present,unless the ego absorbed the knowledge into itself and made it its own.

It is at this point that occult science draws the dividing line between what belongs to the body and what belongs to the soul. It speaks of the astral body as long as it is a question of the gaining of knowledge from an object which is present. But what gives knowledge duration is known as
soul. From this it can at once be seen how close is the connection in man between the astral body and that part of the soul which gives a lasting quality to knowledge. The two are,to a certain extent,united into one principle of human nature. Consequently,this unity is often denoted the astral body. When exact terms are desired,the astral body is called the _soul-body_,and the soul,in so far as it is united with the latter,is called the _sentient soul_.

The ego rises to a higher stage of its being when it centres its activity on what it has gained for itself out of its knowledge of objective things. It is by means of this activity that the ego detaches itself more and more from the objects of perception,in order to work within that which is its own possession. The part of the soul on which this work devolves is called the rational- or intellectual-soul.(3) It is the peculiarity of the sentient and intellectual souls that they work with that which they receive through sense-impressions of external objects of which they retain
the memory. The soul is then wholly surrendered to something which is really outside it. Even what it has made its own through memory,it has actually received from without. But it is able to go beyond all this,and occult science can most easily give an idea of this by drawing attention to a simple fact,which,however,is of the greatest importance. It is, that in the whole range of speech there is but one name which is distinguished by its very nature from all other names. This is the name "I." Every other name can be applied by any one to the thing or being to which it belongs. The word "I," as the designation of a being,has a meaning only when given to that being by himself. Never can any outside voice call us by the name of "I." We can apply it only to ourselves. I am only an "I" to myself; to every one else I am a "you," and every one else is a "you" to me. This fact is the outward expression of a deeply significant truth. The real essence of the ego is independent of everything outside of it,and it is on this account that its name cannot be applied to it by any one else. This is the reason why those religions confessions which have consciously maintained their connections with occult science,speak the word "I" as the "unutterable name of God." For the fact above mentioned is exactly what is referred to when this expression is used. Nothing outward has access to that part of the human
soul of which we are now speaking. It is the "hidden sanctuary" of the soul. Only a being of like nature with the soul can win entrance there. "The divinity dwelling in man speaks when the soul recognizes itself as an ego." Just as the sentient and intellectual souls live in the outer world, so a third soul-principle is immersed in the divine when the soul becomes conscious of its own nature.

In this connection a misunderstanding may easily arise; it may seem as though occult science interpreted the ego to be one with God. But it by no means says that the ego is God,only that it is of the same nature and essence as God. Does any one declare the drop of water taken from the ocean to be the ocean,when he asserts that the drop and the ocean are the same in essence or substance? If a comparison is needed, we may say, "The ego is related to God as the drop of water is to the ocean." Man is able to find a divine element within himself, because his original essence is derived directly from the Divine. Thus man, through the third principle of his soul, attains an inner knowledge of himself, just as through his astral body he gains knowledge of the outer world. For this reason occult science calls the third soul-principle _the consciousness-soul_, and it holds that the soul-part of man consists of three principles, the _sentient-_, _intellectual-_, and _consciousness-souls_, just as the bodily part has three principles, the _physical_, _etheric_, and _astral bodies_.

The real nature of the ego is first revealed in the consciousness-soul. Through feeling and reason the soul loses itself in other things; but as the consciousness-soul it lays hold of its own essence. Therefore this ego can only be perceived through the consciousness-soul by a certain inner activity. The images of external objects are formed as those objects come and go, and the images go on working in the intellect by virtue of their own force. But if the ego is to perceive itself, it cannot merely _surrender_ itself; it must first, by inner activity, draw up its own being out of its depths, in order to become conscious of it. A new activity of the ego begins with this self cognition,--with self-recollection. Owing to this activity, the perception of the ego in the consciousness-soul possesses an entirely different meaning for man from that conveyed by the observation of all that reaches him through the three bodily principles and the two other soul-principles. The power which reveals the ego in the consciousness-soul is in fact the same power which manifests everywhere else in the world; only in the body and the lower soul-principles it does not come forth directly, but is manifested little by little in its effects. The lowest manifestation is through the physical body, thence a gradual ascent is made to that which fills the intellectual soul. Indeed, we may say that with each ascending step one of the veils falls away in which the hidden centre is wrapped. In that which fills the consciousness-soul, this hidden centre emerges unveiled into the temple of the soul. Yet it shows itself just here to be but a drop from the ocean of the all-pervading Primordial Essence; and it is here that man first has to grasp it,--this Primordial Essence. He must recognize it in himself before he is able to find it in its manifestations.

That which penetrates into the consciousness-soul like a drop from the ocean is called by occult science _Spirit_. In this way is the consciousness-soul united with the spirit, which is the hidden principle in all manifested things. If man wishes to lay hold of the spirit in all manifestation, he must do it in the same way in which he lays hold of the ego in the consciousness-soul. He must extend to the visible world the activity which has led him to the perception of his ego. By this means he evolves to yet higher planes of his being. He adds something new to the principles of his body and soul. The first thing that happens is that he himself conquers what lies hidden in his lower soul-principles, and this is effected through the work which the ego carries on within the soul. How man is engaged in this work becomes evident if we compare a high-minded idealist with a person who is still given up to low desires and so-called sensual pleasures. The latter becomes transmuted into the former if he withdraws from certain lower tendencies and turns to higher ones. He thus works through his ego upon his soul thereby ennobling and spiritualizing it. The ego has become the master of that man's soul-life. This may be carried so far that no desire or wish can take root in the soul unless the ego permits its entrance. In this way the whole soul becomes a manifestation of the ego, which previously only the consciousness-soul had been. All civilized life and all spiritual effort really consist in the one work, which has for its object to make the ego the master. Every one now living is engaged in this work whether he wishes it or not,and whether or not he is conscious of the fact.

Again,by this work human nature is drawn upward to higher stages of being. Man develops new principles of his being. These lie hidden from him behind what is manifest. If man is able by working upon his soul,to make his ego master of it,so that the latter brings into manifestation what is hidden,the work may extend yet farther and include the astral body. In that case the ego takes possession of the astral body by uniting itself with the hidden wisdom of this astral principle. In occult science the astral body which is thus conquered and transformed by the ego is called the _Spirit-Self_. (This is the same as what is known as "_Manas_" in theosophical literature,a term borrowed from the wisdom of the East.) In the Spirit-Self a higher principle is added to human nature,one which is present as though in the germ,and which in the course of the work of the human being on itself comes forth more and more.

Man conquers his astral body by pushing through to the hidden forces lying behind it; a similar thing happens,at a later stage of development,to the etheric body: but the work on the latter is more arduous,for what is hidden in the etheric body is enveloped in two veils,but what is hidden in the astral body in only one.(4) Occult science gives an idea of the difference in the work on the two bodies by pointing out certain changes which may take place in man in the course of his development. Let us at first think of the way in which certain soul-qualities of man develop when the ego works upon the soul; how pleasures and desires,joys and sorrows, may change. We have only to look back to our childhood. What gave us pleasure then,what caused us pain? What have we learned in addition to what we knew as children? All this is but an expression of the way in which the ego has gained the mastery over the astral body,for it is this principle which is the vehicle of pleasure and pain,joy and sorrow. Compared with these things,how little in the course of time do certain other human qualities change,for example,the temperament,the deeper peculiarities of the character,and like qualities. A passionate child will often retain certain tendencies to sudden anger during its development in later life.

This is such a striking fact that there are thinkers who entirely deny the possibility of changing the fundamental character. They assume that it is something permanent throughout life,and that it is merely a question of its being manifested in one way or another. But such an opinion is due to defective observation. To one who is capable of seeing such things,it is evident that even the character and temperament of a person may be transformed under the influence of his ego. It is true that this change is slow in comparison with the change in the qualities before mentioned. We may compare the relation to each other of the rates of change in the two bodies to the movements of the hour-hand and minute-hand of a clock. Now the forces which bring about a change of character or temperament belong to the hidden forces of the etheric body. They are of the same nature as the forces which govern the kingdom of life,--the same,therefore,as the forces of growth,nutrition,and generation. Further explanations in this work will throw the right light on these things.

Thus it is not when man simply gives himself up to pleasure and pain,joy and sorrow,that the ego is working on the astral body,but when the peculiarities of these qualities of the soul are changed; and the work is extended in the same way to the etheric body,when the ego applies its energies to changing the character or temperament. This change,too,is one in which every person living is engaged,whether consciously or not. The most powerful incitement to this kind of change in ordinary life is that given by religion. If the ego allows the impulses which flow from religion to work upon it again and again,they become a power within it, which extends to the etheric body and changes it as lesser impulses in life effect the transformation of the astral body. These lesser impulses, which come to man through study,reflection,the ennobling of feeling,and so on,are subject to the manifold changes of existence; but religious feelings impress a certain stamp of uniformity upon all thinking,feeling, and willing. They diffuse an equal and single light over the whole life of the soul.

Man thinks and feels one thing to-day,another to-morrow,the causes of which are of many different kinds; but one who,consistently holding to his religious convictions,has a glimpse of something which persists through all changes,will relate his thoughts and feelings of to-day,as well as his experiences of to-morrow,to that fundamental feeling he possesses. Thus religious belief has the power of permeating the whole of the soul-life. Its influences increase in strength as time goes on because they are constantly repeated. Hence they acquire the power of working upon
the etheric body.

In a similar way the influences of true art work upon man. If,--going beyond the outer form,colour and tone of a work of art,--he penetrates to its spiritual foundations with his imagination and feeling,then the impulses thus received by the ego actually reach the etheric body. When this thought is followed out to its logical conclusion,the immense significance of art in all human evolution may be estimated. Only a few instances are pointed out here of what induces the ego to work upon the etheric body. There are many similar influences in human life which are not so apparent at the first glance. But these instances are enough to show that there is yet another principle of man's nature hidden within him,which the ego is making more and more manifest. Occult science denotes this second principle of the spirit the _Life-Spirit_. (It is the same which in current theosophical literature is called Budhi,a term borrowed from Eastern wisdom.) The expression "Life-Spirit" is appropriate,because the same forces are at work within it as are active in the vital body,with the difference that when they are manifesting in the latter the ego is not active. When,however,these powers express themselves as the Life-Spirit,they are interpenetrated by the ego.

Man's intellectual development,the purification and ennobling of his feelings and of the manifestations of his will,are the measure of the degree in which he has transformed the astral body into the Spirit-Self. His religious experiences,as well as many others,are stamped upon the etheric body,making it into the Life-Spirit. In the ordinary course of life this happens more or less unconsciously; so-called initiation,on the contrary,consists in man's being directed by occult science to the means through which he may quite consciously take in hand this work on the Spirit-Self and Life-Spirit. These means will be dealt with in later parts of this book. In the meantime it is important to show that,besides the soul and the body,the spirit also is working within man. It will be seen later how this spirit belongs to the eternal part of man,as contrasted with the perishable body.

But the work of the ego on the astral and etheric bodies does not exhaust its activity,which is also extended to the physical body. A slight effect of the influence of the ego on the physical body may be seen when certain experiences cause a person to blush or turn pale. In this case the ego is actually the occasion of a process in the physical body. Now if through the activity of the ego in man,changes occur influencing the physical body,the ego is really united with the hidden forces of the physical body,that is,with the same forces which bring about its physical processes. Occult science says that during such activity the ego is working on the physical body. This expression must not be misunderstood. It must on no account be supposed that this work is of a grossly material nature. What appears as gross material in the physical body is merely the manifested part of it; behind this are the hidden forces of its being, which are of a spiritual nature. When the ego puts forth its energies in the manner described,it unites itself,not with the outer material manifestation of the physical body,but with the invisible forces which bring that body into being and afterwards cause it to decay. This work of the ego on the physical body can only very partially become clear to man's consciousness in ordinary life. It can become fully clear only when,under the influence of occult science,man consciously takes the work into his own hands. Then he becomes aware that there is a third spiritual principle within him. It is that which occult science calls the _Spirit-Man_,as contrasted with physical man. (In theosophical literature this "Spirit-Man" is known as Atma.)

Again,with regard to the Spirit-Man,it is easy to make a mistake. In the physical body we see man's lowest principle,and on this account find it hard to realize that the work on that body should be accomplished by the highest principle of the human entity. But just because the spirit active within the physical body is hidden under three veils,the highest kind of human effort is needed in order to make the ego one with that which is the
hidden spiritual energy of the body.

Occult science,therefore,represents man as a being composed of many principles. Those of a bodily nature are:

the physical body,
the etheric or vital body,
the astral body.

The soul-principles are:

thc sentient-soul,
the intellectual- or rational-soul,
the consciousness-soul.

It is in the soul that the ego diffuses its light. Of a spiritual nature are:

the Spirit-Self,
the Life-Spirit,
the Spirit-Man.

It follows from what was said above that the sentient-soul and the astral body are closely united and in a certain sense are one. Similarly,the consciousness-soul and the Spirit-Self form a whole,for in the consciousness-soul the spirit shines forth,and thence irradiates with its light the other principles of the human being. Hence occult science also speaks of man's organization as follows. The intellectual-soul is simply called the ego,because it partakes of the nature of the ego,and in a certain sense is the ego,not yet conscious of its spiritual nature. We thus have seven divisions of man:

(1) physical body;
(2) etheric or vital body;
(3) astral body;
(4) Ego;
(5) Spirit-Self;
(6) Life-Spirit;
(7) Spirit-Man.

Even one accustomed to materialistic habits of thought would not find in this sevenfold organization of man the "fanciful magic" often attributed to the number seven,if one would only keep strictly to the meaning of the above explanations without himself injecting arbitrarily the idea of something magical into the matter. Occult science speaks of these seven principles of man in exactly the same way,only from the standpoint of a higher form of observation of the world,as allusion is commonly made to the seven colours that make up white light,or to the seven notes of the scale (the octave being regarded as a repetition of the keynote). As light appears in seven colours,and sound in seven tones,so is the unity of man's nature manifested in the seven principles described. No more superstition attaches to the number seven in the case of occult science than when associated with the spectrum or with the scale.

On one occasion when these facts were put forward verbally,the objection was made that the statement about the number seven does not apply to colours,since there are others beyond the red and violet rays,invisible to the eye. But even in this respect the comparison with colours holds good,for,in fact,the human being expands beyond the physical body on the one side,and beyond the Spirit-Man on the other; only to the methods of spiritual observation of which occult science here speaks,are these extensions of the human being "spiritually invisible," just as the colours beyond red and violet are physically invisible. This explanation becomes necessary,because the opinion so easily arises that occult science does not seriously apply itself to scientific thinking,but treats such matters unscientifically. However,one who carefully considers the meaning of the statements made by occult science will find that in reality it is never at variance with genuine science; neither when it brings forward the facts of natural science as illustrations,nor when its statements are directly connected with natural research.

CHAPTER III. SLEEP AND DEATH

The nature of waking consciousness cannot be fathomed without observing
that condition which man experiences during sleep,and the problem of life cannot be approached without studying death. Any one failing to perceive the importance of occult science may distrust the manner in which it studies sleep and death. Occult science is,however,capable of appreciating the motives from which such distrust arises. For there is nothing incomprehensible in the assertion that man exists for an active, purposeful life,that his acts depend on his devotion thereto,and that absorption in such conditions as sleep and death can result only from a taste for idle dreaming,and can lead to nothing else than vain imaginings.

The refusal to accept anything of so fantastic a nature may readily be regarded as the expression of a sound mind,while indulgence in such "idle dreaming" is accounted morbid,and a pursuit fit only for people in whom the joy and ardour of life are lacking,and who are incapable of "real work." It would be wrong to set this assertion aside at once as an injustice,for it contains a certain grain of truth. It is one quarter truth,and must be completed by the remaining three quarters belonging to it. Now, if we dispute the one quarter which is right,with one who recognizes that one quarter quite distinctly but who does not dream of the
other three quarters,we only rouse his suspicions. For it must be indeed granted absolutely that the study of that which lies hidden in sleep and death is morbid if it leads to weakness or to estrangement from real life. No less must we admit that much of that which has always called itself occult science in the world,and which is even now practised under that name,bears the impression of what is unhealthy and hostile to life; but

this certainly does not spring from _genuine occult science_.

The real fact of the matter is this,that just as a man cannot always be awake,so neither is he sufficiently equipped for the actual conditions of life,in its entire range,without that which occult science has to offer him. Life continues during sleep,and the forces which work and labour during the waking state draw their strength and refreshment from that which sleep gives them. It is thus with the things under our observation in the manifested world. The boundaries of the world are wider than the field of this observation; and what man recognizes in the visible must be supplemented and fertilized by what he is able to know of the invisible world. A man who did not continually renew his exhausted forces by sleep, would bring his life to destruction; and in the same way a view of the world which is not fertilized by a knowledge of the unseen,must lead to a feeling of desolation.

It is similarly so with regard to death. Living creatures fall a prey to death in order that new life may arise. It is occult science which throws light on Goethe's beautiful phrase: "Nature invented Death in order to have much Life." Just as in the ordinary sense there could be no life without death,so can there be no real knowledge of the visible world without insight into the invisible. All discernment of the visible must plunge again and again into the invisible in order to develop. Thus it is evident that occult science alone makes the life of revealed knowledge possible. When it emerges in its true form it never enfeebles life,but strengthens it and ever renews its freshness and health,when,left to its own resources,it has become weak and diseased.

When a man sinks into sleep the connection between his principles changes,
as described earlier in this work. The part of the sleeping man which lies upon his couch comprises the physical and etheric bodies,but not the astral body and not the ego. It is because the etheric body remains bound to the physical body in sleep that the life-activities continue. For the moment the physical body is left to itself,it must of necessity fall into decay. The things that are extinguished in sleep are ideas,pain, pleasure,joy,grief,the ability to express conscious will,and similar facts of existence. But the astral body is the vehicle of all these things. That the astral body,with all its joy and sorrow,its realm of thought and will,is annihilated in sleep is an opinion that cannot be entertained by an unbiased judgment; it exists still,but in another condition. In order that the human ego and the astral body may not only be endowed with pleasure and pain and all the other things we have named, but
also have a conscious perception of them,it is necessary that the astral body should be united with the physical and etheric bodies. This is the case during waking life,but not in sleep. The astral body has withdrawn itself from the other bodies. It has adopted another kind of existence than that which it possesses while united with the physical and etheric bodies. Now it is the task of occult science to study this other kind of existence in the astral body. During sleep,the astral body withdraws from the possibility of external observation and occult science must trace it in its hidden life,until it again takes possession of its physical and etheric bodies on waking.

As in all cases when knowledge of the hidden things and events of life have to be dealt with,clairvoyant observation is necessary for the discovery of the real facts of the sleep state in its true nature,but if that which may be discovered by this means has once been made clear,it is
comprehensible to really unprejudiced thought without further demonstration. For events in the unseen world show themselves by their effects in the manifested world. If what is revealed by clairvoyant vision is an explanation of visible events,such a confirmation by life itself is

the proof which may rightly be demanded. Even one who will not use the means to be given later for the attainment of clairvoyant vision,may have the following experience: he may,in the first place,take the statements of the clairvoyant for granted,and then apply them to the material events within his experience. He will then find that life thereby becomes clear and comprehensible; and the more exact and minute his observations of ordinary life,the more readily will he come to this conclusion.

Even though the astral body during sleep passes through no experiences, though it is not conscious of pleasure,pain,and the like,it does not remain inactive. On the contrary,it is a fact that active work is its function in the sleep state. For it is the astral body which strengthens and recuperates man's forces,exhausted during waking life.. As long as the astral body is united with the physical and etheric bodies it is related to the outer world through these two bodies. They convey to it perceptions
and representations. Through the impressions which they receive from their
surroundings,it experiences pleasure and pain. Now the physical body can be preserved in the form and shape suitable to the individual only by means of the human etheric body. But this human form can be preserved only
by an etheric body which on its part receives corresponding forces from the astral body. The etheric body is the builder,the architect,of the physical body. It can,however,construct in the true sense only when it receives from the astral body the impulse as to the manner in which it must build. In this latter are contained the models,according to which the etheric body gives the physical body its form. During our waking hours these models for the physical body are not present in the astral body,or, at least,only to a certain extent. For in waking life the soul replaces these models with its own images. When a person directs his senses upon
his environment he thus creates in his ideas pictures which are copies of the world around him. In fact these copies at first disturb the prototypes which give the etheric body the impulse to preserve the physical body. Such disturbance could not be present if a man,by virtue of his own activity,could convey to his astral body those pictures which would give the right impulse to the etheric body. Yet this very disturbance plays an important part in human life,and is able to express itself because the models for the etheric body do not come into full play in the waking life. This fact is revealed by "fatigue." Now,during sleep,no external impressions disturb the force of the astral body. Therefore in this condition it can expel fatigue. The work of the astral body during sleep consists in removing fatigue,and it can accomplish this only by leaving the physical and etheric bodies. During waking life the astral body does its work within the physical body; during sleep it works on the latter from without.

For instance,just as the physical body has need of the outer world,which is of like substance with itself,for its supply of food,something of the same kind takes place in the case of the astral body. Let us imagine a physical human body removed from the surrounding world: it would die. That
shows that physical life is an impossibility without the entire physical environment. In fact,the whole earth must be just as it is if physical human bodies are to exist upon it. For,in reality,the whole human body is only a part of the earth,--indeed,in a wider sense,part of the whole physical universe. In this respect it is related in the same sense as,for example,the finger of a hand to the entire human body. Separate the finger from the hand and it cannot remain a finger: it withers away. Such would also be the fate of the human body were it removed from that body of
which it is a member,--from the conditions of life with which the earth provides it. Let it be raised above the surface of the earth but a

sufficient number of miles and it will perish as the finger perishes when cut off from the hand. If this fact is less apparent in the case of a man's physical organism than in that of his finger and his body,it is merely because the finger cannot walk about on the body as man is able to
do on the earth,and because on that account the dependence of the former
is more obvious.

In the same way that the physical body is embedded in the physical world to which it belongs,so does the astral body form a part of its own world, only it is torn out of it in waking life. We can form a clear idea of what happens by having recourse to an analogy. Imagine a vessel filled with water. No one drop is a separate thing in itself within that entire mass of water. But let us take a little sponge and with it suck up a single drop from the whole mass of water. Something of this kind happens to the human astral body on awaking. During sleep it is in a world resembling its own nature. In a certain sense it forms part of it. On awaking,the physical and etheric bodies suck it up: they absorb it; they contain the organs through which it perceives the outer world. In order to achieve this perception it has to leave its own world,for it is in that world alone that it can receive the models which it needs for the etheric body.

Just as food is supplied to the physical body from its surroundings,so are the pictures of the world surrounding the astral body presented to it during the state of sleep. There,indeed,it lives in the universe,beyond the physical and etheric bodies: in that same universe out of which the whole man is born. The source of the images by means of which man receives
his form is in this universe. He is linked in harmony with it; and when he awakens he rises above the surface of this all-pervading harmony to attain external perception. In sleep his astral body returns to the universal harmony. He brings so much strength from it to his bodies on awaking that
he can once more dispense for a time with sojourning in the realm of harmony. The astral body returns during sleep to its home,and,on awaking,brings back into life freshly invigorated forces. That which the astral body thus gains,and brings with it on waking,finds its outer expression in the refreshment afforded by sound sleep.

Further exposition of occult science will show that this home of the astral body is more extensive than that which belongs to the physical body in the narrower sense of the physical environment. Thus,while man as a physical being is a member of this earth,his astral body belongs to worlds in which other heavenly bodies besides our earth are included. During sleep,therefore,--(this can be made clearas we have said,only by further explanations)--it enters a world to which other stars than the earth belong. In recognition of the fact that man lives during sleep in a world of stars,that is,in an astral world,occult science calls that principle of man which has its real home in that "astral" world and which, every time it returns to the sleep state,draws renewed force from that world,the _astral body_.

It should be superfluous to point out that a misunderstanding might easily arise with regard to these facts; in our time,however,when certain materialistic modes of representation exist,it becomes quite necessary to draw attention to them. In quarters where such representation prevails it may,of course,be said that such a thing as fatigue can be scientifically investigated only in accordance with physical conditions. Even if the learned are not yet unanimous with regard to the physical cause of fatigue,one thing is quite firmly established; we must accept certain physical processes which lie at the root of this phenomenon. It would be well,however,if it were recognized that occult science does not in any way oppose this assertion. It admits everything that is said in this connection,just as it is admitted that for the physical erection of a house one brick must be laid upon another,and that when the house is finished its form and construction can be explained by purely mechanical laws. But the thought of the architect is necessary for the building of the house. This cannot be discovered merely by examination of physical laws.

Just as the thought of the creator of a house stands behind the physical laws which make it explicable,so too,behind what is affirmed,with perfect accuracy by physical science,stands that of which occult science treats. This comparison is of course often put forward when the justification for a spiritual background to the world is in question; and it may be considered a trivial one. But what is important in such matters is not familiarity with certain conceptions,but that the proper weight should be given them in establishing a fact. One may be prevented from doing this simply because contrary ideas have so much power over the judgment that this weight is not felt.

Dreaming is an intermediate state between sleeping and waking. What dream
experiences offer to thoughtful observation is the many-coloured interweaving of a picture-world,which nevertheless conceals within itself some sort of law and order. At first this world seems to have an ebb and flow,often in confused succession. Man in his dream-life is set free from the laws of waking consciousness which bind him to sense-perception and the laws of reason. And yet dreams have some sort of mysterious law, attractive and fascinating to human speculation,and this is the deeper reason why the beautiful play of imagination lying at the root of artistic feeling is always apt to be compared to dreaming. We need only recall a few characteristic dreams to find this corroborated. A man dreams,for example,that he is driving off a dog that is attacking him. He wakes,and finds himself in the act of unconsciously pushing off part of the bedclothes which had been lying on an unaccustomed part of his body and which had therefore become oppressive. What is it that dream-life makes, in this instance,out of an incident perceptible to the senses? In the first place,it leaves in complete unconsciousness what the senses would perceive in the waking state. But it holds fast to something essential--namely,the fact that the man wishes to repel something; and round about this it weaves a metaphorical occurrence.

The pictures,as such,are echoes of waking life. There is something arbitrary in the way in which they are drawn from it. Every one feels that the same external cause may conjure up various dream-pictures. But they give symbolic expression to the feeling that one has something to ward off. The dream creates symbols; it is a symbolist. Inner experiences can also be transformed into such dream-symbols. A man dreams that a fire is
crackling beside him; he sees flames in his dream. He wakes up feeling that he is too heavily covered and has become too warm. The feeling of too
great warmth expresses itself symbolically in the picture. Quite dramatic experiences may be enacted in a dream. For example,some one dreams that
he is standing on the edge of a precipice. He sees a child running toward it. The dream makes him experience all the tortures of the thought--if only the child will not be heedless and fall over into the abyss! He sees it fall,and hears the dull thud of the body below. He awakes,and perceives that an object which had been hanging on the wall of the room has become
unfastened,and made a dull sound by its fall. This simple event is expressed in dream-life by one which unravels itself in exciting pictures. For the present,it is not at all necessary to engage in reflection as to the reason why,in the last example,the moment of the falling of a heavy object expresses itself in a series of events which seem to spread

themselves over a certain length of time; it is only necessary to keep in view that the dream transforms into a picture that which would present itself to the waking sense-perception.

We see that the moment the senses cease their activity,creative power asserts itself in man. It is the same creative power which is present in absolutely dreamless sleep,and at that time recuperates man's exhausted forces. For this dreamless sleep to take place,the astral body must be withdrawn from the etheric and physical bodies. During the dream-state it is so far separated from the physical body as to have no further connection with the organs of sense; but it still maintains a certain connection with the etheric body. The capacity for perceiving the experiences of the astral body by means of pictures is due to this connection which it maintains with the etheric body. The moment this connection also ceases,the pictures sink into the obscurity of unconsciousness and dreamless sleep has set in.

The arbitrary and often nonsensical element in dream-pictures arises from
the fact that the astral body cannot,on account of its separation from the sense-organs of the physical body,relate its pictures to the correct objects and events of the outer environment. It is especially illuminating,in this matter,to examine a dream in which the ego is,as it were,split up; as,for example in the case of a person who dreams that he is a schoolboy and cannot answer the propounded question,while immediately afterward as the teacher,he himself answers it. The dreamer, being unable to make use of his physical organs of perception,is not able to connect both occurrences with himself,as the same individual. Therefore,in order to recognize himself also as a permanent ego,man must
first be equipped with outer organs of perception. Only when he has acquired the faculty of self-consciousness without the aid of such organs will the permanent ego also become perceptible to him outside his physical body. Clairvoyant consciousness has to acquire this faculty,and the method of doing so will be treated in detail later in this work.

Even death takes place for no other cause than a change in the connection
of the principles of man's being. And what is visible to clairvoyant observation with regard to death may also be seen in its effects in the manifested world; in this case also,an unbiased judgment will find the teachings of occult science confirmed by observing external life. The expression of the invisible in the visible is,however,less evident with regard to these facts,and there is greater difficulty in feeling the full importance of that which in the events of outer life endorses the statements of occult science in this domain. These statements may be supposed to be mere pictures of fancy,even more readily than many other things that have been dealt with in this work,if we shut ourselves off from the knowledge that everywhere in the visible is contained an unmistakable foreshadowing of the invisible.

On the approach of sleep,only the astral body is released from its connection with the etheric and physical bodies,which still remain united,whereas at death the separation of the physical from the etheric body takes place. The physical body is abandoned to its own forces,and must therefore disintegrate as a corpse. At death the etheric body finds itself in a condition in which it has never been before during the time between birth and death,--with the exception of certain abnormal conditions
to be dealt with later. That is to say,it is now united with the astral body in the absence of the physical body; for the etheric and astral bodies do not separate immediately after death; they are held together for a time by the agency of a force the presence of which can be easily understood; for were this force not present the etheric body could not

detach itself from the physical body. It would remain bound to the latter, as is shown in the case of sleep,when the astral body is not able to rend asunder these two principles of man's being. This force comes into action at death. It releases the etheric from the physical body,so that the former remains united to the astral body. Clairvoyant observation shows that this connection varies with different people after death. The time of its duration is measured by days. For the present,this period of time is mentioned only for the sake of information.

Subsequently,the astral body is also released from the etheric body and goes on its way alone. During the union of the two bodies,the individual is in a state which enables him to be aware of the experiences of his astral body. As long as the physical body is there,the work of reinforcing the wasted organs has to be begun from without,as soon as the astral body is liberated from it. When once the physical body is separated,this work ceases. Nevertheless,the force which was expended in this way while the man was asleep,continues after death and can now be applied to some other end. It is now used for making the astral body's own experiences perceptible. During his connection with his physical body the outer world enters man's consciousness in images; after the body has been laid aside,that which is experienced by the astral body,when it is no longer connected with sense organs,with this outer physical world, becomes perceptible. At first it has no new experiences. Its connection with the etheric body prevents it from experiencing anything new.

What,however,it does possess,is _memory_ of its past life. The etheric body still being present causes that past life to appear as a vivid and comprehensive panorama. That is man's first experience after death. He sees his life from birth to death spread out before him in a series of pictures. Memory is only present in the waking state,when during life man is united with his physical body,and it is present only to the extent allowed by that body. Nothing is lost to the soul that has made an impression on it during life. Were the physical body a perfect instrument for the purpose,it would be possible,at any moment during life,to conjure up the whole of the past before the eyes of the soul. At death there is no longer any obstacle to this. As long as the etheric body remains,there exists a certain degree of perfection of memory. But this disappears according to the degree in which the etheric body loses the form which it possessed while united with the physical body,and which resembles that body. This is the very reason why the astral body separates,after a time,from the etheric body. It can remain united with the latter only so long as the form of the etheric body corresponds with that of the physical body.

During the period of life between birth and death,separation of the etheric body occurs only in exceptional cases,and for no longer than a brief space of time. If,for example,a man exposes one of his limbs to pressure,part of his etheric body may become separated from the physical one. We say on such occasion that the limb has "gone to sleep," and the peculiar sensation we feel results from the separation of the etheric body. (Of course a materialistic manner of explanation may here again deny the invisible behind the visible and say: all this arises merely from the physical disturbance caused by the pressure.) Clairvoyant vision can see in such a case,how the corresponding part of the etheric body extends beyond the physical limb. Now if a man experiences an unusual shock,or something similar,such a separation of the etheric body from a large part of the physical body may result,for a short time. That is the case when a man,for some reason or other,is suddenly brought face to face with death,--for example when drowning,or threatened by a fatal accident when mountaineering. What is related by people who have had such experiences comes,in fact,very near the truth,and can be ratified by clairvoyant observation. They declare that in such moments their whole lives pass before their minds as though in a huge memory-picture.

Out of the many examples which might here be adduced,allusion will be made to one only,because it originates from a man whose mode of thought
would make everything said here about such things seem pure fancy.(5) Moriz Benedict,the distinguished criminal anthropologist and eminent investigator in many other realms of natural science,relates in his _Reminiscences_ an experience of his own,--to the effect that once,when on
the point of drowning in a bath he had seen his whole life pass before his memory as though in a single picture. If other people describe differently the pictures seen by them under similar circumstances,and even in such a way that they seem to have little to do with the events of their past life,that does not contradict what has been said; for the pictures which arise in the quiet abnormal condition during the separation from the physical body are sometimes at first sight,unintelligible in their relation to life. Correct observation,however,would always recognize this relationship.

Neither is it an objection if,for example,some one who was once on the point of drowning did not experience what has been described; for it must be borne in mind that this can happen only when the etheric body is really separated from the physical body,--when,moreover,the former is still united with the astral body. If,through the fright,a loosening of the etheric and astral bodies also takes place,the experience is not forthcoming,because then complete unconsciousness ensues,as in dreamless
sleep.

Immediately after death the events of the past appear as though compressed
by the memory into a picture. After its separation from the etheric body, the astral body pursues its further wanderings alone. It is not difficult to realize that everything continues to exist which,by means of its activity,the astral body has made its own during its sojourn in the physical body. The ego has to a certain extent elaborated the Spirit-Self, the Life-Spirit,and the Spirit-Man. As far as these are developed,they do not owe their existence to the organs present in the different bodies, but to the ego; and it is precisely this ego which needs no outer organs for perception; nor does it require any such organs in order to retain possession of what it has made one with itself. It might be objected: "Why then is there no perception during sleep of the developed Spirit-Self, Life-Spirit,and Spirit-Man?" For this reason that the ego is chained to the physical body between birth and death. Even though,during sleep,it is out of the physical body with the astral body it nevertheless remains closely connected with the physical body; for the activity of the astral body is directed toward the physical body. On this account the ego is relegated to the outer world of sense for its observations,and cannot receive spiritual revelations in their direct form. Not until death do these revelations come within reach of the ego,because by means of death
the ego is freed from its connection with the physical and etheric bodies. Another world may flash upon the consciousness the moment it is withdrawn
from the physical world which during life monopolizes its activity.

Now there are reasons why even at this juncture all connection with the outer physical world of sense does not cease for man. That is to say, certain desires remain which sustain the connection. There are desires which man creates just because he is conscious of his ego as the fourth principle of his being. These desires and wishes,springing from the

existence of his three lower bodies,can operate only in the external world,and cease to operate when these bodies are cast aside. Hunger is caused by the external body; as soon as that external body is no longer connected with the ego,hunger ceases. Now,had the ego no further desires
than those springing from its own spiritual nature,it might at death draw full satisfaction from the spiritual world into which it is transplanted. But life has given it other desires as well. It has kindled in it a longing for pleasures only to be enjoyed by means of physical organs, although these pleasures themselves do not originate in the nature of those organs. It is not only the three bodies which demand gratification from the physical world,but the ego itself finds pleasures in that world, for the enjoyment of which there exist no means whatever,in the spiritual world.

During life the ego has two kinds of desires: those that spring from the bodies and must therefore be gratified within the bodies,but which must also come to an end with their disintegration; and those that arise from the spiritual nature of the ego. As long as the ego lives in the bodies, those cravings are satisfied by means of the bodily organs. For in the manifestations of the bodily organs the hidden spiritual element is at work,and the senses receive something spiritual as well,in everything of which they are cognizant. That spiritual element is also present after death,although in a different form. Everything spiritual that the ego longs for while in the world of sense,it still possesses when the senses are no longer there.

Now if a third kind of wish were not added to these two,death would mean only a transition from desires which may be satisfied through the senses to such as are fulfilled by the revelation of the spiritual world. The third kind of desire is that which is created by the ego during life in the sense-world,because it finds pleasure in that world,even when no spiritual element is revealed in it. The humblest pleasures may be manifestations of the spirit. The satisfaction afforded a starving creature by taking food is a manifestation of the spirit,for by taking food something is thereupon brought about without which,in a certain sense,the spiritual nature could not develop. But the ego can go beyond the pleasure,which in this case is the outcome of necessity. It may even long for the delicious food quite apart from the service rendered to the spirit by taking nourishment.

It is the same with other things in the sense-world. Desires are created in this way which would never have appeared in the sense-world if the human ego had not been incorporated in it. Neither do such desires arise from the spiritual nature of the ego. The ego must have pleasures of the senses as long as it lives in the body,even though it be for the very reason that its own nature is spiritual. For the spirit manifests in material things,and the ego is enjoying nothing less than spirit when it surrenders itself to that element in the sense-world which is irradiated by the light of the spirit. Moreover,it will continue to enjoy this light even when the senses are no longer the medium through which the spiritual
rays pass. But there is no fulfillment possible in the spiritual world for desires in which the spirit is not living even in the world of the senses.

When death takes place,the possibility of gratifying desires of this description is cut off. Pleasure in good things to eat can be induced only by the presence of the physical organs required for their consumption,--the
palate,tongue,and so forth; but when man has laid aside his physical body he no longer possesses these organs. If,however,the ego still craves that kind of pleasure the craving must remain unsatisfied. As long as this pleasure corresponds to the spiritual need,it is caused only by the presence of the physical organs; but should it happen that the ego has

created the desire without serving the spirit in so doing,it retains it after death in the form of a craving which thirsts in vain for gratification. We can form an idea of what man then experiences only by imagining some one suffering from burning thirst in a region where,far and wide,there is no water to be found. This is the predicament of the ego after death,as long as it retains ungratified desires for the pleasures of the outer world,and has no organs by means of which to satisfy them. Of course the burning thirst,serving as a comparison for the condition of the ego after death,must be thought of as enormously increased,and it must be imagined as extending to all desires still existing,for which all possibility of gratification is lacking.

The next condition of the ego consists in freeing itself from this bond of attraction to the outer world. With regard to this world,it has to attain purification and liberation. It must be cleansed of all wishes which it has created while in the body,and which have no native rights in the spiritual world. As an object is caught and burned up by fire,so is the world of desire,described above,broken up and destroyed after death. A vista is then opened into that world which occult science calls the "consuming fire" of the spirit. This fire seizes upon desires of a sensual nature which however are not rooted in the spirit. Revelations of this kind which occult science is bound to make with regard to such events may
appear hopeless and terrible. It may seem a fearful thing that a hope for the realization of which sense-organs are required,should after death be transformed into despair,and that a wish that can be fulfilled only by the physical world should be changed into torturing deprivation. Yet we can hold such an opinion only as long as we fail to realize that the wishes and desires seized by the "consuming fire" after death do not,in a higher sense,represent forces beneficial to life but destructive to it.

By means of these forces the ego binds itself to the sense-world more closely than is necessary,in order to draw from it all the experience it requires. For the sense-world is a manifestation of the hidden and spiritual world which lies behind it; and the ego could never attain spiritual happiness through the bodily senses,which are the only form in which the spiritual can be manifested,unless it utilized the senses to seek the spiritual element in sense-experience. Nevertheless,the ego loses sight of the true spiritual reality in the physical world to such an extent that it experiences sensual desires irrespective of the needs of the spirit. If sense pleasure,as the expression of the spirit,serves to raise and develop the ego,any pleasure which is not an expression of the spirit warps and impoverishes it. Even though such a desire finds the means of its gratification in the sense-world,still its destructive effect upon the ego is thereby in no way diminished; but it is not until after death that its disastrous effects become apparent.

For this reason a man may,by gratifying such desires,create,during his life,new and similar desires,wholly unaware that he is enveloping himself in a "consuming fire." What becomes visible to him after death is only what already surrounded him during his life,and by thus becoming visible it at once appears in its salutary and beneficent effect. A human being who loves another is certainly not attracted merely by that part of him which is perceptible to the physical senses--the only part which is cut off from observation after death--but after death,just that part of the dear one then becomes visible for the perception of which the physical organs were only the means. The one thing,in fact,which would prevent a man from beholding his friend clearly is the presence of desires which can be satisfied only by means of physical organs. Unless these desires are extinguished,he can have no conscious perception of his friend after death. When looked at in this light,the terrible and hopeless character which after-death experiences might assume for man,according to the descriptions given by occult science,becomes changed into one which is thoroughly satisfying and consoling.

Now the first after-death experiences differ entirely in yet another respect from those during life. During the time of purification man lives, as it were,backwards. He lives over again the whole span of his life since birth; beginning with the events immediately preceding his death, and reversing the order of his experiences,he goes through them again until he reaches back to childhood. In this process he sees with spiritually enlightened eyes all those things which were not inspired by the spiritual nature of the ego,with the difference that he now experiences these things in reverse order.

For instance,a man who died in his sixtieth year,and who at the age of forty had,in an outburst of anger,caused some one either physical or mental pain,will go through this experience again when,on the return journey of existence after death,he reaches that point in his fortieth year; but now he does not experience the satisfaction which his attack had
afforded him during life; instead,he experiences the pain which he inflicted upon the other man. It may at once be seen,however,that whatever pain he feels in the after-death experience is caused by a desire of the ego arising only from the outer physical world; in reality the ego does not only injure another by the indulgence of such a desire,but it also injures itself; although the injury to itself is not apparent during life.

After death,however,the whole of the harmful world of desires becomes visible to the ego,which then feels attracted toward every being or object which had kindled the desire,in order that this may be destroyed in the "consuming fire" by the same means that created it. When man,on his return journey,reaches the moment of his birth,then only have all such desires been purged in the purifying flames,and henceforth nothing remains to hinder him from devoting himself entirely to the spiritual world. He enters upon a new phase of existence. In the same way that he laid aside his physical body at death and,soon afterward,his etheric body,so does that part of his astral body dissolve which can only live in the consciousness of the outer physical world.

Occult science,therefore,recognizes three corpses,--the physical, etheric,and astral. The period at which the last is cast off by man is marked by the time of purification,which amounts to about one third of the time elapsed between birth and death. The reason why this is so can only be explained later,when the course of human life is examined from the standpoint of occult science. To clairvoyant observation,astral corpses,which have been cast off by human beings passing from the state of purification into a higher existence,are constantly visible in the world surrounding man,in exactly the same way that physical corpses,in places inhabited by men,are apparent to physical observation.(6)

After purification an entirely new state of consciousness begins for the ego. Whereas before death the outer perceptions must flow to the ego,in order that upon these perceptions the light of consciousness might be able
to fall,so now in like manner from within,streams a world which attains consciousness. The ego is living in this world also between birth and death; only then this world is clothed in the manifestations of the senses. It is only when the ego,freed from all the ties of sense,turns inward to behold its own "holy of holies," that its true innermost nature, which had hitherto been obscured by the senses,is revealed to it. In the same way that the ego is recognized inwardly before death,so,after death and purification,is the spiritual life inwardly revealed to it in all its fulness. This revelation really takes place immediately after the etheric body is laid aside; but it is obscured by the dark cloud of desires turned toward the outer world. It is as though a world of spiritual bliss were invaded by black demoniacal phantoms,caused by those desires which are

being destroyed by the "consuming fire." Indeed,these desires are not mere phantoms,but real entities,which become apparent immediately after the ego is deprived of physical organs,and is thus able to discern those things which are of a spiritual nature. These entities have the appearance of distorted caricatures of the objects with which the individual had formerly become acquainted through his senses.

Clairvoyant observation shows that this place of purging fire is peopled by beings whose appearance may well seem horrifying and painful to spiritual vision,whose pleasure seems to consist in destruction,and whose passions impel them to evil-doing of such a description that the evil of the physical world seems insignificant in comparison. Whatever desires of the kind described above are brought into that world by man, are looked upon by these beings as food,by means of which their powers are continually strengthened and invigorated.

The picture thus sketched of a world imperceptible to the senses may seem less incredible if we look with an unprejudiced eye on part of the animal world. What is a fierce,devouring wolf,from a spiritual point of view? What does it reveal to us through that which our senses perceive? Nothing else than a soul that lives in desires,and acts by desire. The external form of the wolf may be called an embodiment of those desires; and if man had no organs with which to perceive that form,if its desires appeared invisibly in their effects,--if,therefore,a force invisible to the eye were prowling about,and might be the cause of all that happened through the visible wolf,--he would still be forced to recognize the existence of a creature corresponding to it. Now the beings of the region of purifying fire are not visible to the physical eye,but to clairvoyant sight only; but their effects are clearly apparent. They bring about the destruction of the ego when it gives them nourishment. These effects are clearly visible if what began as a pleasure leads to excess and debauchery.

For even what is perceptible to the senses would attract the ego only in so far as the pleasure had its root in the ego's own nature. The animal is prompted by desire for that in the outer world which its three bodies crave. Man has higher enjoyments,because to the three principles of his bodily nature is added the fourth,the ego. But if the ego seeks a gratification which does not tend toward the maintenance and development of its nature but to its destruction,then such a craving can be neither the effect of its three bodies,nor that of its own nature,but can only be caused by beings,concealed from the senses in their true form,but able furtively to approach that higher nature of the ego,and excite in it desires which,though it is cut off from the senses,can still be satisfied only by means of sense-organs.

For there are beings which feed on passions and desires of a worse kind than those of an animal nature,because they do not expend themselves on objects of the senses but seize upon the spiritual element and drag it down to a sensual level. Therefore the forms of such beings are more hideous,more horrible,to spiritual sight than are the forms of the fiercest animals,in which after all only passions rooted in the senses are incarnated. And the destructive forces of these beings immeasurably surpass any destructive rage existing in the animal world as perceived by the senses. Occult science must in this way enlarge man's view so as to include a world of beings standing,in a certain respect,lower than the visibly destructive animal world.

When man has passed through the world of purification after death,he finds himself in a world the contents of which are spiritual,and which also creates in him longings which can be satisfied only by spiritual things. But even now man distinguishes between that which properly belongs to his ego and what forms the environment of that ego--one might say,its spiritual outer world. Only that,of which he becomes sensible in this environment,pours in upon him in the same way that the perception of his own ego poured in upon him during his sojourn in the body. Whereas man's environment in the life between birth and death speaks to him through his bodily organs,after death when all the bodies are laid aside the language of his new environment penetrates directly into the innermost sanctuary of the ego. Man's whole environment is now filled with beings of a like nature with his ego,for only an ego has access to an ego. Just as minerals,plants,and animals surround man in the sense-world,and compose it,so,after death,is he surrounded by a world composed of beings of a spiritual nature.

Yet he takes something with him into this world which is not part of his environment there; it is what the ego has experienced in the world of the senses. First of all,the sum of these experiences appeared,as a comprehensive memory-picture,immediately after death,while the etheric body was still united to the ego. The etheric body itself is then,indeed, laid aside,but something of the memory-picture remains with the ego as an everlasting possession. Just as though an extract or essence were made out of all the events and experiences which a man encounters between birth and death,so might we describe that which is left behind. It is the spiritual product of life,its fruit. This product is of a spiritual nature. It contains everything spiritual which is revealed through the senses,yet this spiritual treasure could not have been gathered save by life in the sense-world.

This spiritual fruit of the sense-world becomes after death the ego's own inner world. With it the ego enters a world,which consists of beings who reveal themselves in the same and only manner in which man in his innermost depths,can become conscious of his own ego. As a plant seed, which is the essence of the whole plant,grows only when buried in another world,the earth,so now that which the ego brings from the sense-world gradually unfolds itself as a seed under the influence of the spiritual environment in which it has been planted. Occult science can,of course, only portray in pictures what happens in this "spirit-world;" still those pictures present themselves as absolute reality to the clairvoyant's sight,when he investigates invisible happenings,corresponding to those which are visible to the physical eye. Whatever of that world can be described,may be visualized by comparison with the world of the senses for although it is of a purely spiritual nature,it nevertheless resembles the physical world in certain respects. Just as,for instance,in the physical world,a color appears when some object impresses the eye,so in the spirit-world a color appears to the ego when a being acts upon it. But this latter phenomenon is perceived in the same manner as the ego can be perceived inwardly between birth and death. It is not as though the light outside fell within upon the man,but as though another being directly affected the ego,causing the latter to picture this influence in a colour-form.

Thus do all things in the spiritual environment of the ego find expression in a world of coloured rays. As their origin is of a different kind,it goes without saying that these colours of the spiritual world are also of a somewhat different character from physical colours. A similar thing is true of other impressions received by man in the world of sense. But it is the sounds of the spiritual world that most nearly resemble the impressions of the sense-world; and the more at home a man becomes in the spiritual world,the more he realizes it as a life of self-determined motion,which may be compared with the sounds,and the harmony of sounds, of the physical world. Only he does not feel the tones as something approaching an organ from outside,but as a force streaming forth into the outer world through his ego. He feels the sound just as in the sense-world he feels his own speech or song,only he knows that in the spiritual world these sounds,streaming out from him,are at the same time the manifestations of other beings,who are pouring themselves into the world through him.

A still higher manifestation takes place in the spirit-land when the sound becomes the "spiritual word." Then there streams through the ego not only the pulsing life of another spiritual being,but such a being itself communicates its own inner nature to the ego; and then,when the spiritual word streams through the ego,two beings live in one another,without that separating element which every companionship in the sense-world must carry with it. And this is really the nature of the communion of the ego with other spiritual beings after death.

There are three regions in the spiritual world,which may be compared to the three divisions of the physical sense-world. The first region is in a certain respect the "solid land" of the spiritual world,the second the "sphere of ocean and river," and the third the "atmospheric region." That which assumes physical form on earth,so that it can be perceived by physical organs,in accordance with its spiritual nature,is to be seen in the first region of the spirit-world. There,for instance,may be seen the force that fashions the form of a crystal. Only what is there revealed is the opposite of that which appears in the sense-world. In that world the space which is filled by a mass of rock appears to spiritual sight as a kind of hollow space; but round about this hollow is seen the force which fashions the form of the rock. The colour of the rock in the sense-world appears in the spiritual world as its complementary colour; thus a red stone is green when seen from the spirit-world,a green stone is red,and so on. Other qualities also appear in their opposites. Just as stone, masses of earth,and like materials make up the solid land--the continental region of the world of sense--so do the structures described above compose the solid land of the spiritual world.

All that is life in the sense-world belongs to the ocean-region of the spiritual world. To the physical eye,life appears in its effects in plants,animals,and men. To spiritual vision,life is a flowing substance,like oceans and rivers,diffused through the spirit-world. A still better comparison is that of the circulation of the blood in the body; for whereas seas and rivers are seen to be irregularly distributed in the physical world,a certain regularity in distribution of the flowing life reigns in the spirit-world,as in the circulation of the blood. This "flowing life" is simultaneously heard as spiritual sound.

The third region of the spirit-world is its "atmosphere." What is known in the physical world as "feeling" is also present there,permeating everything like the air on the earth. We must imagine a rushing sea of feeling. Pain and sorrow,joy and rapture,flow through this region,like wind and storms in the atmosphere of the physical world. Imagine a battle fought on earth. There confront one another not merely human forms,as seen by the physical eye,but feelings opposed to feelings,passions to passions; pain fills the battlefield just as much as do the forms of men. All that is seething there of passion,pain,and the joy of victory is not only perceptible in its effects as revealed to the physical senses; it may

be seen with the spiritual senses as an atmospheric process in the spirit-world. Such an event in the spiritual world is like a thunderstorm in the physical,and the perception of these events may be compared to the
hearing of words in the physical world. For this reason it is said that as the air envelops and permeates earthly things,so do "interweaving spiritual words" pervade the beings and events of the spirit-world.

And still further observations are possible in this spirit-world. What may be compared to light and heat in the physical world is there too. That which permeates everything in the spirit-world,as earthly things and beings are permeated by heat,is the world of thought itself. There, however,thoughts must be regarded as living and independent beings. What
is understood by man in the manifested world as thought is but a shadow of
what lives as a thought-being in the spirit-world. Imagine thought,as it now exists in man,raised out of him and as an active,energetic being, endowed with an inner life of its own,and you have a feeble illustration of that which fills the fourth region of the spirit-world. In the physical world between birth and death what man understands as thought is but the
manifestation of the thought-world as it is able to mould itself by means of the instruments afforded by the bodies. All such thoughts cherished by man,that carry with them an enrichment of the physical world have their origin in this region. By such thoughts are meant not only the ideas of great inventors and men of genius; but those ideas found in every individual which he does not owe solely to the external world,but through which he,so to speak,transforms that world.

In so far as feelings and passions are concerned,the cause of which lies in the outer world,these feelings are perceptible in the third region of the spirit-world; but everything which so lives in a man's soul as to make him a creator,--influencing,transforming and fertilizing his environment,--is manifest in its original and intrinsic form in the fourth division of the spirit-world.

That which exists in the fifth region may be compared to physical light. In its archetypal form it is wisdom in manifestation. Beings who diffuse wisdom throughout their surroundings,as the sun pours light on physical beings,belong to this realm. Whatever is illuminated by their wisdom stands forth in its true meaning and significance for the spiritual world, just as the colour of a physical object is seen when the light falls upon it. There are still higher regions of the spirit-world,which will be described later in this work.

Into this world the ego is plunged after death,together with the results it carries with it out of physical life. And these results are still united with that part of the astral body which is not cast off at the end of the time of purification. In fact,only that part falls away which,in its desires and wishes,turned,after death,toward physical life. The plunging of the ego into the spiritual world,with what it has acquired in the physical world,may be compared to the planting of a grain of seed in the soil in which it can mature. As the grain of seed draws substances and
forces from its surroundings in order that it may develop into a new plant,so the condition of the ego,when implanted in the spiritual world, is one of development and growth.

Hidden within that which is perceived by an organ,there lies the force whereby that same organ was formed. The eye perceives light; but without
light there would be no eye. Creatures spending their lives in darkness do not develop organs of sight. Thus the whole of man's physical body is

created out of the hidden forces of that of which he becomes conscious through his bodily organs. The physical body is built up by the forces of the physical world,the etheric body by those of the life-world,and the astral body is formed out of the astral world. Now when the ego is transferred to the spirit-world it is met by just those forces which remain hidden to physical perception.

What appear to man's view in the first region of the spirit-world are the spiritual beings that are always surrounding him,and that have built up his physical body. Thus in the physical world man perceives nothing but the manifestations of those spiritual forces which have formed his own physical body. After death he is in the very midst of these moulding forces,which,previously hidden,now appear to him in their true forms. In the same way,in the second region,he is in the midst of the forces by which his etheric body was organized,and in the third region there pour in upon him the potencies out of which his astral body was formed. The higher regions of the spirit-world also direct toward him those forces from which he was built in the life between birth and death.

These denizens of the spiritual world are at present working in co-operation with that which man has brought with him as the product of his last life,which now becomes a germ; and through this co-operation man is,first of all,built up anew as a spiritual being. The physical and etheric bodies are still joined in sleep; the astral body and the ego are, it is true,outside them,but still connected with them. Whatever influences the astral body and the ego receive,in such a state,from the spiritual world,can serve only to recuperate the forces exhausted during the waking state.

But when the physical and etheric bodies have been laid aside,and,after the time of purification,also those parts of the astral body still bound by their desires to the physical world,then everything pouring in upon the ego from the spiritual world is not only a reforming but a reorganizing force. After a certain period,to be dealt with in later chapters,the ego again gathers round it an astral body which will be able to live in such an etheric and physical body as man possesses between birth and death. A man can once more pass through birth and renew his earthly existence,in which,however,will be incorporated the results of his former life. Until the rebuilding of his astral body,man is a witness of his reconstruction. As the powers of the spirit-world are not manifested to him through external organs,but from within outward,like his own ego in self-consciousness,he is able to observe that manifestation as long as his attention is not turned to an outer world of perception. But from the moment that the astral body is reconstituted,his attention is turned outward; the astral body once more craves an outer etheric and physical body. It is thus turned away from the inner revelations. For this reason there is now an intermediate state,during which man is immersed in unconsciousness. Consciousness can emerge again
in the physical world only when the necessary organs for physical perception are formed.

During this period,in which consciousness illuminated by inner perception ceases,the new etheric body begins to link itself to the astral and man can once again enter a physical body. In the linking together of these two bodies only such an ego could consciously take part as had of itself created the Life-Spirit and Spirit-Man out of the creative forces,hidden in the etheric and physical bodies. Until the individual has evolved as far as this,beings further advanced than himself in evolution must guide this linking together. The astral body is guided,by such beings as these, to parents through whom it may be endowed with the appropriate etheric and
physical bodies. Before the attachment of the etheric body takes place, something of very great importance happens to the man who is about to

re-enter physical existence.

In his former life he created disturbing forces,which were revealed to him on the journey retraced after death. Let us again take an example. He caused some pain in an outburst of anger in the fortieth year of his former life. After death,the other's pain came before him as a force which had interfered with the evolution of his ego. It is likewise with all such events of his former life. On his re-entrance into physical life these hindrances to his evolution confront the ego anew. As,on the threshold of death,a sort of memory-picture arose before the human ego, so there now arises a vision of the life approaching. Again he sees a picture,this time showing all the obstacles which he has to clear away, if he is to advance in evolution. And what he thus sees becomes the starting-point for forces which he must bring with him into his new life. The picture of the pain he has caused the other man becomes a force which
impels the ego,on entering life again,to make amends for this pain. Thus the previous life has a determining effect on the new one. The deeds of the new life are in a certain way caused by those of the former life. This connection,following the law,between an earlier and later existence is to be looked upon as the "Law of Destiny"; it has become usual to designate it "Karma," a term borrowed from oriental wisdom.

The building up of a new set of bodies,however,is not the only task incumbent upon man between death and a new birth. While this building up is taking place,man lives outside the physical world. That world, however,continues to evolve during this time. The surface of the earth changes in comparatively short periods of time. What aspect did those regions which are now occupied by Germany bear a few thousand years ago?
When man appears on earth in a new existence,the earth rarely looks the same as it did at the time of his last incarnation. During his absence from the earth all sorts of changes have occurred. Now hidden forces are also at work in this alteration of the face of the earth,proceeding from that very world in which man finds himself after death, and he himself must co-operate with these forces in the transformation of the earth. He can do so only under the direction of Higher Beings until,by the creation of his Life-Spirit and Spirit-Man,he has acquired a clear perception of the connection between the spiritual and its expression in the physical. But he takes part in the transformation of earthly conditions. It may be said that during the period between death and a new birth,man so transforms the earth that its conditions are in keeping with what he has evolved in himself. If we look at a given place on the earth at a definite moment,and see it again after a long lapse of time,under entirely changed conditions,the forces which have wrought the change have proceeded from those who are now dead. And it is this kind of connection which exists between them and the earth until the time of rebirth.

Clairvoyant observation sees in all physical existence the manifestation of a hidden spiritual element. To physical observation it is the light of the sun,climatic changes,and so on,that effect the transformation of the earth,but to clairvoyance it is the force of the dead that acts in the rays of light which fall on the plant from the sun. The clairvoyant sees how human souls hover about plants,how they change the surface of the earth. Not alone upon himself nor upon the preparations for his own new earthly existence,is man's attention bestowed after death,--No,he is called upon then to work upon the outer world,just as he is in life between the time of his birth and death.

Not only does the life of man affect the conditions of the physical world from the spirit-land; but vice versa,activity during physical existence has its effects in the spiritual world. An example may explain what happens in this respect. A bond of love exists between mother and child. This love arises from a mutual attraction caused by the forces of the

sense-world. But in the course of time it changes. A spiritual tie gradually grows out of the sense-bond,and this spiritual tie is not created for the physical world only but for the spirit-world as well. The same applies to other ties. Whatever is created in the physical world by spiritual entities continues to exist in the spiritual world. Friends who were closely united in life belong to each other in spirit-land also,and when their bodies are laid aside they are in much more intimate communion
than during physical life. For as spirits they exist for each other in the same way as,in the above description,spiritual beings reveal themselves to others by inner manifestation; and a tie created between two persons brings them together again in a new life. Thus in the truest sense of the word we may speak of finding one another again after death.

What has once happened to a man between birth and death and from then till
a new birth,repeats itself. Man returns to earth again and again when the fruit he has earned in a physical life has ripened in the spirit-world. It is not,however,a case of repetition without beginning or end; but man has emerged out of other forms of existence and passed into those which run their course in the manner just described,and he will again in the future pass into other forms. A viewpoint of these transition stages will be gained when the evolution of the universe in connection with man is subsequently considered from the standpoint of occult science.

The occurrences between death and a new birth are of course still more concealed from outer sense-observation than is the spiritual foundation underlying manifested life between birth and death. This sense-observation can see only the effects of that portion of the hidden world where they impinge upon physical existence. With regard to this the question must arise whether man,on entering this life at birth,brings with him any results from the events described by occult science as having taken placc between his last death and re-birth. If one finds the shell of a snail in which there is no tracc of the animal he will,in spite of that,recognize that this snailshell was formed by the activity of an animal,and he cannot believe that the shell constructed a form for itself,by means of mere physical forces.

In the same way one who studies a man during life,and finds something in him which cannot be due to _this_ life,might reasonably admit that it arises from what occult science describes,if by doing so an explanatory light is thrown on what is otherwise inexplicable.

Here,too,the unseen causes might appear intelligible to rational sense-observation from their visible effects,and whoever observes life with absolute impartiality will find that,with every fresh observation, this appears to be more and more true. The important question,however,is how to find the right point of view from which to observe their effects in life. Where,for example,are the effects of that to be found which occult science describes as incidents of the time of purification? How are the effects of the experience which,according to occult investigations,man undergoes in purely spiritual regions,manifested after this time of purification?

Problems enough press upon every serious and profound student of life in this domain. We see one man born in want and misery,endowed only with inferior abilities,so that on account of these facts,which are incident to his birth,he appears predestined to a miserable existence. Another, from the first moment of his life,is tended and cherished by loving hands and hearts; brilliant talents are unfolded in him; his gifts point to a successful and satisfactory career. Two opposite views may be taken when
met by such questions as these. The one will adhere to what the senses perceive and what the understanding,relying on these senses,is able to

comprehend. This view will admit no problem in the fact that one man is born fortunate and the other unfortunate. Even if the word "chance" is not used,there will be no question of thinking that such things are brought about through any law of cause and effect. And with regard to talents and abilities,such a view will consider them as "inherited" from parents, grandparents,and other ancestors. It refuses to seek the causes in spiritual events which the man himself met with before birth--regardless of
heredity--and by means of which he shaped his talents and abilities.

Another view would find no satisfaction in such an interpretation. It would assert that even in the manifested world nothing happens in definite places or surroundings without our having to presuppose causes for the event in question. Even though in many cases such causes have not yet been
investigated,they are there. An Alpine flower does not grow in the lowlands. Its nature has something which associates it with Alpine regions. Just so must there be something in a man which determines his birth in a certain environment. Causes belonging to the physical world alone are not sufficient to account for this. To a more profound thinker such an explanation appears in somewhat the same light as when one has dealt another a blow,the motive for which is not attributed to the feelings of the one but is to be explained by the physical mechanism of the hand.

Any explanation of abilities and talents solely by "heredity" is to such a viewpoint equally unsatisfactory. It is true one may say: "See how certain talents are inherited in families." During two and a half centuries musical talents were inherited by members of the Bach family. Eight mathematicians sprang from the Bernouilli family,to some of whom quite different occupations were assigned in their childhood; but the inherited talents always drove them to the family vocation. It may be further pointed out how,by an exact investigation of the line of ancestry of a person in one way or another the gifts of this person have shown themselves in the forefathers,and only represent the sum of inherited talents. Whoever holds the latter of the two views above indicated will be sure not to let such facts pass unnoticed,but to _him_ they cannot mean the same as they do to one who relies for his interpretation on the events of the world of sense alone. The former will point out that inherited talents can no more of themselves,combine into a complete personality than can the metal parts of a watch fit themselves together. And if objection is made that the co-operation of the parents may possibly produce the combination of talents,--that this as it were,takes the place of the watchmaker,--he will reply: "Look impartially at what is new in every child-personality,at that which is absolutely new; that cannot come from the parents,for the simple reason that it does not exist in them."

Inaccurate thinking may create much confusion in this domain. It is still worse when those who hold the second view are set down by the supporters
of the first as opponents of what is,after all,borne out by "ascertained facts." But it may well be that the latter have not the slightest intention of denying the truth or value of those facts. For instance,they see that a definite mental aptitude or predisposition is "inherited" in a family,and that certain gifts accumulated and combined in one descendant result in a remarkable personality. They are perfectly willing to acquiesce when it is said that the most celebrated name seldom stands at
the beginning,but at the end of a line of descent. But it should not be taken amiss if they are compelled to form very different opinions on the subject from those of people who are determined to accept nothing but material evidence. To the latter it may be said that it is true a man shows the characteristics of his ancestors,because the "spirit-soul", which enters upon physical existence at birth,draws its bodily substance

from that which heredity bestows on it. But this says nothing more than that a being shows the peculiarities of the body into which it has descended.

It is no doubt a singular--a trivial--comparison,but the unprejudiced person will not deny its justification,when one says that a human being, who shows the qualities of his forefathers,proves the origin of the personal qualities of that human being as little as the fact that man is wet because he has fallen into the water,proves something regarding his inner nature. And it may further be said that if the most celebrated name stands at the end of a line of family descent,it shows that the bearer of that name needed that particular ancestry to build the body necessary for the expression of his whole personality. But it is no proof that his actual personal qualities were transmitted to him; such a statement is,on the contrary,opposed to sound logic. If personal gifts were inherited, they would be found at the beginning of a line of descent,(7) and starting from that point be transmitted to the descendants. As,however,they stand at the end,it is evident that they are _not_ transmitted.

Now it is not to be denied that those who speak of a spiritual causality in life have contributed no less to bringing about confusion of thought. Far too much generalizing and vague discussion comes from this quarter. To
say that a man's personality is a combination of inherited characteristics may certainly be compared with the assertion that the metal parts of a watch have fitted themselves together. It must also be admitted that,with regard to many assertions about a spiritual world,it is as though some one said that the metal parts of a watch cannot put themselves together in
such a way as to enable the hands to move forward; some intelligence must
therefore be present to effect this forward movement. In face of such an assertion, _he_ certainly builds on a far better foundation who says: "Oh! I care nothing for your 'mystical' beings who move the hands forward. What
I want to know is the mechanical construction by means of which the forward movement of the hands is achieved." It is by no means a question of merely knowing that behind a mechanism,a watch for instance,there is an intelligence (the watchmaker); it can only be of importance to know the ideas in the watchmaker's mind which preceded the construction of the watch. These thoughts may be rediscovered in the mechanism.

Mere dreaming and imagining about the supersensual only result in confusion,for they are not calculated to satisfy opponents. The latter are right in saying that such general allusions to super-physical beings are not at all conducive to an understanding of facts. Of course,such opponents might also say the same of the _exact_ statements of occult science. But,in that case,it may be pointed out that the effects of hidden spiritual causes are seen in manifested life. Let us assume for the moment that what occult science asserts,proven by observation,is correct:--that a man has gone through a time of purification after death, and that during this period he has experienced in his soul how a certain deed,performed by him in a former life,was a hindrance to his progressive evolution. While he was undergoing this experience,the impulse arose in him to make amends for that deed. He brings this impulse
with him into a new life and its presence produces a tendency in his nature which draws him into conditions rendering the amendment possible.--Taking into consideration a number of such impulses,we have the cause for a man's being born into an environment corresponding to his destiny.

We may deal in the same way with another assumption. Let us again accept

as correct the assertion of occult science that the fruits of a past life are incorporated in man's spiritual germ,and that the spirit-land in which man finds himself,between death and a new life,is the region in which these fruits ripen,and are transformed into talents and capabilities which will appear in a new life and will form the personality so that it appears as the effect of what was gained in a former life. It will become evident to any one who accepts these hypotheses and,bearing them in mind,surveys life impartially,that while,by their means,all material facts may be appreciated in their full truth and significance,at the same time everything becomes intelligible which,if only material facts were relied upon,must forever remain incomprehensible to one whose
attention is turned toward the spiritual world. And more important still, that illogical reasoning of the kind indicated above will disappear, namely,--that because the most distinguished name in a line of descent stands at the end of it,its bearer must have inherited his gifts. Life becomes logically comprehensible through the supersensual facts ascertained by occult science.

Yet another weighty objection may be raised by the conscientious seeker after truth who desires to find his way to facts and has no experience of his own in the supersensual world. It may be urged that it is inadmissible to accept the existence of facts,of any kind,simply because by means of them something may be explained which is otherwise unintelligible. Such an objection is meaningless to one who knows the corresponding facts from supersensual experience,and in later chapters of this book the path will be indicated that may be followed in order to gain knowledge not only of the spiritual facts herein described,but also of the law of spiritual causation as a personal experience. Any one,however,who is not willing to enter upon this path may find the above objection important; and what can be said against it is also of value to one who is resolved to follow the path indicated. For if it is received in the right spirit,it is the very best preliminary step that can be taken on this path. It is perfectly true that one ought not to accept a statement about which one is otherwise
ignorant merely because,by means of it,something otherwise inexplicable can be explained,but in the case of alleged spiritual facts the matter is different. If such statements are accepted,the intellectual consequence is not only that,by their means,life becomes intelligible,but that through admitting these hypotheses into the thought-world,experiences of quite a new kind are induced.

Take the following case. Something befalls a man which causes him extremely painful sensations. He may meet the situation in one of two ways. He may submit to the occurrence as something affecting him painfully,and abandon himself to the painful sensation,even becoming absorbed in his grief; or he may meet it in another way. He may say: "It is really I myself who in a former life set the force in motion which has brought me into contact with this thing. I have really brought it on myself." He may then awaken in himself all the feelings which such a thought brings in its train. It goes without saying that the thought must be entertained with perfect seriousness,and with the utmost possible force,if it is to have such consequences in the life of sensation and feeling. One who succeeds in this will meet with an experience which may be best illustrated by a comparison. Let us suppose that two men have each
a stick of sealing wax in his hand. One begins reflecting upon its inner nature. These reflections may perhaps be very wise,but if the "inner nature" did not show itself in any way,some one might easily retort; "That is all imagination." The other,however,rubs the sealing wax with a woolen rag,and then shows that it attracts small particles. There is an important difference between the thoughts which have passed through the
first man's head and his reflections,and those of the second. The

thoughts of the first man had no actual result; those of the second have called out a hidden force,consequently something real.

The same thing happens with regard to the thoughts of a man in whose mind the idea arises that in a former life he has set going within himself the force which causes him to experience a certain event. The mere conception of this stirs up strength within him which enables him to face the event in quite a different manner from that in which he would have met it without entertaining such an idea. It dawns upon him that an event which he would otherwise have looked upon as an accident was really a necessity and he will immediately see that he had the right thought,because this thought had the power to reveal the facts to him. If such inner processes are repeated they will grow into a source of inner power and thus prove their truth by their fruitfulness; and little by little,this truth is found to be powerfully effective. Such processes have a salutary effect on body,soul,and spirit,--nay,they help life forward in every way. Man becomes aware that in this manner he takes the right position with regard to life's continuity; whereas,by taking into consideration only the one life between birth and death,he is the victim of a delusion.

Such an entirely inner proof of spiritual causation can of course be acquired only by each one for himself,in his own inner life. But it is in every one's power to have it. Those who have not acquired it certainly cannot judge of its convincing force; but those who have acquired it can scarcely entertain any further doubt in the matter. And there is no reason for surprise that this should be so. It is only natural that what is so wholly bound up with the constitution of man's inmost being and personality can be adequately proven only by inner experience. On the other hand,it cannot be alleged that because such a matter corresponds to inner experience it must therefore be settled by every one for himself, and that it is no subject for occult science. It is certain that every one must undergo the experience for himself,just as each must see for himself the proof of a mathematical problem. But the path by which such an experience may be gained is open to all,just as the method of proving a mathematical problem is available to every one.

It ought not to be denied--apart from clairvoyant observation of course--that by means of the force producing power of the corresponding thoughts,the just cited proof is the only one which stands firm before all unprejudiced logic. All other considerations are no doubt very important,but in all of them there will be something on which an opponent might seize as a point of attack. Surely one who has acquired a fairly impartial way of looking at things will find something in the possibility and actual fact of man's education,which has the power of logical proof that a spiritual being is struggling for existence within the sheath of the body. He will compare animals with man and say to himself that at the birth of the former there appears certain definite qualities and capacities as something,decisive in itself,which plainly shows how it has been designed by heredity and how it will unfold itself in the outer world. We see how a young chicken carries out life's functions in the appointed way from its birth; but by means of education something comes into touch with man's inner life which is independent of any connection with his heredity,and he may be in a position to assimilate the effects of such external influences. The educator knows that such influences are met by forces coming from man's inner nature. If this is not the case,all instruction and training are meaningless. The unprejudiced educator finds the boundary line between inherited talents and those inner forces of the man himself which shine through them and originate in former lives,to be very sharply marked. It is true,we cannot bring forward such weighty

proofs for things of this kind as we can for certain physical facts,by means of scales; but then these are just the intimate things of life,and one who has the power to appreciate such impalpable proofs will find them
convincing--even more convincing than palpable reality.

That animals may be trained,and thus,to a certain extent,acquire qualities and capacities by education,is no objection to one who is able to see reality,for apart from the fact that transitional stages are met with all over the world,the results of training an animal by no means fade away with its individual existence,as is the case with a man. What is more,the fact has been emphasized that faculties acquired by domestic animals through intercourse with man are transmitted,that is to say, continue in the species,not in the individual. Darwin describes how dogs fetch and carry without having been taught to do so,or without having seen it done. Who would make such an assertion with regard to human education?

Now there are thinkers whose observations have led them beyond the opinion
that a man is built by purely inherited forces from without. They rise to the thought that a spiritual being,an individuality,exists before life in the body,and fashions it; but many of them find it impossible to conceive that there are repeated earthly lives,and that the fruits of former lives are moulding forces during the intermediate state between two
lives. Let us take one instance from among the ranks of these thinkers. Immanuel Hermann Fichte,son of the great Fichte,in his _Anthropology_ (p. 528) gives the observations which led him to the following conclusion:

"Parents are _not_ generators in the full sense of the word. They supply organic substance,and not alone this,but also that intermediate element of mental and sense nature which appears in temperament,colouring of character,definite tendencies,and so on,the common source of which proves to be 'imagination' in the wider sense indicated by us. In all these elements of personality,the mingling and particular combination of the souls of the parents is unmistakable; it is therefore a perfectly well-grounded assertion that this combination is simply the result of procreation,even if we regard procreation,as we must do,as really a soul-process. But the real ultimate centre of the personality is just what is lacking here; for a deeper and more searching observation reveals the fact that even those peculiarities of disposition are but a covering and an instrument for the containing of the individual's really spiritual and ideal capabilities,and are qualified to aid these in their development or to hinder them,but in no wise able to originate them." It is further stated in the same work (p. 532): "Every individual pre-exists as regards the fundamental form of his spirit,for no individual,from a spiritual point of view,resembles another,just as no species of animal resembles another species."

These thoughts reach only far enough to allow a spiritual being to come into the human body; but as the forces shaping such a being are not derived from causes existing in former lives,it would be necessary that, each time a fresh personality appears,a spiritual being should come forth from a Divine First Cause. With this hypothesis there would be no possibility of explaining the relationship which certainly exists between the potentialities struggling out of man's innermost being,and that which is forcing its way thither from his external earthly environment during life. Man's innermost being,issuing in the case of each single person, from a Divine First Cause,would find what confronts him in earthly life quite strange and foreign. Only then would this not be the case--as,in fact,it is not--if there had already been a connection between the inner man and the outer world,and if the inner man were not living in it for the first time.

The unprejudiced educator may undoubtedly observe clearly that he impresses the consciousness of his pupil with something taken from life's experiences which in itself is foreign to his merely inherited qualities, but which,howeverappears to him as if the work out of which these experiences arise,had been done by him in the past. Only repeated lives on earth,in conjunction with the facts set forth by occult science as taking place in spiritual regions between two earthly lives,--only this view can afford a satisfactory explanation of present human life looked at from every side. I say expressly "present" human life,for occult investigation shows that the cycle of earthly life certainly had a beginning,and at that time man's spiritual being,which later entered a bodily frame,existed under different conditions. In the following chapter we shall go back to this primeval condition of human existence. When it has been shown,from the reports of occult science how human beings received their present form in connection with the evolution of the earth, it will also be possible to indicate more precisely how the spiritual germ of man's being descends from superphysical worlds into a bodily form,and how the spiritual law of causation,or "human destiny," is developed.

CHAPTER IV. THE EVOLUTION OF THE WORLD AND MAN

From the foregoing observations it will be seen that man's being is built up of four principles: the physical body,the etheric body,the astral body,and the vehicle of the ego. The ego works within the three other principles,and transforms them. By means of this transformation,are formed on a lower level,the sentient-soul,the rational- or intellectual-soul,and the consciousness-soul: on a higher level of human existence,are formed the Spirit-Self,the Life-Spirit,and Spirit-Man. The relations existing between these human principles and the whole universe are of a most varied character and their evolution is related to that of the universe. By studying this evolution an insight is obtained into the deeper mysteries of man's being.

It is clear that human life is related in the most varied ways to the environment or dwelling place in which it evolves. Physical science, through the facts presented to it,has already been driven to the opinion that the earth itself,man's dwelling place in the broadest sense of the word,has undergone evolution. Science points to former conditions of the earth when man,in his present form,did not yet exist on our planet and it shows how man has slowly and gradually evolved to his present condition
from primitive states of civilization. Physical science,therefore,comes also to the conclusion that there is a connection between man's evolution and that of the heavenly body on which he lives--the earth.

Occult science traces this connection by means of a knowledge which obtains its data from observation quickened by spiritual organs of perception. It traces man backwards in his course of development,and the fact becomes evident to occult science that the real inner spiritual being of man has progressed through a series of lives on this earth. Occult research arrives in this way at an epoch far back in the remote past,when for the first time that inner being of man made its entry into "external life" as we understand it. It was in this first earthly incarnation that the ego began to function in the three bodies--the astral body,the etheric or vital body,and the physical body; and it then carried over the results of that activity into its next life.

If in our investigation we proceed backwards,in the manner indicated,as far as that epoch,we discover that the ego finds an earth condition in which the three bodies,physical,etheric,and astral,are already developed and in which they bear a certain relation to each other. The ego is,for the first time,united with the being composed of these three bodies; and henceforth takes part in the further evolution of the three bodies. Hitherto,up to the stage at which that ego came in touch with them,they had evolved without a human ego.

Occult science must now go back still farther in its researches if it is to answer the questions,"How did the three bodies reach that stage of evolution at which they were able to receive an ego within them?" and "How did that ego itself come into being and acquire the capacity for working within these bodies?"

It is possible to answer these questions only when the gradual development of the earth-planet itself is studied from the occult point of view. By such investigation we arrive at a beginning of the earth-planet. That method of examination which is based only on the facts of the physical senses cannot arrive at conclusions concerning the beginning of the earth. A certain point of view which avails itself of such conclusions arrives at the result that everything material on the earth was formed out of a primeval essence,or vapour. It is not the purpose of this work to enter more fully into such conceptions of our planet's origin; for in occult science the important matter is not merely to inquire into the material processes of the earth's evolution,but first and foremost to discover the spiritual causes lying behind what is material.

If we see before us a man raising his hand,we may consider his action in two different ways: we may examine the mechanism of the arm and the rest of the organism,in order to describe the process as it takes place from the purely physical standpoint,or we may direct the spiritual vision to what takes place in the man's soul and there discover what constitutes the inner motive for raising the hand. In this way an investigator,trained in occult research,sees spiritual processes behind all the events of the physical sense-world. In his eyes all transformations of the material part of the earth-planet are manifestations of spiritual forces lying behind what is material.

But if occult observation of this kind goes farther and farther back in the life of the earth it comes to that point in evolution at which material things first came into being. The material element is evolved out of the spiritual. Up to this point the spiritual element was the only one existing. By occult investigation the spiritual element is perceived,and the observer can see how it becomes partly condensed,as it were,into matter. We have before us a process which is taking place--on a higher level--much as though we were observing a lump of ice being formed by artificial means in a vessel of water. Just as we see the ice being condensed out of what was previously only water,so may we,by means of occult observation,watch the condensation of what was previously entirely spiritual,so to speak,into material things,processes,and beings. In this way the physical earth-planet was evolved out of a cosmic spiritual essence; and everything that is combined materially with the earth-planet has been condensed out of what was previously united with it spiritually. We must not,however,think that _everything_ spiritual was at any one time changed into material form; but,in the latter we have before us merely the transformed portions of what was originally spiritual. Thus, even during the period of material evolution,it is always Spirit that is really the guiding and ruling principle.

It is obvious that the mode of thought which restricts itself to the

processes of physical sense--and to what reason is able to infer from them--is incapable of expressing an opinion about the spiritual element of which we are speaking. Let us assume that a being might exist to whose senses ice would be perceptible,but not the finer condition of water, from which ice is detached by refrigeration. For such a being,water would be non-existent,and could become visible only when parts of it had been transformed into ice. In the same way,the spiritual element behind earthly processes remains hidden from one who only admits the existence of
what is perceptible to his physical senses. And if,from the physical facts which he now perceives,he draws correct conclusions about earlier conditions of the earth-planet,he can penetrate only as far as that point in evolution at which the previous spiritual element was partially condensed into material substance. Such a method of observation no more
discovers the spirit previously existing,than it perceives the spirit which even now rules unseen behind the world of matter.

Not until we come to the last chapters of this work can we deal with those
methods by which man acquires the faculty of looking back,by means of occult perception,upon those earlier conditions of the earth which are now under discussion. For the present we shall merely intimate that the facts concerning the primeval past have not passed beyond the reach of occult research. If a being comes into corporeal existence his material part perishes after physical death. But the spiritual forces,which from out their own depth gave existence to the body,do not "disappear in this way." They leave their traces,their exact images behind them impressed upon the spiritual ground-work of the world. Any one who is able to raise his perceptive faculty through the visible to the invisible world,attains at length a level on which he may see before him what may be compared to a
vast spiritual panorama,in which are recorded all the past events of the world's history. These imperishable traces of everything immaterial are called in occult science the "Akashic Records."

Here it must once more be repeated that investigations of the supersensible realms of existence can be carried on only with the aid of spiritual perception,and consequently can be instituted in the sphere now under consideration,only by reading the Akashic Records above-mentioned. Nevertheless,what was said earlier in this book in a similar instance holds good here. Supersensible facts are only to be investigated by supersensible perceptions; but once investigated and communicated by occult science,they may be grasped by the ordinary powers of thought,if these are honestly exercised without bias. In the following pages the various conditions of the earth's evolution,as given by occult science, will be detailed. The transformation of our planet will be traced down to the conditions of life in which we now find it. Any one who surveys what comes before him at the present time merely through the evidence of his senses,and then lends an ear to what occult science has to say on the subject,namely:--how that which now lies before him has been evolved from
a far distant past,--will be able,if his thought is genuinely unbiased,to say to himself: "In the first place,what occult science reports is quite logical; in the second place,I can,if I assume the reports of occult investigation to be correct,understand how things have become as they now
appear." By "logical" is not meant,in this connection,of course,that errors might not be made from a logical standpoint in some description given by occult research. We are here speaking of "logic" as it is understood in the ordinary life of the physical world. Just as a logical demonstration is accepted there as it is in physical research,even though a single investigator,in a certain domain of facts,may make illogical statements,so is it also with regard to occult science. It may even

happen that an investigator who possesses the power of vision in supersensible spheres may make mistakes in a logical presentment of them, and may be corrected by another who has no supersensible perception, but has,none the less,a capacity for sound thinking. In reality,nothing of any weight can be said against the logical deductions of occult science. And it ought to be unnecessary to insist that nothing can be adduced,on purely logical grounds,against the facts themselves. In the domain of the physical world it can never be proved by logic,but only by ocular demonstration,whether or no there is such an animal as a whale; similarly,supersensible facts can be known only through occult perception.

But it cannot be sufficiently emphasized that an obligation is laid upon the explorer of supersensible regions,before he determines to approach the invisible worlds with his own power of perception,to acquire first of all the aforementioned logical faculty,and this is none the less essential if he recognizes that the world,manifest to his senses,will become comprehensible if he accepts the communications of occult science as correct. All experiences in the supersensible world are nothing but an uncertain--nay,a dangerous--groping in the dark if we despise the method of preparation which has been described. Therefore in this book the facts concerning the supersensible processes of the earth's evolution will first be given,before the path leading to the attainment of supersensible knowledge is dealt with.

We have also,it is true,to take into account that the man who,by sheer thinking,comes to accept what supersensible research has to impart,is by no means in the same position as one who listens to the account of a physical occurrence which he is unable to see. For thinking is in itself a supersensible activity. Materialistic thinking cannot of itself lead to supersensible phenomena. But if thought is directed to supersensible matters through the accounts given of them by occult science,it grows by its own activity into the supersensible world. What is more,one of the very best ways of acquiring supersensible perception is to grow into the higher worlds by meditation upon what has been communicated by occult science. For such a mode of entry insures great clearness of perception. For this reason such thinking is regarded by a certain school of occult investigation as a most valuable first step to take in occult training.

It will be readily understood that it is impossible to mention in this book all the details of the earth's evolution,as it has been spiritually perceived by occultists,in order to illustrate the way in which the supersensible world is reflected in the manifested. Nor was this what was intended when it was said that the unseen may everywhere be demonstrated by its manifest effects. It was meant rather that everything that man encounters may,step by step,become clear and comprehensible if he brings manifested events under the illumination of occult science. Only in a few characteristic instances will reference be made in the following pages to confirmations of the invisible by the manifest,in order to show how this may be done everywhere in the course of practical life,if desired.

Pursuing the evolution of the earth backward according to the above method of scientific spiritual investigations we arrive at a spiritual condition of our planet. But if we go farther back along this path of research,we find that everything spiritual had previously passed through a kind of physical incarnation. Thus we come upon a bygone physical planetary condition,which was afterwards spiritualized,and subsequently transformed into our earth by repeated materialization. Our earth is therefore presented to us as the reincarnation of a very ancient planet. But occult science can go back still farther; and it then finds the whole process twice repeated. Thus,our earth has passed through three previous planetary conditions separated by intermediate spiritual conditions of rest. The physical substance,however,proves to be finer and finer the farther back we follow the incarnations.

Now man,in the form in which he is at present evolving,makes his first appearance upon the fourth of the planetary incarnations which have been described,the Earth proper. And the essential characteristic of his form is that it is composed of four principles,the physical,etheric,and astral bodies and the ego. But that form could not have appeared if it had not been prepared by the preceding events of evolution. The method of preparation was that,in the earlier planetary incarnation,beings were evolved who already had three of the present four principles of man: the physical,etheric,and astral bodies. These beings who,in a certain sense,may be called man's ancestors,had as yet no ego,but they developed the three other principles and their mutual relationship to such a point that they became sufficiently mature to receive an ego. Thus man's ancestor attained to a certain degree of maturity of his three principles during the earlier planetary incarnation. This condition became spiritualized; and out of it a new planetary condition was formed in which man's matured ancestors were contained,as it were,in embryo. Because the whole planet had passed through a process of spiritualization and had appeared in a new form,it offered those embryos,with their physical, etheric,and astral bodies,which were contained therein,not only the opportunity of again evolving up to the level on which they had previously stood,but the further possibility,after having arrived at that level,of reaching out beyond themselves through receiving the ego.

The evolution of the Earth divides itself,therefore,into two parts. During the first period the Earth itself appears as a reincarnation of the previous planetary state. But that recurring state is a higher one than that of the previous incarnation,in consequence of the intervening period of spiritualization. And the Earth contains within itself the germs of man's ancestors belonging to the earlier planet. These were first developed up to the level they had previously reached. The attainment of this level marks the end of the first period. But now,owing to its own higher stage of evolution,the Earth is able to carry the germs still higher,that is,to qualify them for receiving the ego. The second period of the Earth's evolution is that of the development of the ego in the physical,etheric,and astral bodies.

In the same way that man had been thus carried a stage farther by the evolution of the Earth,so also had this been the case during the earlier planetary incarnations. For man had in some measure existed as early as the first of these. Light is therefore thrown on the present constitution of man if his evolution is followed back to the far-remote past of the first of the planetary incarnations mentioned above.

In occult science the first of these is called _Saturn_; the second is termed _Sun_; the third,_Moon_; and the fourth is the _Earth_. It must be distinctly understood that these occult terms are not to be in any way associated with the names used to designate the members of the present solar system.(8) In occult science Saturn,Sun,and Moon are merely names for bygone forms of evolution through which the Earth has passed. In the course of the following account it will be shown what relation these worlds of remote antiquity bear to the celestial bodies composing the present solar system.

The relationship of the four planetary incarnations previously mentioned, can here be only briefly sketched; for the events,the beings and their destiny on Saturn,Sun and Moon were in truth,just as varied as they are on the Earth itself. Therefore only a few characteristics of these conditions can be chosen to illustrate just how these earth conditions have evolved out of earlier ones. In this connection,one should bear in mind that the further back we go the more dissimilar to the present ones do these conditions become. And yet they can only be described by making use of ideas borrowed from existing conditions of the earth. If,for instance,light,heat,etc.,are mentioned in connection with these earlier conditions,it must not be overlooked that they are not exactly the same as that which we now term light and heat. And yet such terminology is accurate,for the clairvoyant observer of earlier stages of evolution perceives something that has developed into the light and heat of the present time. And one who follows the descriptions thus given by occult science will,from the inner relation of these things,easily be able to form such perceptions as correspond to those events which have taken place in a primeval past.

Of course there will be considerable difficulty in treating of those planetary conditions which preceded the Moon incarnation. For during the latter,conditions prevailed which bore,at least to a degree,some resemblance still to earthly conditions. When one attempts to describe these conditions one finds that such resemblances to the present time form
a certain basis on which may be expressed in clear concepts the observations made through clairvoyance. It is quite different when the Saturn and Sun evolutions are to be described. In that case,what lies before clairvoyant observation is utterly different from the objects and beings now belonging to the sphere of human life. And this difference makes it exceedingly difficult to bring the corresponding facts of primeval times within the scope of clairvoyant consciousness at all.

Since however the present constitution of man cannot be understood without
going back to the Saturn state,the description therefore must be given. And surely no one will misunderstand such a description who keeps in view
the existence of the difficulty,and the fact that owing to it much that is said must be in the nature of a suggestion or hint of the facts in question,rather than an exact description of them.

The physical body is the oldest of the present four principles of man's being. It is also the one,which,in its way,has attained the greatest perfection. Occult research shows that this part of man already existed during the Saturn evolution. It will be shown in the following account that the form taken by the physical body on Saturn was,of course, something quite different from the present physical body of man. The earthly physical human body,from its nature,can only exist by being in connection with the etheric and astral bodies and the ego,in the manner described earlier in this book. Such a condition did not as yet exist on Saturn. The physical body was then passing through the first stage of its evolution,without having a human etheric body,an astral body,or an ego incorporated in it.

During the Saturn evolution it was growing ripe for the reception of an etheric body. For that purpose Saturn had eventually to pass into a spiritual condition,and then to be reincarnated as the Sun. During the

Sun incarnation the physical body developed again to the stage it had reached on Saturn as from a germ brought over and only then could it be inter-penetrated by an etheric body. By means of this incorporation of an etheric body,a change took place in the nature of the physical body; it was raised to a second stage of perfection. A similar thing took place during the Moon evolution. Man's ancestor,as he had developed himself when passing from the Sun to the Moon,incorporated in himself the astral body. As a result,the physical body was changed for the second time,and thus raised to its third stage of perfection; at the same time the etheric body was likewise changed,and passed to its second stage of perfection. On the earth the ego was incorporated in man's ancestor,now composed of
the physical,etheric,and astral bodies. Thereby the physical body reached its fourth stage of perfection,the etheric body its third,and the astral body its second stage; the ego is only now at the first stage of its existence.

If we give ourselves up to an unprejudiced examination of man's nature, there will be no difficulty in acquiring a correct idea of these different stages of perfection of his separate principles. For this purpose we have merely to compare the physical with the astral body. It is true,the astral body,as a psychic principle,stands on a higher level of evolution than the physical body. And in future ages,when the former has been perfected,it will be of very much more consequence to man's complete being than the present physical body. Yet,in its own way,the latter has reached a certain high degree of perfection. Consider the marvelous wisdom
with which the structure of the heart is planned,the amazing structure of the brain--nay,even of part of a single bone,such as the upper end of the thigh bone. In the end of this bone we find a net-work or scaffolding, wonderfully constructed and composed of delicate spicules and lamellę. The
whole is so arranged that with the least expenditure of material the most effective action on the joint-surfaces is obtained--hence the most efficient distribution of friction and a proper freedom of movement. Thus wise arrangements are found in the parts of the physical body. And if we go on to observe the harmonious co-operation of the part with the whole, we shall find that it is certainly true that this principle of man's being is perfect and it does not affect the question that in certain parts something apparently useless appears,or that disturbances of structure or
functions may take place. It will even be found that such disturbances are in a way only the necessary shadows of the wisdom-filled light which is poured out over the whole physical organism.

Now compare with this the astral body as the medium or vehicle of pleasure
and pain,desires and passions. What uncertainty rules in it with regard to pleasure and pain; how the desires and passions,of which it is the scene,run counter to the higher goal of man; how senseless they often are. The astral body is only now on its way to attain the harmony and inner poise already possessed by the physical body. Similarly it might be shown that the etheric body is certainly more perfect in its own way than the astral but less perfect than the physical body. And it will equally result from a corresponding study of the ego that this,the real kernel of man's being,is now only at the beginning of its evolution. For how much has already been accomplished of its mission,that of transforming the other principles of man's being in order that they may become a revelation of the ego's own nature?

The result of an outer examination of this kind is intensified for the occult student by something else. It might be pointed out that the physical body is attacked by diseases. Now occult science is in a position to show that a large proportion of all diseases owe their origin to the

fact that the perverse actions and mistakes of the astral body are transmitted to the etheric body,and indirectly through the etheric, destroy the perfect harmony of the physical body. The deeper connection, which can here be only hinted at,and the true cause of many of the conditions of disease,elude that kind of scientific observation which confines itself solely to the facts obtained by means of the physical senses. The connection in most cases comes about in such a way that an injury to the astral body does not cause manifestations of disease in the physical body in the same incarnation in which the injury takes place,but in a later one. Hence the laws now under consideration have a meaning only
for one who is able to admit that human earth-life is repeated again and again. But even if deeper knowledge of this kind is rejected,ordinary observation of life makes it plain that human beings indulge in far too many pleasures and desires which undermine the harmony of the physical body. And the seat of pleasure,desire,passion,is not in the physical but in the astral body. The latter is still so imperfect,in many respects,that it is able to destroy the harmony of the physical body.

It should also be mentioned here that such explanations as these are by no
means intended as proofs of the assertions of occult science about the evolution of the four principles of man's being. The proofs are drawn from spiritual research,which shows that the physical body has behind it a transformation,enacted four times,into higher degrees of perfection,and that man's other principles have been perfected to a lesser degree,as has been described. It is desired merely to indicate here that these communications made by spiritual research relate to facts which are visible in their effects even to ordinary observation,in the degrees of perfection reached by the physical body,etheric body,and so forth.

If we wish to draw an approximately true picture of the conditions prevailing during the Saturn evolution,we must take into account the fact that while it lasted,there were virtually,as yet,none of the things and creatures existing which now belong to the earth and are included in the mineral,vegetable,and animal kingdoms. The beings of these three kingdoms were formed during later periods of evolution. Of all the earthly beings physically perceptible today,man alone existed at that time and of him only the physical body existed as described. But there are at present belonging to the earth not only the denizens of the mineral,vegetable, animal and human kingdoms,but other beings as well,not manifesting in a physical embodiment. Such entities were also present during the Saturn evolution,and their activity on the Saturn scene of action brought about the subsequent evolution of man.

If the organs of spiritual perception are directed,not to the beginning and end,but to the middle period of evolution of this Saturn incarnation, we find there a condition which consists principally of heat. Nothing is to be found composed of gaseous,fluid,or even solid constituents. All these states appear only in later incarnations. Let us assume that a human
being,with the present organs of sense,were to approach the Saturn condition as a spectator. None of the sense-impressions possible to him would confront him there except the feeling of warmth,or heat. Suppose such a being approached this Saturn; he would only sense,upon entering the space occupied by it,that it was in a different degree of heat from the rest of surrounding space. But he would not find that portion of space by any means equally warm throughout,for warmer and colder parts would
alternate in the most complicated manner. Radiating heat would be felt along certain lines. And not only straight lines,but regular figures would be formed by the variation in heat. Something like a cosmic being,

organically constructed in itself, would be discerned, appearing in changing conditions, and consisting only of heat.

It is difficult for a man of the present day to form an idea of anything consisting only of heat, for he is not accustomed to think of heat as something self-existent, but as a perceptible quality of warm or cold gaseous, liquid, or solid bodies. To one who has adopted the physical conceptions of our time it will seem particularly absurd to speak of heat in the foregoing manner. He will, perhaps, say: "There are solid, liquid, and gaseous bodies; but heat only denotes a condition assumed by one of these three bodily forms. If the smallest particles of gas are in motion, the movement will be felt by heat. Where there is no gas, there can be no movement, consequently no heat."

To an occult investigator the fact appears differently. To him heat is something of which he speaks in the same sense as he speaks of gases, of liquids, or of solid bodies. To him it is simply a still finer substance than gas. And gas to him is nothing but condensed heat, in the same sense that liquid is condensed vapour, or a solid body condensed liquid. Thus the occultist speaks of heat bodies just as he does of bodies formed of gas and vapour.

If we are to follow the spiritual investigator into this region, it is however, necessary to admit that there is such a thing as psychic perception. In the world, as it presents itself to the physical senses, heat appears entirely as a condition of solid, liquid, or gaseous bodies; but that condition is merely the outward appearance of heat, or the effect of it. Physicists speak only of this effect of heat, not of its inner nature. Just let us try then to leave entirely out of consideration any effect of heat received through external bodies, and to realize merely the inner experience which comes from saying the words: "I feel warm," "I feel cold." That inner experience is the only thing capable of giving an idea of what Saturn was during its period of evolution described above. It would have been possible to pass right through the portion of space it occupied; no gas would have been there to exercise pressure, no solid or liquid body from which light-impressions could have come; but at every point of space occupied, one would have felt inwardly, without any external impression: "Here there is such and such a degree of heat."

In a cosmic body of this character there are no conditions for the animal, vegetable, and mineral organisms of to-day.(9) The beings whose sphere of action was this Saturn, were at quite a different stage of evolution from that of the present inhabitants of the earth who are perceptible to the senses. In the first place there were beings there who had no physical body like that of contemporary man. We must also guard against thinking of
man's present physical embodiment, when mention is made of a "physical body" in this connection. We should instead carefully distinguish between the physical and the mineral body. A physical body is one governed by the physical laws which are now observable in the mineral kingdom. Now man's
present physical body is not only ruled by those physical laws, but is also permeated with mineral matter. There can be no question as yet on Saturn of a physical-mineral body of this kind. There is only a physical bodily form, governed by physical laws; but these laws are manifested only through the agency of heat.

Therefore the physical body is a fine, subtle, ethereal heat body; and the whole of Saturn consists of such heat bodies. They are the beginnings of the present physical-mineral human body. The latter has been formed out of
the former, because there have become incorporated with the original body the more recently formed gaseous, liquid, and solid substances.

Among the beings of which we are now speaking,who,besides man,were inhabitants of Saturn,there were,for instance,some which did not need a physical body at all. The lowest principle of their nature was an etheric or vital body. On the other hand,they had one principle higher than the human principles. Man's highest principle is the Spirit-Man (Atma); these beings have one still higher. And between the etheric body and the Spirit-Man they have all the principles described in this treatise which are also found in man: the astral body,ego,Spirit-Self,and Life-Spirit. Just as our earth is surrounded by an atmosphere,so too was Saturn; only in this case the "atmosphere" was of a spiritual nature. It really consisted of the beings just named and some others. Now there was constant reciprocal action between the heat bodies of Saturn and the beings we have described. The latter projected the principles of their being down into the physical heat bodies of Saturn. And while there was no life in those heat bodies themselves,the life of their neighbours was expressed in them. They might be compared to mirrors; only there were reflected in them,not the images of the living beings mentioned above,but their conditions of life. Therefore,although nothing living could have been discovered in Saturn itself,yet it had a vivifying effect on its environment in celestial space,because it reflected back into space,like an echo,the life which had been sent down into it. The whole of Saturn appeared as a mirror of celestial life. The very high beings,whose life was reflected by Saturn,are called in occult science "Lords of Wisdom."(10) Their activity on Saturn was not just beginning in the middle period of that evolution,which has been described; in a certain way it had even then already ceased. Before they could be in a position to rejoice in the reflection of their own life from Saturn's heat bodies they had to make those bodies capable of producing such a reflection. Therefore their activity began soon after the beginning of the Saturn evolution. When this happened,the body of Saturn was still chaotic material,which could not have reflected anything.

And in contemplating this chaotic matter,one has transferred himself,by spiritual observation,to the beginning of the Saturn evolution. What is to be observed there does not as yet bear anything of the later character of heat. If we wish to describe it,we can only speak of a quality which may be compared with the human will. From first to last it is nothing but "Will." Therefore it is an entirely spiritual condition that meets us here. If we ask whence came this "Will," we see it proceeding from the effluence of exalted beings,who brought their evolution,by steps only to be dimly conceived,up to such a height that when the Saturn evolution began they were able to pour forth "Will" from their own being. When this effluence had lasted a certain time,the activity of the Lords of Wisdom described above was combined with this Will. Through this means the will, which had hitherto had no attributes,gradually received the quality of reflecting life back into celestial space. In occult science the beings who found their happiness in pouring forth will,at the beginning of the Saturn evolution are called the "Lords of Will."(11)

After a certain stage of the Saturn evolution had been reached,through the co-operation of will and life,begins the influence of other beings, who are also within Saturn's environment. These are the "Lords of Motion."(12) They have no physical or etheric body. Their lowest principle is the astral body. When the Saturn bodies have acquired the capacity for reflecting life,the qualities which have their seat in the astral bodies of the Lords of Motion interpenetrate that reflected life. In consequence of this,it appears as though expressions of feelings,emotions,and similar psychic forces had been cast out of Saturn into celestial space. The whole of Saturn appears like one animated being,manifesting sympathies and antipathies. These psychic manifestations,however,are by no means its own,but merely the activity of the Lords of Motion reflected back.

This also having lasted for a certain period,there begins the activity of yet other beings,that is,of the "Lords of Form."(13) Their lowest principle,too,is an astral body; but that body is at a different stage of evolution from that of the Lords of Motion; whereas the latter communicate only general manifestations of feeling to the reflected life, the astral body of the Lords of Form operates in such a way that the manifestations of feeling are flung out into cosmic space as if they came from individual beings. It might be said that the Lords of Motion make the whole of Saturn appear as an animated being. The Lords of Form separate that life into individual living beings,so that Saturn now appears as a conglomerate of such psychic beings.

Let us imagine,for the sake of illustration,a mulberry or blackberry, made up,as it is,of small individual berries. In a similar manner,to clairvoyant vision,Saturn,during the period of evolution now being described,is made up of individual Saturn beings,which of course have neither life nor soul of their own,but reflect the life and soul of its denizens. Into this condition of Saturn now come beings whose astral body is also their lowest principle,but who have brought it to such a high stage of development that it operates in the same way as the present human ego. Through these beings,the ego in the environment of Saturn looks down on that planet,and imparts its nature to Saturn's individual living beings. Thus something is sent out from Saturn into cosmic space,which has an effect similar to that of human personality in the present conditions of life. The beings causing that effect are designated "Sons of Personality."(14) They confer on the Saturn bodies the appearance of personality. Personality itself,however,is not present on Saturn,but only,as it were,its reflected image,the shell or husk of personality. The real personality of these spirits is in the environment of Saturn. As a result of these Sons of Personality letting their essence stream back from the Saturn bodies in the manner described,that fine substance is bestowed on those bodies which has previously been described as heat. In the whole of Saturn there is no subjectivity; but the Sons of Personality recognize the image of their own subjectivity,when it streams out to them from Saturn as heat.

When all this is taking place,the Sons of Personality are on the same level on which man now stands. They are then passing through their "human" period. In order to look at this fact with an unprejudiced eye,we must imagine it possible for a being to be human without being in the exact form in which man now exists. The Sons of Personality are "human beings" on Saturn. They have as their lowest principle not the physical body,but the astral body with the ego. Hence they cannot express the experiences of their astral body in such physical and etheric bodies as those of contemporary man; they not only _have_ an ego,however,but _are aware_ of the fact,because the heat of Saturn brings that ego streaming back into their consciousness. In fact,they are human beings under different circumstances from those of earth.

As the Saturn evolution progressed,facts follow of a different kind from those already related. Whereas everything hitherto was a reflection of outer life and feeling,there now begins a kind of inner life. In the Saturn world a life of light begins flickering here and there,and growing dim again. A quivering glimmer is seen in some places,something like flashes of lightning in others. The Saturn heat bodies begin to glimmer, to sparkle,and even to emit rays. This stage of evolution having been reached,there again arises the possibility for certain beings to develop their activity. They are those known to occult science as "Sons of Fire."(15) Although these beings have an astral body,they are unable at his particular stage of their existence to stir their own astral bodies; they would not be capable of any feeling or emotion unless they could act upon the Saturn heat bodies which have attained the stage of evolution described. That action affords them the possibility of recognizing their own existence from the effect which they produce. They cannot say to themselves,"I am here"; but rather,"My environment causes me to be here." They have perceptions,and what they perceive is the light-effects in Saturn which have been described. These are,in a certain manner,their ego. This gives them a peculiar kind of consciousness. It is designated "picture-consciousness." It may be represented as having the nature of human dream-consciousness,except that the degree of activity it enjoys must be imagined as being very much greater than it is in human dreams, and also that it is not a question of shadowy dream-pictures floating hither and thither,but of pictures that have a real connection with the play of light on Saturn.

During this reciprocal action between the Sons of Fire and the Saturn heat
bodies,the germs of the human sense organs begin their evolution. The organs,by means of which contemporary man becomes cognizant of the physical world,begin to shine in their first delicate ethereal outlines. Human phantoms,displaying as yet nothing but the primeval light pictures of the sense-organs,become discernible within Saturn to the clairvoyant faculty of perception. Thus these sense-organs are the result of the activity of the Sons of Fire; but they are not the only spirits who shared in their creation. Other beings come upon the scene of Saturn at the same
time as these Sons of Fire,--beings so far advanced in their evolution that they are able to make use of the germs of the human sense-organs for beholding the cosmic events taking place in the Saturn life. They are the "Lords of Love."(16) If they were not there,the Sons of Fire could not have the consciousness described above. They behold the events on Saturn
with a consciousness which makes it possible for them to convey these events as pictures to the Sons of Fire. They themselves forego all the advantages which might accrue to them from contemplating events on Saturn;
they renounce all joys and pleasures; they give up all these in order that the Sons of Fire may come into possession of them.

A new period of Saturn's existence succeeds these occurrences. Something
else is added to the play of light. If what here presents itself to clairvoyant perception be reported,it may seem an absurdity to many. Within Saturn,intermingled sensations of taste seem to be surging. Sweet, bitter,sour,etc.,are perceived throughout the interior of Saturn; while without,in cosmic space,all this expresses itself as tone,as a kind of music.

In the course of these processes there are again certain beings who find it possible to develop activity on Saturn. These are the "Sons of Twilight,or Life."(17) They enter into reciprocal action with the forces of taste surging up and down within Saturn. By this means their etheric or vital body attains a state of such activity that it may be called a kind of metabolism. They bring life into the interior of Saturn. Hence processes of nutrition and excretion take place. This inner life makes it possible for yet other beings to come into the planet,the "Lords of Harmony."(18) They bestow a dim kind of consciousness on the Sons of Life,
which is even more vague and dim than the dream-consciousness of

contemporary man. It is of the kind that now comes to man in dreamless sleep,and is,indeed,of such a low order that it does not,so to speak, "enter into his consciousness." Yet it is there. It differs from waking consciousness in degree and also in its nature. Plants,too,have this dreamless-sleep consciousness at the present time. Even though it does not bring about any perceptions of an external world,in the human sense of the word,yet it regulates the life processes and brings them into harmony with the processes of the outer world.

This adjustment cannot be perceived by the Sons of Life at the stage of Saturn's evolution now being described; but the Lords of Harmony perceive it,and therefore it is they who really do the adjusting. All this life is enacted within the human phantoms already described. To clairvoyant vision they consequently appear animated; yet their life is only a semblance of life. It is the life of the "Sons of Life," who,so to speak,make use of the human phantoms in order to manifest themselves.

Let us now turn our attention to the human phantoms with their semblance of life. During the Saturn period described,their form is constantly changing. Sometimes they bear one aspect,sometimes another. In the further course of evolution,their forms become more definite,and occasionally permanent. This is due to their becoming interpenetrated by the action of the Spirits described at the beginning of the Saturn evolution,--the Lords of Will (the Thrones). The consequence is that the human phantom itself is endowed with the simplest,dullest form of consciousness. This must be thought of as still duller than the consciousness of dreamless sleep. Under present conditions,minerals have that consciousness. It brings the inner being into harmony with the outer physical world. On Saturn it is the Lords of Will who regulate that harmony. And thus man appears as a copy of the Saturn life itself. That life which is on a large scale on Saturn,is at this stage on a small scale in man. Thus the first germ is prepared for that which is still only a germ in contemporary man the "Spirit-Man" (Atma). This dull human will (within Saturn) is manifested to clairvoyant faculty by effects which may be compared with odours. Outside in celestial space,there is a manifestation like that of a personality,which however is not directed by an inner ego but is regulated from without,like a machine. Those who regulate it are the Lords of Will.

It will become evident,from a survey of the foregoing,that starting from the previously described middle period of the Saturn evolution,the following steps of that evolution can be characterized by comparing their effects with the sense-perceptions of the present time. It might be said that the Saturn evolution manifests as heat; then a play of light is added; then an appearance of taste and sound; finally something emerges which manifests within the interior of Saturn as sensations of smell,and without,as a human ego acting mechanically.

What have the Saturn revelations to say about what preceded the heat condition? Now this is something that cannot be compared with anything accessible to outer sense-perception. A state of things precedes the heat condition,which contemporary man experiences only in his inner being. When he gives himself up to ideas which he forms in his own soul,without having any inducement brought to bear on him by an external impression, then he has something within himself which cannot be perceived by any physical sense,but is only accessible to the perception of the higher clairvoyant vision. Manifestations precede the heat condition of Saturn, which can only be perceived by a clairvoyant. Three such conditions may be mentioned: pure psychic warmth,not outwardly perceptible; pure spiritual light,which is outward darkness; and lastly,something of a spiritual

essence which is complete in itself,and needs no outer being in order to become self-conscious. Pure,inner heat accompanies the appearance of the
Lords of Motion; pure,spiritual light,that of the Lords of Wisdom; pure inner being is linked with the first emanation of the Lords of Will.

Thus,with the appearance of heat on Saturn,our evolution comes forth out of the inner life of pure spirituality into outwardly manifested existence. It will be particularly difficult for present-day consciousness to accept this,if it must be said in addition that at the same time,with the advent of the Saturn heat condition,what we call "Time" also makes its first appearance. That is to say,the previous conditions have nothing to do with time. They belong to that sphere which may be called,in occult science,"duration." Consequently,everything that is said in this book about the conditions existing in the "Sphere of Duration" must be understood in such a way that when expressions referring to time conditions are used,they are only to be accepted for the sake of comparison and explanation. That which,in a certain sense,precedes "time," can be expressed in human language only by terms which imply the idea of time. Even if we are aware that the first,second,and third Saturn conditions were not enacted "one after the other," in the present sense of the word,yet we cannot do otherwise than describe them one after
the other. Indeed,in spite of their duration or coexistence in time,they are so dependent on one another that this very dependence may be compared
with sequence,in time.

This indication of the first conditions of evolution on Saturn also throws light on any further questions that may be asked as to the origin of those conditions. From the purely intellectual point of view,it is,of course, quite possible,when dealing with the source of anything,to inquire after "the source of the source." But in the face of facts,this is not possible. A comparison,however,will help us to realize this. If we find ruts on a road we may ask,"To what are they due?" And the reply may be, "To a carriage." It may further be asked: "Whence did the carriage come? Whither is it going?" An answer founded on fact is again possible. We may then proceed to ask,"Who occupied the carriage? What purpose had the person in using it? What was he,or she,doing?" At last,however,we shall reach a point at which inquiry by means of facts finds its natural limit; and on inquiring further we get away from the original questions. We only continue the inquiry mechanically,as it were.

In such matters as the one brought forward as a comparison,it is easy to see where facts demand the end of the inquiry. It is not so evident when we are face to face with great cosmic questions. But as the result of really exact observation,it will nevertheless be seen that all inquiry as to origins must come to an end at the Saturn condition portrayed above. For we have reached a region in which beings and events are no longer justified by that from which they proceed,but by themselves.

As a result of the Saturn evolution it appears that the human germ developed up to a certain point. It attained the low,dim state of consciousness described above. We must not imagine that its evolution does
not begin until the last of the Saturn stages. The Lords of Will carry on their work through all conditions. Only the result is most striking to clairvoyant perception in the last period. There is nothing like a fixed boundary between the activities of the several groups of beings. If it is said that the Lords of Will work first,then the Lords of Wisdom,and so on,it is not meant that they are working only at that time. They are working all through the Saturn evolution; only their activity can best be observed during the periods specified. The several groups have,as it were,the leadership at those times.

Thus the whole Saturn evolution appears as a working out of what streamed forth from the Lords of Will through the Lords of Wisdom,Motion,Form, and the rest. Through this process those spiritual beings themselves experience evolution. For instance,after they have received their life reflected back from Saturn,the Lords of Wisdom stand on a different level than before. The result of that activity exalts the faculties of their own being. The consequence is that,on the completion of such activity, something similar to human sleep comes upon them. To their periods of activity in connection with Saturn succeed other periods,during which they live,as it were,in other worlds. At these times their activity is withdrawn from Saturn. On this account clairvoyant perception sees an ascent and a descent in the Saturn evolution that has been described. The ascent lasts until the formation of the heat condition. Then,with the play of light,the ebb-tide sets in. When the human phantoms have assumed form through the Lords of Will,the spiritual beings have also gradually withdrawn themselves. The Saturn evolution dies away; as a phase of evolution,it disappears. A kind of resting pause occurs.

The human germ at the same time enters upon a state of dissolution; not, however,a state in which it passes away,but one like that of a plant seed,resting in the earth in order that it may ripen into a new plant. Thus the human germ reposes,until a new awakening,in the depth of the cosmos. And by the time the moment of awakening has arrived,the spiritual beings described above have acquired,under other conditions,the faculties by means of which they can further advance the human germ. The Lords of Wisdom have,in their etheric body,gained the faculty not only of enjoying the reflection of life as they did on Saturn,but of pouring life forth from themselves,and endowing other beings with it. The Lords of Motion are now as far advanced as were the Lords of Wisdom on Saturn.
Then the lowest principle of their being was the astral body; they now possess an etheric,or vital body; and in a corresponding degree the other spiritual beings have reached a further stage of evolution. All these spiritual beings are therefore able to work at the further evolution of the human germ in a different way than on Saturn.

But the human germ was dissolved at the end of the Saturn evolution. In order that the more highly evolved spirit-beings might resume their work where they had left it off,the human germ must once more briefly recapitulate the stages through which it had passed on Saturn. This,in fact,is what appears to clairvoyant faculties of perception. The human germ comes forth out of its retirement and begins to develop by its own ability,by means of the forces which had been implanted within it on Saturn. It comes forth out of the darkness as a "being of Will," and assumes the appearance of life,of soul qualities,etc.,up to that mechanical manifestation of personality which it possessed at the end of the Saturn evolution.

The second of the great periods of evolution that have been mentioned,the "Sun period," effects the raising of man's being to a higher stage of consciousness than that which it had attained on Saturn. Compared with man's present state of consciousness,the Sun condition might certainly be termed "unconsciousness," For it is approximately that condition which contemporary man experiences during absolutely dreamless sleep. Or it might be compared to the low degree of consciousness in which our vegetable world now slumbers. For occult science there is no such thing as unconsciousness,but only different degrees of consciousness. Everything in the world is conscious.

In the course of the Sun evolution,the human being attains a higher degree of consciousness through the incorporation within it of the etheric,or vital body. Before this can take place the Saturn conditions must be recapitulated in the manner described above. This recapitulation has quite a definite meaning. That is to say,when the period of rest which was spoken of in the foregoing statement has come to an end,that which was formerly Saturn issues forth,out of "cosmic sleep," as a new celestial body,the Sun. But the conditions of evolution have meanwhile changed. The spiritual beings,whose activity on behalf of Saturn we have portrayed,have progressed onward into different conditions. Yet at first the human germ appears on the newly formed Sun in the form it possessed on Saturn. It has first of all so to transform the various stages of evolution through which it has passed on Saturn that they may suit the new conditions on the Sun. Consequently,the sun epoch begins with a recapitulation of the occurrences on Saturn,adjusted to the changed conditions of Sun life. Now when the human being has advanced so far that the stage of evolution it reached on Saturn has been adapted to the Sun conditions,the Lords of Wisdom already mentioned,begin to let the etheric,or vital body,pour into the physical body. The higher stage which man reaches on the Sun may therefore be characterized in this way: the physical body,already formed in the germ-state on Saturn,is raised to a second stage of perfection by becoming the vehicle of an etheric or vital body. This last-named etheric body attains its first degree of perfection on its own account during the Sun evolution. In order,however, that the second degree of perfection for the physical and the first for the etheric body may be reached,the intervention of still other spirit-beings is necessary during the further course of the Sun life,in a similar manner to that which has been described as taking place during the Saturn stage.

When the Lords of Wisdom begin to stream forth their etheric body,the Sun,previously dark,begins to shine. At the same time the first appearances of inner activity are seen in the human germ; life has begun. What had to be described as a semblance of life on Saturn now becomes actual life. The influx lasts for a certain time,at the end of which an important change for the human germ sets in--that is to say,it organizes itself into two parts. Whereas up to this point the physical and etheric bodies formed an intimately connected whole,the physical body now begins to detach itself as a separate part. Yet even that separated physical body is still pervaded by the etheric body. Therefore we have now to do with a human being composed of two principles. One portion is a physical body permeated by an etheric body; the other is an etheric body and nothing else. This separation comes to pass,however,during a period of rest in the Sun life. During this pause the shining,which had begun to appear, dies away. The separation takes place during a "cosmic night," as it were. Yet this interval of rest is much shorter than the one between the Saturn and Sun evolutions mentioned above. At the expiration of the rest period the Lords of Wisdom work for a while on the two-fold being of man,just as they had previously done on the undivided being. Then the Lords of Motion begin their activity. They cause their own astral body to stream through the human etheric body. By this means man acquires the capacity for executing certain inner movements in the physical body. These movements may be compared with those of sap in a plant of our own time.

The Saturn body consisted exclusively of heat substance. During the Sun evolution that heat substance is condensed into a state which may be compared with that of our present-day gas or steam. In occult science "air" is the name ordinarily used for this condition. The first beginnings of such a state are seen after the Lords of Motion have begun their activity. The following spectacle is presented to clairvoyant consciousness. Within the heat substance there appears something like delicate formations which are set in rythmic motion by the forces of the etheric body. These formations represent the human physical body at the stage of evolution now attained by it. They are permeated through and through with heat,and are also wrapped,as it were,in a heat envelope. From a physical point of view,man's nature may now be said to be composed
of heat structures with air forms embedded in them--the latter in regular motion. Hence,if we wish to retain the foregoing comparison with a plant of the present day,we must remember that it is not a solid plant organism which we have to consider,but an air or gas form,(19) the movements of which may be compared with the circulation of the sap in plants of to-day.

The evolution thus indicated continues. After a certain time another interval of rest sets in; after this the Lords of Motion go on working until their activity is supplemented by that of the Lords of Form. The effect of the latter is that the gas structures,which before were constantly changing,now assume lasting form. This,too,happens because the Lords of Form cause their forces to flow in and out of the human etheric body. When the Lords of Motion alone were acting on the gaseous organisms,these were in perpetual motion,not keeping their form for an instant. Now,however,they temporarily assume distinguishable shapes. Again,after a certain period,there occurs a time of rest; and then once more the Lords of Form continue their activity. But the conditions within the Sun evolution are now entirely changed. For the point has been reached
when the Sun evolution has attained its zenith. This is the time at which the Lords of Personality,who attained their human stage on Saturn,ascend to a higher degree of perfection. They advance beyond the human stage; they attain a form of consciousness which contemporary man does not yet
possess in his normal course of development on the earth. He will acquire it when the earth--the fourth of the planetary stages of evolution--has reached its goal and has entered upon the next planetary period. Then man
will not only perceive around him what his present physical senses enable him to apprehend,but he will be able to see in images the inner psychic conditions of the beings surrounding him. He will have a (clairvoyant) picture-consciousness,although retaining complete self-consciousness. There will be nothing dream-like or vague in his clairvoyance,but he will perceive what is psychic,in pictures certainly,but in such a way that these images will be the expression of realities,as physical colours and sounds are now. Man,at present,can attain to this degree of clairvoyance only through occult training,which will be treated later in this book.

Now this clairvoyance is attained by the Sons of Personality,as a gift of their normal evolution,midway in the Sun period; and it is just on this account that they become capable of acting on the newly formed etheric body of man during the Sun evolution,in a way similar to that in which they acted on the physical body on Saturn. Just as there the heat reflected their own personality back to them,so do the gaseous organisms now reflect back to them,in gleams of light,the images of their clairvoyant consciousness. They clairvoyantly behold what is taking place on the Sun. And this vision is by no means mere observation; it is as though something of the force which mortals call love made itself felt in the images which stream forth from the Sun. If a clairvoyant looks more closely,he will find the cause of this phenomenon. Exalted beings have blended their activity with the light that is being radiated from the Sun.

They are the Lords of Love (the Christian Seraphim) already mentioned. Henceforth they act,together with the Sons of Personality,on the human etheric,or vital body. By means of that activity the etheric body advances a step farther along its path of evolution. It acquires the capacity not only of transforming the gaseous forms within it,but of so elaborating them that the first indications of a propagation of living human beings appear. Emanations,so to speak,are driven out (as though exuded) from the gaseous organisms that take on shapes resembling their
mother-forms.

In order to describe the further course of the Sun evolution,reference must be made to a fact in the formation of worlds which is of the greatest
possible significance. It is this,--that by no means every being attains the goal of its evolution in the course of one epoch; there are some that fall short of that goal. Thus,during the Saturn evolution,not all of the Sons of Personality actually reached the human stage for which,as described above,they were destined; and just as little did all the physical human bodies,developed on Saturn,attain the degree of maturity which qualifies them to become vehicles of an independent etheric body on the Sun. The consequence is that beings and organisms are present on the
Sun which are not in harmony with their environment. These must now make
up,during the Sun evolution,for what they failed to attain on Saturn. The following may,therefore,be clairvoyantly observed during the Sun period. When the Lords of Wisdom begin their pouring in of the etheric body,the Sun body is to some extent darkened. Structures are mingled with
it which,properly speaking,belong to Saturn. They are heat organisms which are not able to condense themselves into air in the proper manner. These are the human beings left behind in the Saturn stage. They are not able to become vehicles of a normally developed etheric body.

Now the heat substance of Saturn,which has thus been left behind,splits into two parts on the Sun. One part is absorbed,as it were,by human bodies,and henceforward forms a kind of lower nature within man's being. Thus something,which really corresponds to the Saturn stage,is incorporated in the bodily part of man on the Sun. Now just as the Saturn body of man made it possible for the Sons of Personality to raise themselves to the human stage,the Saturn part of man performs the same
office on the Sun for the Sons of Fire. They raise themselves to the human
stage by letting their forces flow in and out of the Saturn part of man, as did the Sons of Personality on Saturn.

This also happens during the middle period of the Sun evolution. The Saturn part of the human being is then so far matured that with its help the Sons of Fire (Archangeloi) are able to pass through their human stage. Another part of the Saturnian heat substance becomes detached and attains
an independent existence alongside of and among the human beings on the
Sun. This forms a second kingdom by the side of the human kingdom,a kingdom which develops on the Sun only a perfectly independent physical body,like a heat body. In consequence of this,the fully evolved Sons of Personality are not able to direct their activity toward any independent etheric body in the manner before described. But there were also certain Sons of Personality left behind at the Saturn stage who fell short of the human stage. A bond of attraction exists between them and the second Sun
kingdom which has become independent. They must now act toward the

backward kingdom on the Sun as their advanced brethren did on Saturn in regard to human beings. The latter had only their physical body perfected here. But there is no possibility on the Sun for such a work on the part of the backward Sons of Personality. They therefore separate themselves from the Sun body,and form an independent celestial body outside it. This body,accordingly,withdraws from the Sun,and from it the backward Sons of Personality act on the beings of the second Sun kingdom which have been
described. In this way two world-organisms have been formed out of the one
which was previously Saturn. The Sun has now in its environment a second
celestial body,one which exhibits a kind of re-birth of Saturn,a new Saturn. From this Saturn the character of personality is conferred on the second Sun kingdom. Therefore within this kingdom we have to do with beings which have no personality on the Sun itself. Yet they reflect back to the Sons of Personality on the new Saturn the special personality of those spirits. Clairvoyant consciousness is able to observe among the human beings on the Sun,heat forces which act upon the regular course of
Sun evolution,and in which the sway of the spirits described as belonging to the new Saturn is to be seen.

We notice the following facts about man's being during the middle period of the Sun evolution. It is divided into a physical body and an etheric body. Within these the activity of the advanced Sons of Personality plays, conjointly with that of the Lords of Love. Now part of the backward Saturn
nature is mingled with the physical body. In this plays the activity of the Sons of Fire. We now see in everything which the Sons of Fire effect on the backward Saturn nature,the forerunners of the present human sense-organs. It has been shown how these Sons of Fire were already at work on the elaboration of the sense-germs in the heat substance on Saturn. The first outline of the present human glands is to be recognized in what is accomplished by the Sons of Personality conjointly with the Lords of Love (Seraphim).

But the above described is not the whole of the activity of the Sons of Personality dwelling on the new Saturn. They not only extend their activity to the second Sun kingdom mentioned above,but they also establish a kind of connection between that kingdom and the human senses.
The heat substances of this kingdom flow in and out of the germs of the human sense-organs. By this means the human being on the Sun acquires a
kind of perception of the lower kingdom situated outside him. That perception is naturally a dim one,closely corresponding to the dull Saturn-consciousness previously described. And it consists essentially of varied heat effects.

Everything here described as taking place in the middle of the Sun evolution continues for a certain definite period. Then a time of rest again occurs. After that,things continue for a while in the same manner up to a certain point of evolution,at which the human etheric body is so far matured that a united action of the Sons of Life (Angeloi) and the Lords of Harmony (Cherubim) can set in. To clairvoyant consciousness, certain manifestations now appear within man's being,which may be compared with perceptions of taste,and which are made known externally as
sounds. A similar thing has already been stated about the Saturn evolution. But here on the Sun the processes relating to human beings are more from within and are full of more independent life.

The Sons of Life thereby acquire that dim picture-consciousness which the Sons of Fire had already attained on Saturn. In this the Lords of Harmony are their helpers. They really behold clairvoyantly what is now being enacted within the Sun evolution; only they give up all the results of that contemplation,and the enjoyment of those revelations of Wisdom that arise from it,and allow them to stream,like splendid visions of enchantment,into the dream-like consciousness of the Sons of Life. The latter again work these pictures of their visions into the etheric body of man,so that it attains higher and higher stages of development.

Again an interval of rest ensues,again everything is awakened from "cosmic sleep"; and after further lapse of time the human being is sufficiently advanced to use its own forces. These forces are the same that were poured forth into man's being by the "Thrones" during the latter part of the Saturn period. This human being now evolves an inner life, which,in its manifestation to clairvoyant consciousness,may be compared with an inner perception of smell. But outside,in the direction of celestial space,man's being is manifested as a personality,though not one directed by an inner ego. It appears more like a plant with the character of a personality. It has been stated that at the end of the Saturn evolution personality is manifested somewhat machine like. And just as then,the first germ was developed of that which still remains a germ in contemporary man,--the Spirit-Man (Atma),--so at this point there is formed a similar first germ of the Life-Spirit (Budhi).

When all this has continued for some time,an interval of rest again occurs. Following this,as in previous instances,the activity of the human being is resumed for a while. Then conditions commence,which mark a new intervention of the Lords of Wisdom. By its means human nature becomes capable of feeling the first traces of sympathy and antipathy for its environment. In all this there is still no real sensation but only a premonition of sensation. For the inner life-activity,which might be characterized in its manifestation as perception of smell,is revealed externally as a kind of primitive language. If the human being is inwardly conscious of a useful smell--or taste,or glitter,--it is manifested outwardly by a sound; and the same thing happens,in a corresponding way, with an inwardly uncongenial perception. Through all the events described, the real meaning of the Sun evolution for the human being is indicated. The human being has reached a higher stage of consciousness than that of the Saturn period. It is the consciousness of sleep.

After a time,the point of evolution is also reached at which the higher beings connected with the Sun stage must pass into other spheres in order to work out that with which they have endowed themselves by their work on the human being. A long period of rest sets in,one similar to that between the Saturn and Sun evolutions. Everything that has been perfected on the Sun passes into a condition which may be compared with that of a plant when its powers of growth are resting in the seed. But just as those powers of growth appear again in a new plant,so does everything that was living on the Sun come forth again,after the period of rest,from the cosmic depths,to begin a new planetary existence.

The meaning of such a term of rest,or "cosmic sleep," will readily be understood if we will only direct our spiritual vision to one of the orders of beings already mentioned,for instance,to the Lords of Wisdom.

They were not far enough evolved on Saturn to be able to ray forth an etheric body from themselves. They were only prepared for this after they had gone through their experiences on Saturn. During the rest (Pralaya) they transform into actual capacity what has been previously only prepared
within them. Thus on the Sun they are evolved far enough to pour forth life from themselves,and to endow the human being with an etheric body of
its own.

After the interval of rest,that which had previously been the Sun comes forth again out of the "cosmic sleep." That is,it again becomes perceptible to the clairvoyant faculties which had been able to observe it before,but had lost sight of it during the resting period. There are now two points to be observed with regard to the newly appearing planetary organism,which may,in occult science,be denoted the "Moon" (and this must not be confused with that portion of it which is now the earth's moon). In the first place,that which had detached itself during the Sun period as a "new Saturn" is once more within the new planetary body. This Saturn has therefore been again united with the Sun during the term of rest. Everything which was in the original Saturn reappears at first as one world-organism. Secondly,the human etheric bodies which had been formed on the Sun have been absorbed,during the resting period,by that which constitutes the spiritual sheath of the planet. At this point of time,therefore,they do not make their appearance united with the corresponding physical human bodies,but these latter at first appear separately. They contain everything which had been gained for them on Saturn and the Sun,but they are without the etheric,or vital body. Indeed,they cannot incorporate that etheric body within themselves immediately,for it has also been passing,during the period of rest, through an evolution with which they are not yet harmonized.

What occurs at the beginning of the Moon evolution,in order to bring about this adjustment,is,first of all,another recapitulation of the Saturnian events. The physical part of man passes once more through the stages of the Saturn evolution,but under greatly altered circumstances. On Saturn there were only the forces of a heat body at work within him; now there are also those of the gas body that has been elaborated. These latter forces do not,however,appear quite at the beginning of the Moon evolution. Then everything appears as though man's being were composed only of heat substance,and as though the gas forces were lying dormant within that substance. Then comes a time when the first indications of these forces make their appearance; and lastly,in the latest period of the Saturn recapitulation,man's being has the same appearance as during the animated period of his Sun existence. Yet,all life still proves to be but a semblance of life.

Next occurs a period of rest similar to the short periods of rest of the Sun evolution. Then the pouring in of the etheric body,for which the physical body has now become ripe,begins anew. As in the case of the recapitulation of Saturn,this influx takes place in three distinct periods. During the second of these,man's being is so far adjusted to the new Moon conditions that the Lords of Motion are able to bring into play the faculty they have acquired. This faculty consists in pouring the astral body out of their own being into man's being. They prepared themselves for this work during the Sun evolution,and during the time of rest between the Sun and Moon they transformed what had been prepared into
the faculty alluded to. This influx lasts for a while,then one of the shorter intervals of rest sets in. After that the influx continues until the Lords of Form begin their activity. In consequence of this pouring of the astral body into the human being by the Lords of Motion,man acquires

his first psychic qualities. He begins to develop sensations in connection with the processes which take place within,through the possession of an etheric body,and which during the Sun evolution were still of a plant-like nature; these processes now give him sensations of pleasure and displeasure. But it is nothing more than a constant inner ebb and flow of such pleasure and displeasure,until the Lords of Form intervene. Then these changing feelings are so transformed that there appear in man's being what may be regarded as the first signs of wish or desire. The human being strives after a repetition of what has once caused pleasure,and tries to avoid what has been felt as antipathetic. However,since the Lords of Form do not give up their own nature to the human being,but merely let their forces stream in and out,desire is wanting in depth of feeling and independence. It is directed by the Lords of Form,and has an instinctive character.

The human physical body on Saturn was a heat body; on the Sun a condensation into the gaseous state,or into "air," has taken place. Now, as during the Moon evolution,the astral element is rayed into the physical part,which at a definite moment attains a further degree of condensation and arrives at a state which may be compared with that of a liquid substance of today. In accordance with the usage of occult science this state may be called "water." By water,is not meant only the water we now have,but this term applies to every liquid form in existence. The physical human body now gradually assumes a form composed of three kinds of material structures. The densest is a "water body"; through this flow air currents; and all of this again is permeated by manifestations of warmth.

Now all the organisms do not attain full,adequate maturity during the Sun stage. Therefore there are organisms to be found on the Moon which are only at the Saturn stage,and others which have only reached the Sun stage. In this way two other kingdoms arise by the side of the normally evolved human kingdom. One consists of beings which have stopped short at the Saturn stage,and therefore have only a physical body,which even on the Moon is not yet able to become the vehicle of an independent etheric body. This is the lowest of the Moon kingdoms. A second consists of beings which have been left behind at the Sun stage,and which therefore do not mature sufficiently on the Moon to take on an independent astral body. These form a kingdom between the one just mentioned and the regularly developed human kingdom.

But there is still something else taking place; The substances containing only heat forces and those containing only air forces,permeate these human beings. Thus it happens that the latter have within them on the Moon both a Saturnian and a solar nature. In this way a kind of cleavage has taken place in human nature; and by means of this cleavage,something very momentous is called forth within the Moon evolution after the activity of the Lords of Form has begun. The first evidences of a cleavage in the cosmic body of the Moon becomes then apparent. One part of its substances and beings separates from the other; two heavenly bodies are formed out of one. One of these becomes the abode of certain higher beings who were previously more closely connected with the undivided celestial body; while the other is occupied by human beings,the two lower kingdoms described above,and certain higher beings who did not pass over to the first celestial body.

The first heavenly body,with the higher beings,appears like a reborn but refined Sun; the other is really the new formation,the "old Moon." The regenerated Sun,on going out,takes with it only "heat" and "air" from the substances which have been formed on the Moon; on what is left as the Moon there is the liquid condition as well as the other two substances. As a result of this separation the beings which have withdrawn with the newborn Sun are not,in the first place,hampered in their further evolution by the denser Moon beings. Thus they are able to continue their own progress without hindrance. But thus they attain just that much more power to act now upon the Moon beings from their Sun. And they in turn also acquire thereby new possibilities of evolution. Most important of all,the Lords of Form are still in union with them. These accentuate the passions and the desire-nature,and this expresses itself gradually also in a further condensation of the physical human body. What was previously nothing but liquid in that body assumes a densely viscous form; and the air-like and heat-like formations are correspondingly condensed. Similar processes take place in the two lower kingdoms.

The result of the separation of the Moon-body from the Sun-body is that the former bears the same relation to the latter as the Saturn-body once did to the whole cosmic evolution surrounding it. The Saturn-sphere was formed out of the body of the "Lords of Will" (the Thrones). From out its substance emanated back into cosmic space everything which the above-mentioned spiritual beings in the environment of Saturn experienced. And this radiation by degrees awakened independent life,by means of the subsequent processes. All evolution is due to the fact that independent beings differentiate themselves from their environment,then this environment like a reflection stamps itself upon those differentiated beings who then evolve further independently. The Moon-body,having likewise separated from the Sun-body,reflects at first the life of the latter. If nothing further had then happened,the following cosmic process would have taken place: There would have been a Sun-body in which spiritual beings adapted to that body would have lived through their experiences in the elements of heat and air.

Set over against this Sun-body would have been a Moon-body,in which other beings of like nature with the Sun-beings would have undergone their experiences in the conditions of heat,air,and water. The progress from the Sun-incarnation to that of the Moon would have consisted in the Sun-beings seeing their own life,as in a reflection of the events on the Moon. They would have thus been able to enjoy it,something which they were still incapable of doing during the Sun incarnation. But evolution did not remain at this stage. Something occurred which was of the deepest significance for all future evolution. Certain beings adapted to the Moon-body,take possession of the element of will (the heritage of the Thrones) which was at their disposal,and by its means develop a life of their own,which takes shape independently of the Sun-life. Alongside of those Moon experiences which are entirely under the influence of the Sun, there arise independent Moon experiences,and,at the same time,states of rebellion or mutiny against the Sun-beings. And the various kingdoms which had arisen on the Sun and Moon,first and foremost of which was the kingdom of man's ancestors,are drawn into these conditions. In this way the Moon-body contains within it,spiritually and materially,two kinds of life; one that is in inner union with the Sun-life,and another which has "fallen away" from it and goes its own way independently. This division into a twofold life appears in all subsequent events of the Moon incarnation.

What presents itself to clairvoyant consciousness in this period of evolution may be realized from the following pictures. The whole basic mass of the Moon is formed of a semi-animated substance which at one time moves sluggishly,at another quickly. This is not yet a mineral mass like the rocks and constituents of the earth upon which present day humanity walks. We might call it a kingdom of plant-minerals,only we have to imagine that the main body of the Moon consists wholly of this plant-mineral substance,as the earth today consists of rock,soil and other substances. Just as now we have towering masses of rock,so there were then harder portions embedded in the Moon's bulk; these may be compared with hard wooden structures or formations of horn; and as plants now arise out of mineral soil,so the surface of the Moon was covered and penetrated by the second kingdom,consisting of a kind of plant-animal. Their substance was softer than the general mass of the Moon,and more mobile. This kingdom extended over the other,like a viscous sea.

Man himself at that time may be called animal-man. He had in his nature the component parts of the other two kingdoms; but his being was thoroughly interpenetrated by an etheric and an astral body,upon which the forces of higher beings worked,issuing from the severed Sun. His form was thus brought to greater perfection. While the Lords of Form were giving him a form which adapted him to Moon life,the Sun-Spirits were giving him a nature which lifted him beyond that life. He had the power of ennobling his own nature with the faculties given him by these Spirits,--in fact,of raising what was akin to the lower kingdoms to a higher level.

Seen spiritually,the events now under consideration may be described in the following way. Man's ancestor had been brought to greater perfection by beings who had fallen away from the Sun kingdom. This improvement extended especially to everything that could be experienced in the element of water. Over that element the Sun-beings,who were rulers in the elements of heat and air,had less influence. The consequence of this was that in the organism of man's ancestor two kinds of beings manifested themselves. One part of the organism was wholly interpenetrated by the influences of the Sun-beings. In the other part,the rebellious Moon-beings were operative. Owing to this,the latter part was more independent than the former. In the former there could only arise states of consciousness in which the Sun-beings lived; in the latter there lived a kind of cosmic consciousness,such as was typical on Saturn,only now upon a higher level.

Man's ancestor consequently felt himself to be an "image of the universe," whereas his "Sun-part" felt itself to be only an "image of the Sun." The two beings now came to a kind of conflict in man's nature. A settlement of this conflict was brought about by the influence of the Sun-beings, through which the material organism which made the independent universal consciousness possible,was rendered frail and perishable. From time to time this part of the organism had to be thrown off. During and also some time after the separation,man's ancestor was a being wholly dependent on the Sun influence. His consciousness became less independent; he lived within it,entirely surrendered to Sun-life. Then the independent portion of the Moon was once more renewed. After some time this process was repeated. Thus man's ancestor lived on the Moon in alternating conditions of clearer and duller consciousness; and the alternation was accompanied by a change of his being in a material respect. From time to time he laid aside his Moon-body and resumed it later. Seen physically,great variety appears in the kingdoms of the Moon above mentioned. The mineral-plants, plant-animals and animal-men are differentiated into groups. This will be understood when it is borne in mind that as a result of certain organisms having been left behind at each of the earlier stages of evolution,forms possessing most varied qualities took physical shape. There are formations still retaining the qualities of the early Saturn period,others showing those of the middle period and again others of the closing period of Saturn. A similar statement is true of all the stages of the Sun evolution.

As organisms belonging to the evolving planet are left behind,so is it also with certain beings connected with that evolution. Through the progress of evolution up to the Moon period,different grades of such beings have already arisen. There are the Sons of Personality who not even on the Sun have attained their human stage; but there are also others who then caught up with evolving humanity. A number of the Sons of Fire,who should have attained humanity on the Sun,fell behind. Now,just as during the Sun evolution certain of the Sons of Personality withdrew from the Sun and caused the reappearance of Saturn as a separate body,so it also happens that in the course of the Moon evolution the beings described above separate and form individual celestial bodies. So far we have mentioned only the separation into Sun and Moon; but for the reasons already given,other world-organisms detached themselves from the Moon-body,which made its appearance after the great interval between the Sun and Moon.

After a certain time we have a system of cosmic bodies the most advanced of which,as can easily be seen,must be called the New Sun. And just such a bond of attraction as was described above for the evolution as existing between the backward Saturn kingdom and the Sons of Personality on the new Saturn,is formed between each of these bodies and the corresponding Moon-beings. It would take us much too far to follow up in detail all the celestial bodies that come into existence. It must suffice to have pointed out the reason why a succession of them arises by degrees from the undivided world-organism which appears as Saturn at the beginning of human evolution.

After the intervention of the Lords of Form,on the Moon,evolution proceeds for a while in the manner described. At the end of this time there is again a pause. While it lasts,the coarser portions of the three Moon kingdoms are in a sort of resting state,but the finer parts,in particular the human astral body,extricate themselves from those coarser organisms. They reach a condition in which the higher forces of exalted Sun-beings are able to act upon them very powerfully. After the interval of rest they again interpenetrate those parts of man's being which are composed of the coarser substances. Because they received such powerful forces during the pause--in a free state--they are able to make those coarser substances ripe for the influence,after a certain time,of the Sons of Personality and the Sons of Fire,who have progressed normally.

In the meantime these Sons of Personality have raised themselves to a level upon which they possess the "consciousness of inspiration." Here they are not only able--as was the case with clairvoyant picture-consciousness--to observe the inner state of other beings in images,but to apprehend the inner nature itself of those beings,as though in a spiritual tone-language. But the Sons of Fire have risen to that height of consciousness possessed on the Sun by the Sons of Personality. Thus both kinds of spirits are able to influence the now more developed life of the human being. The Sons of Personality act on the astral body,the Sons of Fire on the etheric body of this human being. The astral body thereby acquires the character of personality. It now not only experiences pleasure and pain,but relates them to itself. It has not arrived at a complete ego-consciousness,that says to itself,"I am here"; but it feels itself upheld and protected by other beings in its environment. When looking,as it were,up to these,it is able to say, "This,my environment,keeps me alive."

The Sons of Fire now work upon the etheric body. Under their influence the
movement of forces in that body becomes more and more an inner function of
life. What then results finds physical expression in a circulation of fluids and in phenomena of growth. The gaseous substances have become condensed into liquid substances; we may speak of a kind of nutritive process,in the sense that what is received from without becomes transformed and elaborated within. Perhaps if we think of something intermediate between nutrition and respiration in the present meaning of the terms,we may get an idea of what then happened in this respect. The nutritive matter was drawn from the animal-plant kingdom by the human being. We must think of those animal-plants as floating or swimming--or even lightly attached in an element surrounding them,as the lower animals of the present time live in water,or land animals in air. Yet the element is neither water nor air in the present sense,but something midway between the two,a kind of thick vapour in which most heterogeneous substances move hither and thither,as though dissolved in currents flowing in all directions.

The animal-plants appear only as condensed regular forms of this element, often differing little physically from their environment. The process of respiration exists alongside of the process of nutrition. It is not as it is upon the earth,but like a drawing in and a streaming out of heat. To clairvoyant observation it is as though during those processes,organs opened and closed,through which a warming current passed in and out,and through which airy and watery substances were also carried in and out. And
since man's nature at this stage of evolution already possesses an astral body,respiration and nutrition are accompanied by feelings,so that a sort of pleasure ensues when materials which promote the upbuilding of man's nature are taken in from without. Aversion is caused if injurious substances flow in,or even if they merely approach.

Just as during the Moon evolution the respiratory and the nutritive processes were closely connected,as has been described,so was the process of perception in close connection with reproduction. No immediate
effect was produced on any of the senses by the things and beings in the environment of Moon humanity. Perception was,on the contrary,of such a nature that the presence of things and beings called up pictures in the dull,dreamy consciousness. These pictures were much more closely connected with the real nature of the environment than the present sense-perceptions,which record in colour,sounds,smell etc.,so to speak,only the outside of things and beings.

In order to get a clearer idea of the human consciousness on the Moon,let us imagine human beings immersed in the vaporous environment described
above. Most varied processes take place in this vapour-element. Materials unite,substances break asunder one from the other; some parts become condensed,others rarified. All this happens in such a way that human beings do not see or hear anything of it directly,but it calls up

pictures in their consciousness. These may be compared with the images of
our present dream-consciousness,as for instance when an object falls to the ground,and a sleeping man does not discern what has really happened but perceives it in the form of a picture; let us say he thinks that a shot has been fired. However,the pictures in the Moon-consciousness are not arbitrary,as is the case with such dream-pictures; although they are symbols,not representations,yet they correspond with outer events. A definite outer event can call up only one definite picture. The Moon-being is therefore in a position to regulate his conduct by means of these pictures,as present-day man does by means of his perceptions. We must nevertheless be careful to notice that conduct,regulated by perception, is governed by choice whereas action,under the influence of the pictures we have described,takes place as if prompted by some dim instinct.

It is by no means as though only outer physical processes become perceptible through this picture-consciousness,but it is through the pictures that the spiritual beings,who rule behind the physical facts together with their activities,become likewise perceptible. Thus the Lords of Personality become visible,so to speak,in the phenomena of the animal-plant kingdom; the Sons of Fire appear behind and in the mineral-plant beings; and the Sons of Life appear as beings whom man is able to imagine unconnected with anything physical,--whom he sees,as it were,as etheric-psychic organisms.

Though these pictures of the Moon-consciousness were not representations,
only symbols of outer things,they nevertheless had a much more important
effect on the inner nature of man than the images now caused by perception. They were able to set the whole inner being into motion and activity. The inner processes were moulded in conformity with them. They were genuine formative forces. Man's being became what those formative forces made it; it became,to a certain extent,a representation of the events of its consciousness.

The further evolution progresses in this manner,the more it results in a deeply incisive change in man's being. The power issuing from the pictures in the consciousness gradually becomes unable to extend over the whole human bodily frame,which divides into two parts,or two natures. Members are formed subject to the shaping influence of the picture-consciousness, and they become to a great extent a copy of that life of imagination in the way just described. Other organs escape such an influence. They are, as it were,too dense,too much determined by other laws,to conform themselves to the picture-consciousness. These organs withdraw from the
human influence; but they come under another,that of the exalted Sun-beings themselves. A period of rest,however,is first seen to precede this stage of evolution. During this pause,the Sun-Spirits are gathering force to influence the Moon-beings under quite new circumstances.

After this term of rest,man's being is distinctly divided into two natures. One of these is withdrawn from the independent action of the picture-consciousness; it assumes a more definite form,and comes under the influence of forces which,though issuing from the Moon body,are only called forth there through the influence of the Sun-beings. This part of the human being shares more and more in the life which is stimulated by the Sun; the other part rises,like a kind of head,out of the first one.
It is flexible,can move itself,and takes shape in conformity with the life of dull human consciousness. Yet the two parts are closely connected with each other; they send one another their vital fluids,and members extend from one into the other.

An important harmony is now attained by the working out,during the time in which all this happened,of such a relation between the Sun and Moon as is in keeping with the aim of this evolution. It has already been intimated in a former passage how the advancing beings throughout their stages of evolution,shape their celestial bodies from out the general cosmic mass. They emanate,as it were,the forces which govern the aggregation of the substances. The Sun and Moon have thus separated from each other,as was necessary for the preparation of the right abodes for their respective beings. But this regulation of material and its forces by the spirit is carried very much farther. The beings themselves condition as well,certain movements of the heavenly bodies,and the definite revolutions of them around each other. In consequence,those bodies occupy changing positions with regard to each other. And if the position or situation of one body relative to another is altered,the effects of their respective inhabitants upon each other also change. So it is with the Sun and Moon. Through the movement of the Moon around the Sun,which by this time had come about,the human beings come alternately at one time more into the sphere of the Sun's influence,at another they are turned away from it and are then thrown back more on their own resources. The movement is a consequence of the "fall" of certain Moon-beings,as already described,and of the settlement of the conflict which was thereby brought about. It is the physical expression of the new relation of spiritual forces created by this falling away. As a consequence of the rotation of the one sphere round the other the beings inhabiting these heavenly bodies experience the alternating conditions of consciousness above described. We may put it thus,that the Moon alternately turns its life toward the Sun and away from it. There is a Sun time and a planetary time and during this latter,the Moon-beings develop on the side of the Moon which is turned away from the Sun.

It is true however,that so far as the Moon is concerned,in addition to the movement of the celestial bodies,still something else must be considered. That is to say,clairvoyant consciousness,on looking back, can plainly see the Moon-beings wandering around their own planet,at quite regular periods of time. Thus at certain times they seek localities where they can give themselves up to the Sun influence; at other periods they wander to places where they are not subject to that influence,and where they can,as it were,reflect upon their own being.

In order to complete the picture of these events,we must further notice that the Sons of Life attain their human stage during this period. Man's senses,the beginnings of which already existed on Saturn,cannot even yet,on the Moon,be used for his own perception of external objects. But at the Moon stage those senses become the instruments of the Sons of Life, who make use of them in order to perceive through them. These senses, belonging to the physical human body,enter thereby into reciprocal relations with the Sons of Life,by whom they are not only used but improved.

Through the changing relations of the Sun,there appears now in the human being himself,as has been already indicated,a change in the conditions of life. Things so shape themselves that when the human being is dominated by the Sun influence,he devotes himself more to the Sun life and its phenomena than to himself. At such times he feels the greatness and glory of the universe; he,so to speak,absorbs them. Those very exalted beings who dwell on the Sun then influence the Moon,which again influences human beings. This influence,however,does not extend to the whole of man,but chiefly to those parts which have thrown off the influence of their own picture-consciousness. It is then that especially the physical and the etheric bodies attain a definite size and form. On the other hand,the phenomena of consciousness retire into the background. But when the human being is turned away from the Sun,it is occupied with its own nature; an inner activity begins,especially in the astral body while the outer form, on the contrary,becomes more insignificant,and less perfect in form.

Thus during the Moon evolution there are two states of consciousness to be clearly distinguished,alternating with each other; duller during the Sun period and clearer during the time when life is left more to its own resources. The first state though duller,is on the other hand more unselfish; man then lives a life more devoted to the outer world,to the universe. It is an alternation of states of consciousness,which on one hand may be compared with the alternation of sleeping and waking in present day humanity,as well as with his life between birth and death,on the other hand with the more spiritual existence between death and a new birth. The awakening on the Moon,when the Sun period gradually ceases, might be described as something intermediate between the awakening of contemporary man each morning,and his being born. And in the same way the gradual dulling of consciousness at the approach of the Sun period resembles a condition midway between falling asleep and dying. For on the old Moon there was not yet such a consciousness of birth and death as man now possesses. Man gave himself up to the enjoyment of the universe in a kind of Sun life. During this period he was carried beyond his own life; he lived more spiritually. We can only attempt an approximate description, by way of comparison,of what man experienced during such times. He felt as though the forces of the universe were streaming into him,pulsing through him. He felt as though intoxicated with the harmonies of the universe which he thus experienced.

As such times his astral body was as though set free from the physical body; also part of the etheric body went with it out of the physical body. This organism,consisting of the astral and etheric bodies,was like a delicate,wonderful musical instrument,from the strings of which the mysteries of the universe reverberated. And the members of that part of the human being on which consciousness had but slight influence were shaped in accordance with the harmonies of the universe. For the Sun-beings worked in those harmonies. Thus this part of man was given its form by the spiritual sounds of the universe; and at the same time the alternation between the clearer state of consciousness during the Sun period,and the duller one,was not so abrupt as was that between the waking state and that of absolutely dreamless sleep in contemporary man.
The picture-consciousness was not so clear as the present waking consciousness; but on the other hand,the other consciousness was not so dull as the dreamless sleep of the present day.

Thus the human being had a conception,even though dim,of the play of the cosmic harmonies in his physical body and in that part of his etheric body which had remained united with the physical body. During the time when,so to speak,the Sun did not shine on humanity,the picture-concepts replaced these harmonies in man's consciousness. There was then a revival particularly of those parts of the physical and etheric bodies which were

under the immediate power of consciousness. On the other hand,other parts
of the human being,now not exposed to the formative forces streaming from
the Sun,underwent a kind of hardening and drying up process. When the Sun
period again drew near,the old bodies decayed; they fell away from the human being,and as though from the grave of his old bodily form,the rejuvenated human being appeared,who even in this new form,was still uncomely.

A renewal of the life-process had taken place. By the operation of the Sun-beings and their harmonies,the new-born body shaped itself again in its perfection,and the process described above was repeated. Man felt that renewal as if it were the putting on of new garments. The kernel of his being had not passed through an actual birth or death; it had only passed from a spiritual tone-consciousness,in which it was given over to the outer world,to one of a more inner nature. It had sloughed off its skin. The old body had become useless; it was thrown off and renewed. This
then more clearly describes what has been characterized above as a kind of
reproduction,and which as has been said,is closely connected with perception. Man's being has brought forth his likeness with respect to certain parts of the physical and etheric bodies. However a being totally different from the parent being does not come into existence,but the kernel of the parent-being passes over into the offspring. No new being arises,but the same one in a new form.

Thus the Moon human being experiences a change of consciousness. When the
Sun period draws near,his pictured images become dimmer and dimmer, and
blissful devotion takes possession of him; the harmonies of the universe resound in his peaceful inner being. Toward the end of this time the images of the astral body begin to be animated; he begins to be more conscious of himself and able to experience sensation. Man experiences something like an awakening from the bliss and tranquility in which he was wrapped during the sun period.

At the same time another important experience begins. With this new clearing up of the picture-consciousness the human being sees himself as though enveloped in a cloud,which has descended upon him like a being from the cosmos.

And he feels that being as something belonging to him,as a completion of his own nature; he feels it as that which gives him existence,as his "ego." That being is one of the Sons of Life. Man feels toward him somewhat like this: "I have lived in this being,even when I was given up to the glory of the universe in the Sun period,--only then he was not visible to me; now he is." And it is also this Son of Life from whom proceeds the force which,during the Sunless period,acts upon the body of man. Then when the Sun period again approaches,man feels as though he himself became one with the Son of Life. Even if man does not see him,he nevertheless feels closely united with him.

Now the connection with the Sons of Life was such that not every individual human being had a Son of Life to himself,but an entire group of people felt such a being belonging to them. Thus people on the Moon lived segregated into groups,and each group felt in one of the Sons of Life its common "group-ego." The etheric body of each particular group had
a specific form,in this way these groups differed from each other. But as the physical bodies shaped themselves in conformity with the etheric

bodies,the differences of the latter were also stamped upon the former; and the individual groups of human beings appeared as so many species of people. As the Sons of Life looked down on the human groups belonging to them,they saw themselves to a certain extent reproduced in manifold individual human beings. And therein they felt their own egohood. They,so to speak,mirrored themselves in man. This was indeed the mission of the human senses at that time. It has already been shown that the senses did not as yet transmit objective perceptions. But they reflected the nature of the Sons of Life. What those Sons of Life perceived through reflection, gave them their "ego-consciousness." What was aroused in the human astral body by this reflection was the dull dim pictures of the Moon-consciousness. By thus acting conjointly and reciprocally with the Sons of Life,the human beings laid the foundations of the nervous system within their physical bodies. The nerves appear,one might say,as continuations of the senses,directed inwardly into the human body.

It is evident,from this description,in what manner the three kinds of Spirits,those of Personality,of Fire,and of Life,act upon Moon-humanity. If we look back upon the most important,namely the middle period of the Moon evolution,we may say that the Sons of Personality are at that time implanting in the human astral body independence and the character of personality. It is owing to this fact that man can turn his attention inwards and work upon himself during those times when the Sun is not shining upon him.

The Sons of Fire act upon the etheric body in so far as the independent formation of the human being becomes imprinted upon it. Through their means it comes to pass that human beings are again conscious of themselves,as such,every time the body is renewed. Thus a kind of memory is bestowed on the etheric body through the Sons of Fire.

The Sons of Life act on the physical body in such a way that it is able to become the expression of the astral body which has now become independent. They thus make it possible for the physical body to become a physiognomic copy of its astral body. On the other hand,higher spiritual beings,in particular the Lords of Form and of Motion,reach down into the physical and etheric bodies,as far as these are developing during the Sun periods, regardless of the independent astral body. Their intervention comes from the Sun,in the manner described above.

Under the influence of such facts,the human being gradually matures to a point where it can develop within itself the germ of the Spirit-Self just as during the second half of the Saturn evolution it developed the germ of the Spirit-Man and on the Sun that of the Life-Spirit. Thereby all the Moon conditions are changed. Human beings have not only become more noble and refined through successive transformations and renewals,but they have also gained in power. For this reason the picture-consciousness was more and more maintained during the Sun periods. It also gained influence in the formation of the physical and etheric bodies,which hitherto had been formed entirely by the action of the Sun-beings.

What took place on the Moon through human beings and the Spirits connected with them became more and more like that which had formerly been effected by the Sun with its higher beings. The consequence was that those

Sun-beings were able more and more to concentrate their forces on their own evolution. By this means the Moon became,after a time,mature enough
to be again re-united with the Sun. To spiritual vision,these occurrences take place as follows: The "rebellious Moon-beings" had been gradually overcome by the Sun-beings and compelled to submit to them in such a manner,that their activities became a part of and subordinate to the activities of the Sun-beings. It is true that this happened only after the lapse of long ages during which the Moon periods had become shorter and shorter,and the Sun periods longer and longer. Now there again comes an evolution during which the Sun and Moon form one world-organism. By this
time the physical human body has become quite etheric.

When it is said that the physical body has become etheric,it must not be imagined that under such circumstances there is no existing physical body. What was formed as a physical body during the Saturn,Sun,and Moon periods,still exists. It is important to recognize the physical element even where it is not externally and physically manifested. It may also be present in such a way that it shows outwardly an etheric or even an astral
form. We must distinguish between the outward appearance and the inner
law. What is physical may become etheric and astral,at the same time retain in itself the physical law. That is the case when the physical body of man has attained a certain degree of perfection on the Moon. It becomes
etheric in form.

But when clairvoyant observation,which can perceive such things,is directed toward an etheric body of this kind,that body is seen to be ruled by physical,not etheric,laws. The physical element has in this case been taken into the etheric world,there to rest and to be nurtured as though in a mother's tender care. Later it again emerges in a physical form,but at a higher stage. If Moon-humanity had kept its physical body in its coarse physical form,the Moon would never have been able to unite itself with the Sun. By accepting the etheric form,the physical body becomes more closely related to the etheric body,and by this means can again be more closely interpenetrated with those parts of the etheric and astral bodies which had been forced to withdraw from it during the Sun periods of the Moon evolution. Man,who appeared as a being with a two-fold nature during the separation of Sun and Moon,again becomes an undivided being. The physical becomes more psychic. Therefore the psychic also becomes more closely connected with the physical.

Now the Sun-Spirits,into whose immediate sphere this undivided human being has entered,are able to act upon it in quite a different manner from their previous influence from without on the Moon. Man is now in a more psycho-spiritual environment. Owing to this,the Lords of Wisdom are able to effect something momentous. They imbue and inspire him with wisdom. He thereby becomes in a certain sense an independent soul. And to
the influence of these beings is added that of the Lords of Motion. They act principally on the astral body,so that under their influence it produces psychic activity,and an etheric body filled with wisdom. The latter is the foundation of that which has been described above as the rational or intellectual soul in contemporary man,whereas the astral body,inspired by the Lords of Motion,is the germ of the sentient soul. And because all this is effected in man's being in his progressed condition of independence,these germs of the rational and sentient soul appear as the expression of the Spirit-Self. In this connection the mistake must not be made of thinking that at this period of evolution the Spirit-Self was something separate from the intellectual and sentient souls. The latter are only the expression of the Spirit-Self,which

signifies their higher unity and harmony.

It is especially significant that the Lords of Wisdom intervene at this period in the manner described. For they do this not only with regard to humanity but also for the benefit of the other kingdoms which have been elaborated on the Moon. Upon the reunion of Sun and Moon these lower kingdoms are drawn into the Sun sphere. Everything in them which was physical becomes etheric. There are,therefore,minela-plants and plant-animals now in the Sun,just as there is humanity there. But those other creatures are still endowed with their own laws of being. They therefore feel like strangers in their environment. They came upon the scene with a nature but little in harmony with their surroundings. But as they have become etheric,the activity of the Lords of Wisdom may also extend to them. Everything which has come from the Moon into the Sun now becomes pervaded with the forces of the Lords of Wisdom. Hence what is developed out of the Sun-Moon organism during this period of evolution may be called in occult science the "Cosmos of Wisdom."

When,therefore,after an interval of rest,our Earth system appears as the successor of this Cosmos of Wisdom,all the beings newly emerging on the earth,developing out of their Moon-germs,prove to be filled with wisdom. And this is the reason why earthly man when contemplating the things around him,is able to discover the wisdom concealed in their inner nature. The wisdom in each leaf of a plant,in every bone in animal and man,in the marvelous structure of the brain and heart,fills us with admiration. If man requires wisdom to understand things,and therefore gathers wisdom from them,this shows that there is wisdom in the things themselves. For however much man might have striven to understand things by means of wise perceptions,he could not draw wisdom from them unless it had first been put into them. He who tries by means of wisdom to understand things,assuming at the same time that wisdom had not first been concealed within them,may just as reasonably believe that he can empty water out of a glass into which it has not first been poured. As will be shown later in this book,the Earth is the "old Moon" risen again. And it appears as an organism full of wisdom,because it was permeated by the Lords of Wisdom and their forces during the epoch that has been described.

It will easily be understood that this description of the Moon condition could take account only of certain temporary forms of evolution. It was necessary to pause at certain things in the progress of events,and single them out for delineation. It is true that this kind of description gives only isolated pictures,and it may be deplored for this reason,that in the foregoing account the evolutionary scheme was not brought down to a system of precise and definite concepts. But in the face of such an objection it may be well to point out that the description was intentionally given in less clearly defined outlines. For it is not of so much consequence here to give speculative ideas and to construct theories as to represent what really passes before the spiritual eyes of clairvoyant consciousness,when looking back upon these events. With regard to the Moon evolution this cannot be done in such sharp and definite outlines as are characteristic of earthly perceptions. In the Moon period we are mainly concerned with variable,changing impressions, with shifting,moving pictures and their transitory stages. We have, moreover,to bear in mind that we are contemplating an evolution continuing through long,long periods of time,and that out of all that presents itself,it is possible to seize upon only momentary pictures and fix them for delineation.

The Moon period actually reached its highest point at the time when the astral body,implanted in man,had brought him so far along the evolutionary path that his physical body afforded the Sons of Life the possibility of attaining their human stage. Man had then attained all that this epoch could give him for himself,for his inner nature on the upward path. The following,or second half of the Moon evolution may therefore be termed the "ebb-tide," or wane. But even during this ebb-tide one sees a most important thing taking place with regard to man's environment,and even with regard to himself. It is now that wisdom is implanted in the Sun-Moon body. It has been shown that during the ebb-tide the germs of the intellectual and sentient souls are implanted. But the development of these,as well as of the consciousness-soul and with it the birth of the "Ego"--the free self consciousness--does not ensue until the Earth period.

At the Moon stage the intellectual- and sentient-souls have as yet no appearance of being used by human beings as a means of expression; they appear rather as instruments of those Sons of Life who belong to humanity.
Were we to describe the feeling of the human dweller on the Moon in this respect,we should have to say that he experiences the following: "The Son of Life lives in and through me; he surveys through me the environment of the Moon; in me he reflects upon the things and beings of that environment." The Moon human being feels himself overshadowed by the Son of Life,and looks upon himself as the instrument of that higher being. During the time of the separation of Sun and Moon he felt a greater measure of independence when the Sun was turned away from him; but at the same time he also felt as though the ego belonging to him,which had disappeared from the picture-consciousness during the Sun period,now became visible. It was,for Moon-humanity,what may be described as a change in the states of consciousness,so that the Moon-being had this feeling: "In the Sun period my ego wafts me away into higher regions,into the presence of exalted beings;and when the Sun disappears it descends with me into lower worlds."

The actual Moon evolution was preceded by a preparatory stage. In a certain way the Saturn and Sun evolutions were recapitulated. Now,after the reunion of Sun and Moon,during what we have termed the ebb-tide, two epochs may be distinguished one from the other. In the course of these, even physical condensation occurs to a certain degree. Therefore psycho-spiritual conditions of the Sun-Moon organism alternate with others of a more physical nature. In such physical epochs human beings and those of the lower kingdoms appear as though they were preparing,in stiff not yet self-reliant forms,the type of what they were to become in a more independent manner during the Earth period. We may therefore speak of two preparatory epochs in the Moon evolution,and of two others during the ebb-tide. In occult science such epochs may be termed cycles.(20) In that period which follows the two preparatory epochs,and precedes those of the ebb-tide--that is to say,during the time of the separation of the Moon--three epochs can again be distinguished. The middle period is the time when the Sons of Life reached the human level. It is preceded by a period in which all conditions lead up to that crowning event; and it is followed by one which may be called a time of adaptation and of perfecting the new creations.

In this way the middle period of the Moon evolution is again divided into three epochs,which,with the two preparatory periods and the two during the ebb-tide make up seven Moon cycles,or rounds. It may therefore be said that the whole Moon evolution passes through seven cycles,or rounds.

Between them are intervals of rest,which have been mentioned repeatedly in the above description. Yet we can approach a true concept of these facts only if we do not think of the changes between the periods of activity and those of rest,as sudden ones. For instance,the Sun-beings little by little withdraw their activity from the Moon. A time begins for them which,viewed from without,appears to be their resting period, whereas in reality an intense,independent activity still continues on the Moon itself. Thus the active period of one kind of being repeatedly extends into the resting time of another. If we take account of such things we may speak of a rhythmic ascent and descent of forces in cycles.

Indeed,similar divisions are to be recognized even within the seven Moon cycles mentioned. We may then call the whole Moon evolution one great cycle,and the seven divisions,or rounds,within it,"small" cycles; and again,the separate parts of these,"smaller" cycles. This systematic arrangement into seven times seven divisions is also noticeable in the Sun evolution and can be indicated during the Saturn period. Yet we must bear in mind that the boundaries between the divisions are somewhat obliterated even in the Sun,and still more so in Saturn. These boundaries become more and more defined the nearer evolution advances to the Earth period.

At the close of the Moon evolution,which has been sketched in the foregoing pages,all the beings and forces connected with it enter upon a more spiritual form of existence. This is on quite a different plane from that of the Moon period,and also from that of the Earth evolution which follows. A being possessed of faculties so highly developed as to enable him to perceive all the details of the Moon and Earth evolutions need not necessarily be able to see what happens during the interval between the two periods. For one possessing such vision,beings and forces would,at the end of the Moon period,disappear,as it were,into nothingness; and after an interval they would issue forth again from the dusky twilight of the cosmic depths. Only a being endowed with considerably higher faculties would be capable of following up the spiritual events which take place during this interval.

When this interval is over,the beings who took part in the evolutionary processes on Saturn,Sun,and Moon reappear endowed with new faculties. Beings of a higher order than man have,by their former achievements,won the power of bringing man's evolution forward to a point at which he would be able to unfold in himself,during the Earth period,a form of consciousness which stands a step higher than the picture-consciousness he had possessed during the Moon period. But man must first be prepared to receive this gift.

During the Saturn,Sun,and Moon evolutions,he incorporated within his being the physical,etheric,and astral bodies. But those bodies were only endowed with such faculties and powers as enabled them to have a picture-consciousness; the organs and forms by means of which they could attain to a cognizance of a world of outer sense-objects,such as is requisite for the Earth stage,were still wanting. Just as the new plant unfolds only what is concealed in the seed originating from the old plant, so do the three principles of man's nature appear,at the beginning of the new stage of evolution,with such forms and organs as will enable them to develop only a picture-consciousness. It is necessary first to prepare them for the unfolding of a higher state of consciousness.

This takes place in three preliminary stages. During the first,the physical body is raised to a level at which it becomes able to undergo the necessary remodeling which is to serve as a basis for consciousness of outer objects. This is one of the preliminary stages of the actual earth evolution,and may be called a recapitulation of the Saturn period on a higher level. For during this period,as during the Saturn period,higher beings are working only on the physical body. When the latter has progressed far enough in its evolution,all beings must first again pass into a higher form of existence before the etheric body can also progress. The physical body must,as it were,be recast,in order to be able,in its remodeled state,to receive the more highly constituted etheric body. After this interval devoted to a higher form of existence,a kind of recapitulation of the Sun evolution on a higher level,occurs for the purpose of shaping the etheric body. And after another interval,a similar thing occurs for the astral body,by means of a recapitulation of the Moon evolution.

Let us now turn our attention to the evolutionary processes taking place after the close of the third recapitulation described. All beings and forces have passed again into a state of spiritualization. During that state they ascended into higher worlds. The lowest of the worlds,in which something of them is still to be perceived during this spiritualizing epoch,are the same in which contemporary man sojourns between death and a
new birth. These are the regions of the spirit-world. Thence the beings and forces gradually descend again into lower worlds. Before the physical Earth evolution begins they have so far descended that their lowest manifestations are to be seen in the astral or psychic world.

Everything human existing at that period is still in its astral form. In order to understand this condition of humanity,attention should be paid especially to the fact that though man has within him the physical, etheric and astral bodies,yet the physical and etheric bodies are not present in their own forms but in astral form. It is not physical form that makes the physical body physical,but the fact that it embodies physical laws,although possessing an astral form. It is a being in a psychic form with a physical law of existence. The etheric body is in a similar position.

To spiritual vision the Earth at this stage of evolution appears at first as a heavenly body all soul and spirit,in which,therefore,even physical and life forces appear in a psychic form. In this world-organism everything which will subsequently be moulded into the creatures of the physical earth is contained in a germinal state. The globe is luminous; but its light is not yet such as could be seen by physical eyes,supposing even that they had then existed. The globe shines only in psychic light to the opened vision of the seer.

A process now takes place on this globe which may be designated "condensation." The result of this is that after a time a fiery form appears in the midst of the psychic globe; this condition was similar to that of Saturn in its densest state. This fiery form is interpenetrated by the action of the various beings who are taking part in the evolution. The reciprocal action which is to be observed between those beings and the planetary body is like a rising out of and a diving into the earth's fiery globe. Hence the earth's globe is by no means a homogeneous substance, but
has somewhat the character of an ensouled and spiritualized organism. The

beings destined to become human on the earth in man's present form are as yet in a condition which renders them the least capable of sharing in the activity of plunging into the fiery globe. They remain almost entirely in the uncondensed environment. They are still living in the bosom of the higher spiritual beings. At this stage they come in contact with the fiery earth at only one point of their psychic form,and this causes one part of their astral form to be densified by the heat. Thus earth-life is enkindled in them. They therefore still belong to psycho-spiritual worlds with regard to the greater part of their nature,but by coming in contact with the earth's fire,vital heat plays around them.

If we wish to draw a material,yet supersensible,picture of these human beings in the very beginning of the earth's evolution,we must imagine a psychic ovoid,or egg,contained within the circumference of the earth, and enclosed on its lower surface,as an acorn is by its cup. The substance of the cup,however,consists solely of heat or fire. The process of being enveloped by heat not only causes the kindling of life in the human being,but a change appears simultaneously in the astral body. In this body becomes incorporated the first germ of what afterwards becomes the sentient-soul. We may therefore say that man at this stage of his existence consists of the sentient-soul,the astral body,the etheric body,and the physical body,which latter is formed out of fire. Those spiritual beings who participate in human existence surge through the astral body. Man feels himself bound to the earth body by the sentient-soul. He has therefore at this time a preponderating picture-consciousness,in which are manifested those spiritual beings in whose bosom he reposes; and the feeling of his own body seems to be merely a point within that consciousness. He looks down,so to speak,from the spiritual world upon earthly possession,which he feels belongs to him.

Further and further the condensation of the earth now proceeds and at the same time the differentiation of the various parts of man,as has been described,becomes more and more defined. From a definite point of evolution onward,the earth is so far condensed that only part of it is fiery; another part has assumed a substantial shape,which may be termed "gas" or "air." A change also takes place now in man. He is not only brought into contact with the heat of the earth,but the air substance is incorporated in his fire-body. And as heat kindled life in him,the air playing around him creates an effect within him which may be called (spiritual) sound. His etheric body begins to resound. Simultaneously,a part of the astral body becomes separated from the remainder; this part is the germ of the intellectual-soul which appears later.

In order to bring before our eyes what takes place in the human soul at this time,we must notice that the beings superior to man are surging through the airy-fiery body of the earth. In the fire-earth it is at first the Sons of Personality who are of importance to man,and when man is stirred into life by the heat of the earth his sentient soul says to itself,"These are the Sons of Personality." In the same way the beings called "Archangels" earlier in this book (in accordance with Christian esotericism) appear in the air-sphere. It is their influences which man feels within him as sound,when the air plays around him. And the intellectual-soul then says to itself,"These are the Archangels." Thus what man at this stage perceives,through his connection with the earth, is not as yet a collection of physical objects,but he lives in sensations of heat which rise up to him,and in sounds; in those heat currents and sound waves,however,he feels the Sons of Personality and the Archangels. It is true that he cannot perceive those beings directly,only,as it were,through a veil of heat and sound. While these perceptions are penetrating from the earth into his soul,there continue to ascend and descend within it the images of those higher beings in whose tender care he feels himself to be.

Now evolution takes a further step,which is once more expressed in condensation. Watery substance is incorporated into the Earth-body,so that now the latter consists of three parts,--igneous,aeriform,and aqueous. Before this happens,something of great importance takes place. An independent celestial body is split off from the fiery-aeriform earth; this new body becomes in its later development our present sun.(21) Previously,earth and sun had formed one body. After the sun had been split off,the earth still has at first everything within it which is in and on the present moon. The separation of the sun takes place because higher beings could no longer carry on their own evolution as well as their task on Earth within this atmosphere,now densified to the consistency of water. They separate from the general mass of the Earth the
only substances useful to them,and fare forth to make a new abode for themselves in the sun. They now influence the earth from the sun,from outside. Man,however,needs for his further evolution an environment in which matter becomes still more condensed.

With the incorporation of watery substance in the earth-body a change also
takes place in man. Henceforth not only does fire stream into him and air play around him,but watery substance is incorporated into his physical body. At the same time his etheric part changes: that is,it is now perceived by man as a fine light-body. Previous to this,man had felt currents of heat rising up to him from the earth: he had felt air surrounding him through tones; now,the watery element also penetrates his
fire-air body,and he sees its ebb and flow as the alternate flaring up and dimming of light. But a change has also taken place in his soul. To the germs of the sentient and intellectual souls is added that of the consciousness-soul. The "Angels" work in the element of water: they are also the real producers of light. It was as though they appeared to man in light.

The higher beings who were previously in the Earth-planet itself,now influence it from the sun. On this account all effects produced on the earth are changed. The human being chained to earth would no longer be able to feel the influence of the sun-beings within him,if his soul were unceasingly turned toward the earth,from which his physical body is taken. A change now appears in the conditions of human consciousness. At
certain times the sun-beings wrest the soul of man from his physical body, so that man is now alternately purely psychic,in the bosom of the sun-beings,and,when united with the body,in a condition in which he receives earth influences. When in the physical body,heat currents stream up to him; a sea of air is sounding round him and water pours into and out of him. When man is out of his body the images of the higher beings in whose care he is,float through his soul.

The earth passes through two periods at this stage of its evolution. During one of these it allows its substances to circulate around the human
souls and clothe them with bodies; during the other,the souls have withdrawn from it,and only the bodies are left and the human beings are in a condition of sleep. It is speaking quite in conformity with facts to say that in those times of a remote past the earth passed through a day and a night time. (Expressed in terms of physical space this means that through the reciprocal action of the sun-beings and the earth-beings,the earth is brought into a movement in relation with the sun; thus there is brought about the alternation of day and night periods described above.

The day period is when the surface of the earth,on which man is evolving, is turned toward the sun; the night period,the time when man leads a purely psychic existence,is when the earth's surface is turned away from the sun. Now it must not,of course,be imagined that in that far-off time the earth's motion around the sun was like its present motion. The conditions were still utterly different. But even at this early point it is helpful to realize that the motions of the celestial bodies are a consequence of the mutual relations of the spiritual beings inhabiting them. Spiritual-psychic causes produce in the celestial bodies positions and motions which permit the manifestation of spiritual conditions on the physical plane.)

If our gaze were turned upon the earth during its night period,its body would appear like a corpse. For it consists to a great extent of the decaying bodies of those human beings whose souls are in another state of existence. The organized watery and aeriform structures of which human bodies were formed become disintegrated,and dissolve into the rest of the earth's substance. Only that part of man's body which was formed from the very beginning of the earth evolution by the co-operation of fire and the human soul,and which subsequently became denser and denser,continues to exist as an insignificant looking embryo. Now when the day period begins, the earth once more participates directly in the sun influence,and human souls press forward into the sphere of physical life. They come in contact with the embryos,and cause them to spring up and assume an external form, which appears like an image of man's psychic being. Something like a delicate fertilization then takes place between the human soul and the bodily embryo.

The souls thus embodied now begin once more to attract the aeriform and watery substances and incorporate them in their own bodies. Air is expelled and absorbed by the organized body,--the first beginning of that which later appears as the respiratory process. Water too is absorbed and expelled; the nutritive process in its original form has begun. But these processes are not yet perceived as external ones. A kind of external perception takes place in the soul only by means of the already characterized kind of fertilization. Here the soul vaguely feels its awakening to physical existence when it comes in contact with the embryo which is held toward it from the earth. It then feels something which may be put into words thus: "This is my form." And such a feeling,which might even be called a dawning consciousness of self,abides within the soul through this union with the physical body. But the soul still feels the process of absorbing air in an absolutely psycho-spiritual way,as an image,which appears in the form of tone-pictures surging up and down; these give form to the embryo which is being incorporated within them. The soul everywhere feels itself in the midst of sound waves,and that it is fashioning the body in accordance with those tone forces. Thus are human forms developed at that stage of evolution. They cannot be observed in any external world by our present consciousness. They evolve like vegetable or flower forms of fine substance,therefore appear like flowers waving in the wind.

During his Earth period,man experiences the blissful feeling of being fashioned into such forms. The absorption of the watery parts is felt in the soul as an accession of force,or inner strength. From without it appears as growth of the physical human structure. As the direct influence of the sun decreases,the human soul also loses the power of controlling these processes. By degrees they are cast aside. Only those parts are left which allow the embryo,above described,to mature. But man leaves his body,and returns to the spiritual form of existence. (As not all parts of the earth's body are employed in building up human bodies,we must not imagine that during the earth's night period,it is composed exclusively of disintegrating corpses and embryos waiting to be awakened. All these are imbedded in other structures,which are formed out of the earth's substances. The status of those structures will be explained later.)

Now,however,the process of condensing the earth's substance continues. To the watery element is added the solid or "earthly" substance ("earthly" in the sense of occult science). And when this happens man also,during his earth period,begins to incorporate the earthly element in his body. As soon as this incorporation begins,the forces which the soul brings with it out of the disembodied state,no longer have the same power as before. Previously,the soul had fashioned its body out of the igneous, aeriform,and watery elements,in accordance with the tones which resounded and the light-pictures which played around it. The soul cannot do this with regard to the solidified form. Other forces now interpose to shape it. What is left behind of man,when the soul withdraws from the body,is not only an embryo to be fanned into life by the returning soul, but a structure containing in itself reanimating power. The soul,at its departure,not only leaves its image behind on earth but sends down some of its animating power into that image.

Now on its reappearance on earth the soul alone no longer suffices to awaken the image to life; reanimation must take place in the image itself. The spiritual beings influencing the earth from the sun now uphold the reanimating force that is in the human body,even though man himself is not upon the earth. Thus,during its incarnation,the soul is not only sensible of the sounds and light-pictures floating around,in which it feels the beings next above it,but,through receiving the earthly element,it comes under the influence of those still higher beings who have taken up their abode on the sun. Previously,man felt that he belonged to the psycho-spiritual beings with whom he was united when free from the body. His ego was still within them. Now that ego confronts him during physical incarnation,quite as much as everything else which is around him during that period. Independent images of the psycho-spiritual being of man were henceforth on the earth. These structures,in comparison with the present human body,were of a finer material. For the earthly part mixed with them only in its finest state,much in the same way as when man of the present day absorbs the finely distributed substances of an object through his organ of smell. Human bodies were like shadows. But as they were distributed over the whole earth they came under earth influences,which varied in their nature on different parts of the earth's surface. Whereas formerly bodily images corresponded to the human soul animating them,and on that account were essentially alike over the whole earth,differences now appeared between human forms. In this manner the way was prepared for what appeared later as differences of race.

When the human body became independent,the previous close union of the earth-man with the psycho-spiritual world was to a certain extent dissolved. Henceforth,when the soul left the body,the latter,in a way, continued to live. If evolution had gone on advancing in this manner,the earth would have hardened under the influence of its solid elements. To the eyes of the seer who looks back on those conditions,human bodies, when abandoned by their souls,appear to become more and more solidified.

And after a time the human souls returning to earth would have found no available material with which to combine. All the substances available for man would have been used up in filling the earth with the hardened, wood-like remains of incarnations.

Then an event took place which gave a new turn to the whole evolution. Everything in the solid earthly substance which could contribute to permanent induration was eliminated. At this point our present moon left the earth. And what had previously directly conduced to a moulding of permanent forms,now operated from the moon indirectly and in a diminished degree. The higher beings,on whom that moulding of forms depended,had resolved to exercise their influences upon their earth no longer from its interior,but from without. By this means there was brought about in the bodily structure of man a difference which must be called the beginning of the separation into a male and a female sex.

The finely constituted human forms which formerly inhabited the earth,had produced through cooperation of the two forces within themselves,that of the embryo and that of the animating force,the new human form,their descendant. These descendants are now transformed. In one group the animating power of the psycho-spiritual element was paramount; in another the animating germinal force. This was caused by the weakening of the power of the solid element in consequence of the moon's leaving the earth.

The reciprocal action of these two forces now became more delicate than it had been before--when it occurred within one single body,consequently the descendant also became more delicate and fine. He entered the earth in a delicate condition,and only gradually incorporated more solid parts within him. In this way the possibility of union with the body was once more given to the human soul returning to earth. It no longer animated the body from without,because that animation took place on the earth itself; but it became united with the body,and enabled it to grow. Of course a certain limit was set to that growth. Through the separation of the moon, the human body had for a time become supple; but the more it continued to grow on the earth,the more the solidifying forces got the upper hand. At length the share borne by the soul in the organization of the body grew less and less,and the body disintegrated when the soul ascended to psycho-spiritual modes of existence. One can trace how the forces gradually acquired by man during the Saturn,Sun,and Moon evolutions take part more and more in the progress of man during the described formative periods of the earth. The first part to be kindled by the earth's fire is the astral body,still containing within it the etheric and physical bodies in a state of solution. Then the astral body is organized into a more subtle astral part,the sentient soul,and into a grosser etheric part,which henceforth is in contact with the earth-element; when this occurs,the etheric or vital body,already fore-shadowed,makes its appearance. And while the intellectual and consciousness-souls are being evolved in the astral man,there are incorporated into the etheric body those coarser parts which are susceptible to sound and light.

At the time when the etheric body still further densifies and changes from a light-body into a fire or heat-body,the stage of evolution has been reached at which,as described above,parts of the solid earth-element are incorporated into man. Because the etheric body has condensed to the consistency of fire,it is now able,by means of the forces of the physical body previously implanted in it,to combine with those substances of the physical earth attenuated as far as the fire-state. But by itself

it would no longer be able to introduce air substances into the body which has meanwhile become more solidified. Then,as indicated above,the higher beings dwelling on the sun interpose,breathing air into the body. While man,by virtue of his past,is able of himself to become permeated with earthly fire,higher beings direct the breath of air into his body. Heretofore the etheric body of man,as a receiver of sound,had been the director of the air current. It permeated man's physical body with life. Now the physical body gets life from without. The result is that this life becomes independent of the soul part of man. On departing from the earth the soul leaves behind not only the seed of its form,but also a living image of itself. The Lords of Form now remain united with that image,and the life they have bestowed,they transfer to man's descendants,when his soul has left the body. Thus comes about what may be called heredity,and when the human soul once more appears on earth it feels that it is in a body animated by the life of its ancestors. It feels itself especially attracted to just that kind of a body. In this way something like a _memory_ is formed of the ancestor with whom the soul feels itself to be
at one. This memory passes through the line of descendants in the form of
a consciousness possessed in common. The ego thus flows down through the
generations.

At this stage of evolution man,during his life on earth,was conscious of himself as an independent being. He felt the inner fire of his etheric body to be combined with the external fire of the earth. He could feel the heat that was streaming through him as his own ego. In those heat currents,interwoven with life,are to be found the first beginnings of the circulation of the blood. But in what flowed into him as air,he did not exactly feel as his own being. Indeed,it was the forces of the higher beings we have described that were working in that air. But still there was left to him,within the air that flowed through him,that part of the active forces which belonged to him by virtue of his previously formed etheric powers. He was master in one part of those air currents. And to that extent,it was not only the higher beings who were shaping him,but he himself. He formed the air parts of his being in accordance with the images of his astral body. While air was thus flowing into his body from without,a process which became the basis of respiration,part of the air was formed within him into an organism which became fixed and was the basis of the subsequent nervous system. Thus man at this period was connected with the external earth by heat and air.

On the other hand,he was not conscious of the introduction within himself of the solid element of the earth. Although it contributed to his own embodiment,he could not perceive directly what was being supplied but could only do so through a dim consciousness in the image of the higher beings who were active in the process. In the same kind of picture-form, as an expression of the beings above him,man had previously perceived the introduction of the fluid element into the earth. Through the densification of his earthly form the pictures have now undergone a change
in his consciousness. The solid element has been mixed with the fluid. This incoming of the solid element must also be seen to be the work of higher beings operated from without. It is no longer possible for the human soul to have the power of directing the supply for that supply has now to serve his body,which is being built up from without. He would spoil its form if he were to direct the influx himself.

What,therefore,reaches him from without appears to him to be directed by
authoritative orders issuing from the higher beings who are at work on the
shaping of his body. Man feels himself to be an ego; he has within him,as

part of his astral body,his intellectual-soul,through which he inwardly perceives,in the form of pictures,what is happening externally,and by means of which he permeates his delicate nervous system. He feels himself
to be descended from ancestors,by virtue of the life flowing down through the generations. He breathes,and feels it to be the effect of the higher beings who have been described as the Lords of Form. He is likewise subject to their impulses in all that which comes to him from the outside (as his food). What he finds most obscure is his origin as an individual. As to that,he only knows that he has been under the influence of the Lords of Form expressing themselves in earth-forces. In his relations with the outer world,man was guided and ruled. This finds expression through the fact that man has a consciousness of the psycho-spiritual activities operating behind his physical environment. It is true that he does not see the spiritual beings in their own form,but he is conscious in his soul of sounds and colors. He knows,however,that it is the actions of spiritual beings that are realized through that world of images. What those beings communicate to him,reaches him as sound; their manifestations appear to him in light-pictures.

The innermost concepts,of which earthly man becomes conscious,are those
conveyed to him by the element of fire or warmth. He can already distinguish between his own inner heat and the heat currents of the earth's periphery. In these latter are manifested the Sons of Personality. But man has only a dim consciousness of what is behind the currents of external heat. It is in those very currents that he feels the influence of the Lords of Form. When powerful effects of heat are produced in man's environment,the soul feels that spiritual beings are now heating the earth's circumference--beings,from whom a spark has been detached, which
warms his inner being.

In the effect of light,however,man does not yet distinguish in quite the same manner between the outer and the inner. When light-pictures appear
around him,they do not always produce the same feeling in the soul of the earth-man. There were times when he felt them as external images. This was
during the period when he had just descended from the disembodied state into incarnation. It was the period of his growth on earth. As the time approached for the embryo to be developed those images faded,and man only
retained something like inner memory-pictures of them. The actions of the Sons of Fire (Archangels) were contained in those light-pictures,which appeared to man to be the servitors of the Fire-spirits who sent down a spark into his own inner being. When their outer manifestations died away, man felt them inwardly in the form of images (memories). He felt himself united with their forces. And so indeed he was. For by means of what he had received from them,he was able to work upon his surrounding atmosphere. This,under his influence,began to emit light.

At that time nature forces and human forces were not as yet separated from
each other as they subsequently became. What happened on earth still emanated to a great extent from human forces. Viewing nature processes on
the earth from the outside,one would then have seen in them not only something independent of man,but also the effect of human activity within those processes. Sound-perceptions assumed a still more different form to
the earth-man. From the beginning of earth-life they had been perceived as outer tones. Whereas the external air pictures were perceived up to the middle of earth existence,the external tones could be heard even after

that middle period. And only toward the end of his life did the earth-man become insensible to them. But the memory-pictures of those sounds remained. In them were contained the manifestations of the Sons of Life (Angels). When,toward the end of his life,man felt himself inwardly united with those forces,he was able,by imitating them,to produce mighty effects in the earth's watery element. The waters surged in and above the earth under his influence. Man had perceptions of taste only during the first quarter of his earth-life,and even then they seemed to the soul like a memory of the experience of his disembodied state. As long as they lasted,his body continued to grow more and more solid by assimilating external substances. In the second quarter of earth life growth still continued,but the form was already fully developed. At this time man could perceive other living beings near him only through their heat,light,and sound effects; for he was not as yet capable of imagining the solid element. During the first quarter of his life he received the taste-impressions described,only through the watery element.

Man's external bodily form was an image of this inner psychic condition. Those parts were most fully developed which contained the first fore-shadowing of the later form of the head. The other organs appeared only as appendages. These were shadowy and indistinct. Yet earth-beings varied with regard to form. There were some in whom the appendages were
more or less developed,according to the earth-conditions under which they lived. This varied with people's different dwelling places on the earth. Where they were more involved in the things of earth,the appendages became more prominent. Those human beings who at the beginning of physical
development on earth were the ripest,owing to their previous evolution, having come in contact with the fire-element at the very beginning before the earth had been condensed into air,were those now able to develop the first beginnings of the head most completely. They were those persons possessing most inner harmony.

Others were ready for contact with the fire-element only when the earth had already evolved air within it. They were more dependent upon outer conditions than the first mentioned,who distinctly felt the Lords of Form through heat,and during their earth-life felt as though they retained a memory of having belonged to those spirits and of having been connected with them in the disembodied state. The second species of human beings only had the memory of the disembodied state to a more limited degree; they were conscious of their fellowship with the spiritual world chiefly through the light-influences of the Sons of Fire (Archangels). A third type of human beings was still more entangled in earthly existence. It was they who were unable to come in contact with the fire-element until the earth was separated from the sun and had absorbed the watery element within itself. Their feeling of fellowship with the spiritual world was especially slight at the beginning of earth-life. Only when the activities of the Archangels,and more especially of the Angels,influenced the inner imaginative life,did they feel this connection to any degree. On the other hand,at the beginning of the earth-period they were full of active impulses for performing deeds which can be accomplished under earthly conditions only. In them the extremities were particularly strongly developed.

When the Moon-forces,before the separation of the moon from the earth, tended more and more to harden the latter,it happened that among the descendants of the embryos left behind upon the earth by man,there were some in whom human souls returning from the disembodied state could no
longer incarnate in consequence of the Moon-forces. The form of these descendants was too much solidified and through the Moon-forces,had become too unlike the human form to be able to reassume it. Consequently

certain human souls no longer found it possible,under these circumstances,to return to earth. Only the ripest and strongest of these souls felt competent to transform the earth-body during its growth,so that it could blossom into a human form. Only a portion of the bodily descendants of man became the vehicles of earthly human beings. Another part,because of its solidified form,was able to receive only souls on a lower level than those of men. But there was one group of human souls, however,which was prevented from participating in the earth-evolution of that time. In this way they were driven to embark on another course.

There were souls who,as far back as the separation of the sun from the earth,found no place on the latter. For their further evolution they were removed to a planet which,under the guidance of cosmic beings,was detached from the universal world-substance,--that substance of which the earth formed a part at the beginning of its physical evolution,and from which the sun had separated. This planet,in its physical expression,is the one known to outer science as "Jupiter." (Here we are speaking of celestial bodies,planets,and their names exactly in the sense of a more ancient science,and as is in harmony with occult science. Just as the physical earth is only the physical expression of a great psycho-spiritual organism,so is every other celestial body. And as the seer does not denote only the physical planet by the word "earth," nor only the physical fixed star by "sun," so when speaking of "Jupiter," "Mars," and the other planets,he signifies far-reaching spiritual relationships. The form and mission of the heavenly bodies have,in the nature of things,been essentially changed since the times of which we are here speaking,--in a certain respect even their position in celestial space has been changed. It is possible only for one who follows with the seer's vision the evolution of those celestial bodies back to remote ages of the past,to apprehend the connection of contemporary planets with their predecessors.)
On Jupiter the souls that have been described continued their evolution.

And later,when the earth was tending more and more toward solidification, still another abode had to be prepared for souls who even though they were able to occupy the solidified bodies for a time,could no longer do so when this solidification had progressed too far. An appropriate place for their further evolution was prepared on "Mars." Even as far back as the time when the soul was still united with the sun,and was incorporating the sun's air elements within itself,certain souls were proving unfit to participate in the earth's evolution. They were too powerfully affected by the earthly bodily form. Accordingly,even at that time,they had to be withdrawn from the direct influence of the Sun-forces. These had to influence them from without. The planet Saturn became the scene of their further evolution.

Thus,in the course of the earth's evolution,the number of human forms decreased,and forms appeared which had not embodied human souls. These were able to receive only astral bodies as the human physical and etheric bodies on the old Moon had done. While the earth was becoming depopulated as far as human beings were concerned,these other beings were colonizing it. Eventually all human souls would have been compelled to leave the earth if,by detaching the Moon from it,a way had not been provided to preserve those human bodies which at that time could still harbor human souls. It was made possible for these,during their earth life,to withdraw the human ego from the effects of the Moon-forces coming directly from the earth,thus allowing it to mature sufficiently within themselves until it could be exposed directly to those forces. As long as the embryo was developing within man,it was under the influence of those beings who, under the leadership of the mightiest of their number,had detached the moon from the earth in order to conduct the evolution of the latter over a critical point.

When the earth had developed the air element within it,astral beings were present as described above,who had belonged to the old Moon and who had been left behind. They had fallen short even of the lowest human souls in their evolution. They became the souls of those forms which already before the separation of the Sun had to be abandoned by man. These beings are the ancestors of the animal kingdom. As time went on,they developed especially those organs which in man thus far only existed as appendages. Their astral body had to work on the physical and etheric bodies in the same way as did the human astral body during the old Moon-period. Now the animals which had thus come into existence had souls which could not dwell in the individual animals. The soul extended its being also to the descendant. Virtually,animals descended from one form have a soul in common. Only when the descendant diverges from the ancestral type through special influences,does a new animal soul become incarnated. In this sense,in accordance with occult science,we can speak of a species or group-soul,in animals.

Something of a similar nature took place at the time of the separation of sun and earth. There came forth from the watery element,forms no further evolved than man was before the old Moon-evolution. They could only receive an impression from anything of an astral nature when the latter influenced them from without. This could not happen until after the departure of the sun from the earth. Whenever the sun-period of the earth set in,the astral element in the sun stimulated these forms in such a way that they formed their vital body out of the etheric part of the earth. When the sun turned away from the earth,that etheric body was again dissolved into the common earth-life. And as a result of the co-operation of the astral part of the sun with the etheric part of the earth,there emerged from the watery element those physical forms which became the ancestors of the present vegetable kingdom.

Man became an individualized soul-being on earth. His astral body,which had been poured into him on the Moon through the Lords of Motion,now became organized on earth into the sentient-intellectual-and consciousness-souls. And when the consciousness-soul had progressed so far that it was able to form for itself during earth-life,a body adapted to that life,the Lords of Form endowed that body with a spark from their fire. The "ego" was enkindled within it. Every time man left the physical body he was in the spiritual world,in which he met the beings who,during the Saturn,Sun,and Moon evolutions,had given him his physical,etheric, and astral bodies,and who had developed them as far as the earth-stage. Since the spark of ego had been enkindled during earth-life,there had also come about a change in the disembodied life. Up to this point of evolution,man had had no independence in the spiritual world. Within that world he did not feel himself a separate being,but as though he were a member of the exalted organism which was composed of the beings superior to him. The "ego experience" on earth now takes effect also in the spiritual world. Henceforth man feels himself to be,to a certain degree, a unit in that world. But he feels also that he is unceasingly linked with it. In the disembodied state he again finds the Lords of Form,in a higher aspect,and this aspect he had perceived in their manifestation on earth by means of the spark of his ego.

At the separation of the moon from the earth,the disembodied soul began to have experiences in the spiritual world which were connected with that separation. To develop such human forms upon earth which could receive soul individuality,only became possible through the fact that a part of the shaping forces passed over from the Earth to the Moon. Thus human individuality came within the sphere of the Moon-beings. And in the disembodied state the reminiscence of earthly individuality could only operate because,even in that state,the soul remained within the sphere of those mighty spirits who had brought about the separation of the moon. The process worked in such a manner that immediately after leaving the earth-body the soul could only see the exalted Sun-beings as though in a lustre reflected from the Moon-beings. And it was only when sufficiently prepared by gazing at that reflected splendor,that the soul attained to the vision of the exalted Sun-beings themselves.

The mineral kingdom of the earth also arose out of what was ejected from human evolution in general. Its structures are what remained solidified after the moon was detached from the earth. The only soul-element which felt attracted to those structures was that which had been left behind at the Saturn stage,and was therefore only adapted for developing physical forms. All the occurrences treated of here and in what follows were enacted in the course of exceedingly long periods. But the question of chronology cannot be entered into here.

The events described,present the evolution of the earth from without. Seen spiritually from within,the facts present themselves as follows: The spiritual beings who drew the moon out of the earth and incorporated their own existence with the moon,--thus becoming earth-moon beings,--brought about a certain formation of the human organism by means of the forces which they sent to the earth from the moon. Their influence affected the "ego" which man had acquired,and made itself felt in the interplay of that "ego" with the astral,etheric,and physical bodies. They made it possible for man to reflect within himself consciously and to reproduce within his cognition,the wisdom revealed in the cosmos. It will be remembered that during the old Moon-period man,owing to the separation from the sun at the time,acquired a certain independence in his organism, a more unfettered stage of consciousness than that which he had been able to derive directly from the Sun-spirits. This free,independent consciousness--a heritage from the old Moon-evolution--appeared again during the earth-period in question. But it was just this consciousness which, through the influence of the described earth-moon beings,could again be brought into union and harmony with the universe and be made a reflection of it. This would have happened if no other influence had asserted itself. Without that influence,man would have become a being whose consciousness would not have reflected the world in pictures of cognition,through his own free volition,but through natural necessity. But things did not happen in this way. At the time when the moon split off,certain spiritual beings interposed in human evolution who had retained so much of their Moon nature that they could not take part in the exodus of the sun from the earth,and were shut out from the influence of the spirits who from the earth-moon had exerted their activity upon the earth. These spirits

with the old Moon nature were,so to say,banished to the earth,but with an irregular development. In their Moon-nature was that which had rebelled
against the Sun-spirits during the old Moon-evolution,and which had so far been a blessing to man that it had led him to a free,independent state of consciousness. The consequences of the peculiar development of these spirits during the earth-period entailed their becoming adversaries of the spirits who,acting from the moon,desired to make human consciousness an automatic reflector of the universe. What had helped man
to a higher state of development of the old Moon,proved to be in opposition to the possibilities which had arisen through the evolution of the earth. The opposing forces had brought with them from their Moon nature the power of working upon the human astral body,namely,--as above
indicated,--the power of making it independent. They exercised that power by giving the astral body a certain degree of independence--even throughout
the earth-period--compared with the automatic (involuntary) state of consciousness which had been brought about by the spirits of the earth-moon.

It is difficult to express in the language of to-day the effects on man, in that far-off time of the spiritual beings referred to. They must not be thought of as analogous to natural influences of the present time,nor yet as similar to the influence of one human being on another,when the first awakens in the second inner powers of consciousness by words which help
the second person to understand something,or which stimulate him to virtue or vice. The effect referred to as operative in that primeval age was not a force of nature but a spiritual influence,conveyed in a spiritual way,which descended upon man as a spiritual influx from higher spirits,conformable with man's state of consciousness at that time. If we think of this influence as a force of nature we altogether miss its essential reality. If we say that the spirits with the old Moon nature tempted man in order to lead him astray for their own ends,we are using a
symbolical expression,which is good as long as we remember that it is but a symbol and are at the same time clear in our minds that a spiritual fact underlies the symbol.

The influence brought to bear on man by the spirits who had remained behind during the Moon-evolution had a two-fold result. Man's consciousness was divested of the character of being merely a mirror of the universe,because the possibility was aroused in the human astral body of regulating and controlling,by means of this astral body,the images in the consciousness. Man became the ruler of his own knowledge. But on the
other hand it was the astral body that was the starting point of that rulership,and consequently the ego set over the astral body came to be continually dependent upon it. Hence man was from this time forth exposed
to the lasting influences of a lower element in his nature. It was possible for him in his life to sink below the height on which he had been placed by the spirits of the earth-moon in the course of the world's progress. And subsequently he was open to the lasting influence on his nature of the irregularly evolved Moon-spirits. We may call these Moon-spirits Luciferian,to distinguish them from the other spirits who, from the earth-moon,made consciousness into a mirror of the universe, without bestowing free will. The Luciferian spirits endowed man with the possibility of developing free activity in his consciousness,and at the same time created the possibility of error and evil.

As a result of these events man was brought into a different connection

with the Sun-spirits from that which had been destined for him by the spirits of the earth-moon. These wished to develop the reflecting human consciousness in such a manner that within the whole life of the human soul,the influence of the Sun-spirits would have become dominant. These purposes were thwarted,and an opposition was thus created in human nature
between the influence of the Sun-Spirits and that of the spirits who were irregularly developed on the old Moon. Owing to this opposition,the inability to recognize the physical Sun-influences as such also arose in man; they were hidden by the earthly impressions of the outer world. Filled with these impressions,the astral part of man was drawn into the sphere of the ego. This ego,--which otherwise would have felt only the spark of fire bestowed on it by the Lords of Form,and which would have submitted to the bidding of those spirits in everything that had to do with external fire,--henceforth worked upon external heat phenomena through
the element with which it had itself been inoculated. A bond of attraction was thereby established between the ego and the earth-fire.

In this way man became more involved in earthly materiality than had been ordained for him,which was effected through the earth-moon spirits in man's body. The real individual ego was thereby set free from the mere earth-ego so that although man during earth-life only partially felt himself to be an ego,he at the same time felt his earth-ego to be a continuation of that of his ancestors through the generations. The soul was conscious of a kind of "group-ego" in earth-life,dating back to remote ancestors; man felt himself to be a member of this group. Only in the disembodied state could the individual ego be conscious of itself as a separate being. But this state of isolation was impaired because the ego was still burdened with a memory of the earth-consciousness (earth-ego.) This memory clouded its vision of the spiritual world,which began to be covered as with a veil between death and birth just as it is hidden from physical vision upon earth.

The many changes which took place in the spiritual world while human evolution was passing through the conditions just described,found physical expression in the gradual adjustment of the mutual relations existing between the sun,moon,and earth (and,moreover,between other celestial bodies).

The alternation of day and night stands out as one result of those relations. (The motions of celestial bodies are regulated by the beings who inhabit them. The earth's motion,of which day and night are the result,was induced by the mutual relations of various spirits superior to man. The moon's motion had been brought about in the same way,in order that after the separation of the moon from the earth,the Lords of Form might,by means of the revolution of the former around the latter,work upon the human physical body in the right way,and with the right rhythm.) The ego and astral body of man now worked within the physical and etheric
bodies by day; at night that activity ceased: for the ego and the astral body then left the physical and etheric bodies and came wholly within the sphere of the Sons of Life or Angels,the Sons of Fire or Archangels,the Sons of Personality,and the Lords of Form. Besides the Lords of Form,the Lords of Motion,of Wisdom and the Thrones also included the physical and etheric bodies in their sphere of influence at this time. The injurious effects produced on man by the errors of his astral body during the day, could thus be counter-balanced.

As people upon Earth now again multiplied there was no reason why human
souls should not incarnate in their descendants. The earth moon-forces now
acted in such a way that under their influence the human bodies became

entirely capable of incarnating human souls. The souls who had previously removed to Mars,Jupiter and the other planets were now guided to earth, and there was thus a soul ready for each human being born in the physical line of descent. This went on through long periods so that the immigration of souls to earth corresponded to the increase of human beings. Souls now leaving their bodies at physical death retained the echo of their earthly individuality as a memory in the disembodied state. This memory acted in such a way that whenever a body was born on earth suitable for them, they again incarnated it. Consequently there were among the human descendants some whose souls came from without and who appeared on earth for the first time since its very earliest periods,and there were others whose souls had continually incarnated on the earth. In subsequent periods of earthly evolution the number of young souls appearing for the first time grows ever smaller and smaller,and the reincarnated souls become more and more numerous; yet for long ages the human race was composed of the two types of beings conditioned by these facts.

Henceforth man on earth felt himself united with his forefathers through the group-ego which he had in common with them. On the other hand,the experience of the individual ego was all the stronger in the disembodied state between death and a new birth. The souls which entered human bodies from celestial space were in a different position from those which had one or more earthly lives behind them. The former,as souls entering upon the physical earth-life,brought with them only the conditions to which the higher spiritual world and their experiences outside the sphere of earth had subjected them. The others had,by their actions in former lives, added conditions of their own. The fate of the first was determined only by facts lying outside of the new earth-conditions; that of the reincarnate souls is also determined by what they themselves have done in former lives under earthly conditions. Individual human Karma makes its first appearance simultaneously with reincarnation.

Because the human etheric body was withdrawn from the influence of the astral body in the manner above indicated,the generative faculty was not included in the sphere of human consciousness,but was under the sway of the spiritual world. When the time had come for a soul to descend to earth,procreative impulses arose in the human being. The entire process, to a certain degree was veiled in mysterious obscurity as far as earthly consciousness was concerned. The consequences of this partial separation of the etheric from the physical body were felt during earthly life also. The qualities of the etheric body were capable of being especially heightened by spiritual influence. In the life of the soul this expressed itself through a special perfection of memory. Independent logical thought was at this period only in its most rudimentary stage in man; on the other hand,the faculty of memory was almost unlimited. Externally it appeared as though man had direct knowledge of the working forces of every living being. He had at his disposal the vital and generative forces of the animal and,more especially,of the vegetable kingdom. He was able,for instance,to draw out of a plant the force which impels it to grow,and to use that force,just as we now use the forces of inanimate nature; for example,the power dormant in coal which is extricated and used for propelling engines.(22)

The inner soul life of man was also transformed in many different ways by the Lucifer influence. Many kinds of feelings and emotions due to it might be instanced. Of these only one can be mentioned. Previous to this influence,the human soul acted,in that which it had to shape and to do, according to the purposes of higher spiritual beings. The plan of everything that was to be carried out was determined from the beginning. And in proportion to the degree to which human consciousness was evolved, it was able to foresee how things must develop in the future in accordance with that preconceived plan. That consciousness of the future was lost when the veil of earthly perceptions was woven across the manifestations of higher spiritual beings and in these the real forces of the Sun-spirits were hidden. Henceforth the future became uncertain,and in consequence of this the possibility of fear was implanted in the soul. Fear is a direct result of error.

It is however evident that through the Luciferian influence,man became independent of certain definite forces to which he had previously submitted without the exercise of his will. Henceforth he was able to form resolutions of his own. Freedom is the result of the Luciferian influence, and fear and similar feelings are only the phenomena attendant on the evolution of human freedom.

Spiritually seen,fear makes its appearance in this way. Within the earth-forces,under whose influence man had come by means of the Luciferian powers,other beings were operating,which had developed irregularly much earlier in the course of evolution than the Luciferian powers. With the earth-forces man admitted into his nature the influence of these other beings. They gave the quality of fear to feelings,which without them would have operated quite differently. They may be called Ahrimanic beings. They are the same that Goethe calls Mephistophelian.

Although the Luciferian influence manifested itself at first only in the most advanced individuals,it soon spread to others. The descendants of the advanced individuals intermingled with the less progressive described above,and in this way the Luciferian force was conveyed to the latter. But the etheric body of these souls returning from the different planets could not be protected to the same extent as that of the descendants of those who remained on earth. The protection of the etheric body of these descendants emanated from an exalted Being in Whom was vested the leadership of the cosmic when the separation of the sun from the earth took place. That Being is the Ruler of the Kingdom of the Sun. With him those lofty spirits,whose cosmic development was sufficiently matured, departed for their dwelling-place in the Sun. But there were other beings who had not reached such a height at the separation of the sun; these were obliged to seek other spheres. It was through their instrumentality that Jupiter and other planets became detached from that general cosmic substance of which,at the outset,the earthly physical organism consisted. Jupiter now became the abode of those beings who were not highly enough developed to live on the sun,and the most advanced of these became the leader. As the Leader of the Sun evolution became the "higher ego" which worked in the etheric body of the descendants of those who had remained on earth,so the Jupiter leader became that "higher ego" which manifested as a common consciousness in certain other human beings. Those were the human beings descending from the intermixing of those who had only appeared on earth at the time of the air-element and had gone over to Jupiter. These human beings may be called,in conformity with occult science,"Jupiter-humanity." They were scions of the human race which had adopted human souls far back in that ancient time; but who,at the beginning of earthly evolution,were not yet mature enough to take part in

the first contact with fire. They were souls midway between the human and
animal soul-kingdoms.

Now there were other beings who,under the leadership of the greatest one
among them had detached Mars from the general cosmic substance,to make it
their dwelling place. Under their influence there arose a third kind of humanity,formed by interbreeding,--the "Mars-humanity." (This knowledge throws light upon the origin of the formation of the planets of our solar system; for all the members of that system originated through the various stages of maturity reached by the beings inhabiting them. But of course it is not possible to enter into all the details of cosmic differentiation here.) Those people who felt in their etheric body the influence of the exalted Sun-being Himself may be called "Sun-humanity." The Being Who lived in them as the Higher Ego--of course only in the race,not in the individual,--is the same to Whom various names were given in later times, when man had gained conscious knowledge of Him. It is he Who appears to
the human race today as the Christ.

"Saturn-humanity" is also to be distinguished at that time. The "higher ego" of this race appeared as a being who,with his associates,had been forced to leave the general cosmic substance before the separation of the Sun. In these individuals not only the etheric body but also the physical body was partly exempt from the Luciferian influence. But the etheric body
was nevertheless not well enough protected in the less developed races of mankind to be able to sufficiently resist the influences of the Luciferian beings. These individuals could arbitrarily use the spark of the ego within them to such a degree that they were able to call forth mighty and destructive effects of fire around them. The result was a mighty terrestrial catastrophe. A large part of the inhabited earth was wrecked by fiery storms,and with it the human beings that had fallen into sin. Only a very small part of those who had remained untouched by sin,were able to take refuge in a region which had so far been shielded from the fatal human influence.

The country occupying that part of the earth now covered by the Atlantic Ocean proved to be peculiarly well fitted for the abode of the new human race. Thither that part of humanity repaired which had preserved purity. Only stray groups of humanity inhabited other regions. Occult science gives the name of "Atlantis" to that part of the earth which once existed between the present continents of Europe,Africa,and America. (This particular stage of human evolution has its special nomenclature in theosophical literature. The period preceding the Atlantean is called the Lemurian age,whereas that during which the Moon-forces had not yet fully developed is called the Hyperborean age. This is preceded by yet another, which coincides with the earliest period of the evolution of the physical earth. Biblical tradition describes the period before the influence of the Lucifer-beings came into play as the Paradise time,and the descent to earth,or entanglement of humanity in the sense-world,as the expulsion from Paradise.)

The Atlantean period of evolution was the real time of separation into the Saturn,Sun,Jupiter,and Mars humanities. Up to that time only predispositions for this separation had been developed. The division between the state of waking and sleeping had special consequences,which appeared particularly in the Atlantean race. During the night the human astral body and ego were in the sphere of the beings superior to man,as far up as the Sons of Personality. Man could perceive the Sons of Life (the Angels) and the Sons of Fire (the Archangels) through that part of his etheric body which was not united with the physical body. For he was able to remain united,during sleep,with that part of his etheric body which was not interpenetrated by the physical body. It is true,his perception of the Sons of Personality was vague,owing to the Luciferian influence; but not only the Angels and Archangels became visible to man in this condition but also those beings who were not able to enter upon earthly existence because they had lagged behind on the Sun or Moon,and were therefore obliged to remain in the psycho-spiritual world. But man, by means of the Luciferian influence,drew them into his soul which was separated from his physical body during sleep. Thus he came in contact with beings whose influence was highly corrupting. They increased in his soul the propensity for error; especially the tendency to misuse the powers of growth and reproduction,which since the separation of the physical and etheric bodies were now under his control.

Certain human beings of the Atlantean period however became entangled in
the sense world only to a very limited degree. Through them,the Luciferian influence became,instead of a hindrance to human evolution,a means of further progress. It enabled them to develop knowledge of earthly
matters sooner than would otherwise have been possible. They sought to expel error from their imaginative life and to interpret,by means of cosmic phenomena,the original purposes of spiritual beings. They kept themselves free from those impulses and desires of the astral body which were directed merely toward the sense-world. Hence they became more and
more free from the errors of the astral body. This resulted in a condition through which they were able to confine their perceptions to that part of the etheric body which was separated from the physical body in the manner
described above. Under these conditions the capacity of the physical body for perception was practically extinguished and the physical body itself was as though dead. For through the etheric body,these individuals were wholly united with the kingdom of the Lords of Form,and were able to learn from them how they were being guided and directed by that exalted Being the "Christ," who was the Leader at the time of the separation of sun and earth. These people were Initiates. But since human individuality had been brought into the sphere of the Moon-beings,as described above, these Initiates could not as a rule come into direct contact with the Christ-Being,they could only see it as a reflection,shown them by the Moon-beings. Thus they did not see the Christ-Being directly,but only the reflection of its glory.

They became leaders of the rest of humanity,to whom they were able to impart the mysteries they had seen. They attracted disciples,to whom they
communicated the methods for attaining the condition which leads to Initiation. Only those could attain knowledge of the Christ who belonged to the Sun-humanity mentioned above. They cultivated their mystic learning,and the occupations which promoted it,at a particular spot which,in occult science terminology may be called the Christ oracle,or Sun oracle,the term "oracle" being used to denote a place where the purposes of spiritual beings are unveiled.

Other oracles were called into being by the members of the Saturn,Mars, and Jupiter humanities. The intuitive vision of their Initiates was confined to seeing those beings who were revealed to them in their etheric
bodies as their respective "higher egos." Thus adherents of the Saturn, Jupiter,and Mars wisdom arose. Besides these methods of Initiation,there were others for those who had assimilated too much of the Luciferian spirit to allow as large a part of the etheric body to be separated from the physical body as was the case with the Sun humanity. Nor could they be

brought to the revelation of the Christ through these conditions. Because their astral body was more influenced by the Lucifer principle,they were obliged to undergo a more difficult preparation,and then,in a less disembodied state than the others,they were able to receive the revelation,not indeed of the Christ Himself,but of other exalted beings.

There were beings who,although they had left the earth at the separation of the sun,did not stand on such a high level that they were able to continue taking part in the Sun evolution. They formed an abode for themselves away from the sun,after its separation from the earth: this was Venus. Their leader was the being who now became a "higher ego" to these Initiates and their adherents. A similar thing happened with the leading spirit of Mercury for another group of people. In this way the Venus and Mercury oracles arose. One kind of human beings,who had most
completely absorbed the Luciferian influence,could reach only one of the higher beings who,with his associates,had been the first to be expelled from the Sun evolution. This being has no particular planet in cosmic space,but still lives within the periphery of the earth,with which he was once more united after the return from the sun. The group of people, to whom this being was revealed as its "higher ego" may be called the followers of the Vulcan oracle. Their attention was more directed to earthly phenomena than that of the other Initiates. They laid the first foundations of what afterwards became the human arts and sciences. On the
other hand,the Mercury Initiates established the study of the more super-sensible things; and the Venus Initiates did this to a still greater extent.

The Vulcan,Mercury,and Venus Initiates differed from those of Saturn, Jupiter,and Mars in the manner of receiving their Mysteries; the latter received them more as a revelation from above,and in a more finished state; whereas the former gained their knowledge more in the form of their
own thoughts--in the form of ideas. The Christ Initiates occupied a middle position. While having a direct revelation,they acquired the capacity for clothing their Mysteries in a human form of conception. The Saturn, Jupiter,and Mars Initiates were obliged to express themselves more in symbols; the Christ,Venus,Mercury,and Vulcan Initiates were able to impart their knowledge more through ideas or concepts.

Whatever knowledge of this kind reached Atlantean humanity came indirectly
through the Initiates. But the rest of mankind also received special faculties through the Lucifer principle; for,through the intervention of lofty cosmic beings,what otherwise might have wrought ruin was transformed into good. One of these faculties was that of speech. This was
brought about by the condensation of man's physical body and by the separation of part of his etheric from his physical body. For some time after the separations of the moon,man felt himself connected with his physical ancestors through the group-ego. But this common consciousness,
linking posterity with its ancestors,was gradually lost in the course of generations. Later descendants had an inner memory of only their more recent ancestors,no longer of their earlier forefathers. It was only in conditions akin to sleep,during which mankind came in contact with the spiritual world,that the remembrance of one ancestor or another again emerged. Then people thought of themselves as one with that ancestor whom
they believed to be reappearing in them. This was an erroneous idea of reincarnation,which arose especially in the later Atlantean period. The true doctrine of reincarnation could be learned only in the schools of the Initiates. They could see how the human soul passes through the

disembodied state on its way from one incarnation to another,and they alone were able to impart the real truth of the matter to their disciples.

In the remote past which is now under consideration,man's physical form was very different from his present form. It was still,to a great extent, the expression of the qualities of his soul. Man was composed of a softer and more delicate substance than that which he has since acquired. That which is now solidified in the limbs was then soft,flexible,and plastic. The bodily structure of the more psychic and spiritual human beings was delicate,supple,and expressive. These less evolved spiritually possessed coarser,heavier,less mobile bodily structures. A high degree of psychic maturity contracted the extremities,and the Stature remained small; backwardness of the soul and entanglement in sensuality were outwardly expressed by gigantic size. While man was growing to maturity his body was being formed in accordance with what was developing in his soul,in a way which would appear incredible and fabulous to contemporary ideas. Depraved passions,impulses,and instincts brought in their train a colossal increase of matter. Man's present physical form has come about through a contraction,thickening,and consolidation of the Atlantean human form. And whereas man,before the Atlantean period,had been an exact image of his soul-nature the events of the Atlantean evolution bore within them the causes which lead to the formation of post-Atlantean man,whose physical form is solid and comparatively independent of the qualities of the soul. (The forms of the animal kingdom had solidified during far more remote Earth periods than those of man.) The laws now governing the shaping of forms in the kingdom of nature certainly did not prevail in the remote past.

Toward the middle of the Atlantean evolution a calamity gradually befell humanity. The Mysteries of the Initiates had to be carefully kept secret from those who had not purified their astral bodies from sin. Had they gained insight into that hidden knowledge,into the laws by means of which higher beings directed the forces of nature,they would have employed those forces thus placed at their disposal for their own perverted needs and passions. The danger was all the greater because mankind was coming, as has been described,into the sphere of lower spiritual beings,who could not take part in the regular evolution of the earth and were therefore working against it. These persistently influenced humanity in such a way as to instil into it interests which were actually directed against human welfare. But mankind still had the power to employ the forces of growth and reproduction belonging to animal and human nature in their own service.

Not only humanity in general,but even some of the Initiates yielded to temptation from low spiritual beings. They were induced to employ the supersensible forces mentioned above for a purpose which ran counter to human evolution. And for this purpose they sought out associates who were not initiated,and who made use of the secrets of the supersensible forces of nature for low ends. The result was a great corruption of human nature. The evil spread further and further; and since the forces of growth and generation,if torn from their original sphere and used independently, have a mysterious connection with certain forces working in air and water, there were thus unchained,through human action,mighty,destructive natural forces which led to the gradual ruin of the Atlantean territory by the agency of air and water catastrophes. Atlantean humanity was obliged to migrate--i. e.,that portion of it which did not perish in the storms.

In consequence of these storms the surface of the earth was altered. On one side,Europe,Asia,and Africa gradually assumed their present shape; on the other,America appeared. Great migrations took place to these countries. Those migrations which were directed eastward from Atlantis are especially important for us of today. Europe,Asia,and Africa were gradually colonized by the descendants of the Atlanteans. Various peoples fixed their abode in these continents. They were at different stages of development,and also at different levels of corruption. And with them came the Initiates,guardians of the oracle-Mysteries. They established sanctuaries in various parts,in which the cults of Jupiter,Venus,etc., were cultivated sometimes in a good,sometimes in an evil manner. The betrayal of the Vulcan Mysteries exercised an especially unfavourable influence,for the attention of their adherents was mostly centered on earthly matters. By this betrayal,mankind was made dependent on spiritual beings who,as a result of their past evolution,rejected everything emanating from the spiritual world which had been evolved through the separation of the earth from the sun. In accordance with the tendency they had thus developed,they worked upon just that element in man which was formed through his having perceptions of the sense-world,behind which the spiritual world lies hidden. Henceforth beings acquired great influence over many of the human inhabitants of the earth,and indeed their influence asserted itself more and more by depriving mankind of the feeling for spiritual things.

Since the size,form,and flexibility of the physical human body were still largely affected by the qualities of the soul,the consequence of the betrayal of the Mysteries also appeared in changes of the human race in these respects. Wherever the corruption of humanity manifested itself especially in the abuse of supersensible powers for the satisfaction of lower inclinations,desires and passions,unsightly human shapes, grotesque in form and size were the result. These were not able to survive the Atlantean period,and became extinct. Post-Atlantean humanity was formed physically from those Atlantean ancestors in whom such a solidification of the bodily form had taken place that it no longer yielded to those powers of the soul which had now become perverted.

There was a certain period in the Atlantean evolution during which,by means of the law ruling in and around the earth,just those conditions prevailed which tended to solidify man's bodily form. Those human racial types which had been solidified before this period could,it is true, reproduce themselves for a long time,yet the souls incarnating in them gradually became so cramped that they had to die out. It is true that some of these race-types survived into the post-Atlantean times; those which had remained sufficiently agile lasted even for a very long time in modified form. Human forms which had remained flexible,after the period just described,became bodies for such souls as had,in a large measure, undergone the pernicious influence of the betrayal described above. These forms were destined to speedy extinction.

In consequence of what had thus happened,beings had brought their influence to bear upon human evolution,since the middle of the Atlantean period,beings whose influence tended to make mankind live in the physical sense world in an unspiritual manner. This went so far that,instead of man's seeing the real form of that world,phantoms,hallucinations,and illusions of every kind appeared to him. Mankind was exposed not merely to the Luciferian influence but to that of those other beings mentioned above,whose leader may be called Ahriman,according to the appellation given him later in the Persian civilization. (He is the same as Mephistopheles.) Through this influence man was subject,after death,to

powers which made him appear even then as a being adhering only to material earthly conditions. He lost more and more the unobstructed vision
of the events of the spiritual world. He was forced to feel himself in Ahriman's power,and to a certain extent shut out from intercourse with the spiritual world.

There was one oracle-sanctuary of special importance,which in the universal decline had preserved the ancient cult in its purest form. It was one of the Christ oracles,and on that account it was able to preserve not only the Christ Mystery itself but those of the other oracles as well. For in the manifestation of the loftiest of the Sun-spirits,were also revealed the regents of Saturn,Jupiter,and the other planets. In the Sun oracle the secret of producing in some particular human being,such human etheric bodies as had been possessed by the best of the Jupiter,Mercury, and other Initiates was known. By means of the methods used for this purpose,which cannot be further dealt with here,impressions of the best etheric bodies of the ancient Initiates were preserved,in order that they might subsequently be stamped upon suitable individuals. The same process
could be employed with the astral bodies of the Venus,Mercury,and Vulcan Initiates.

At a certain time the Leader of the Christ Initiates found Himself isolated with a few associates,to whom He was able to impart,to a very limited extent only,the mysteries of the cosmos. For those associates were individuals who were endowed with the natural ability to permit the least possible degree of separation between the physical and etheric bodies. They were altogether,at that time,the best possible individuals for promoting the further progress of humanity. Their experiences in the realm of sleep had become rarer and rarer. The spiritual world was more and more closed to them. Therefore they were also lacking in the comprehension of all that had been revealed to man in ancient times when he was not in his physical,but only in his etheric body. Those immediately surrounding the leader of the Christ oracle were the farthest advanced with regard to the union of the physical body with that part of the etheric body which had previously been separated from it. This union came about in the human being little by little,as a result of the transformation which had taken place in the Atlantean continent and the earth in general.

The physical and etheric bodies of man fitted more and more into each other. Hence the memory lost its former unlimited capacity,and the human life of thought began. That part of the etheric which was united with the physical body transformed the physical brain into an actual instrument of thought,and man from this time,first really felt his "ego" within his physical body. Self-consciousness awoke. This was at first the case with only a limited number of the human race,pre-eminently with the associates of the leader of the Christ oracle. The bulk of humanity,scattered over Europe,Asia,and Africa,retained in varying degrees the remnant of the old conditions of consciousness. Hence they had direct experience of the supersensible world.

The associates of the Christ Initiate were people of highly developed intelligence but of less experience in supersensible spheres than any of their contemporaries. The Initiate journeyed with them to a country in central Asia. He wished them to be guarded as much as possible from contact with those of less developed consciousness. He instructed his followers along the lines of the mysteries which had been revealed to him and especially did he do this with their descendants. Thus he gathered round him a people who had received into their hearts the impulses corresponding to the Mysteries of the Christ Initiation. Out of this company he chose the seven best,that they might be endowed with the etheric and astral bodies which bore the impress of the etheric bodies of

the seven best Atlantean Initiates. Thus he educated a successor to each of the Christ,Saturn,Jupiter,etc.,Initiates. These seven Initiates became the teachers and leaders of the people who,in the post-Atlantean period,had colonized the south of Asia,especially ancient India. Since these great teachers were endowed with the etheric bodies of their spiritual ancestors,the contents of their astral body,that is,the science and knowledge they themselves had worked out,was far below what
was revealed to them through their etheric body. Therefore if these revelations were to speak within them,they were obliged to impose silence on their own science and knowledge. Then the exalted beings who had also spoken to their spiritual ancestors spoke out of and through them. Except during the times when these beings were speaking through them,they were
simple people,endowed with the measure of intelligence and feeling which they had cultivated and worked out for themselves.

There lived at this time in India a race of people who had retained a particularly vivid remembrance of the ancient soul-condition of the Atlanteans,which permitted experiences in the spiritual world. Moreover, the heart and soul of a great number of these people were powerfully attracted by such experiences. By a wise decree of fate,the majority of the race had come to southern Asia from among the best portions of the Atlantean population. Besides this majority,other Atlanteans had migrated thither at different times. The Christ Initiate,referred to above, appointed his seven great disciples to be the teachers of this association of people,to whom they imparted their wisdom and precepts. Many of these
ancient Indians needed but little preparation for reviving within them the scarcely extinct faculties leading to observation of the supersensible world. For longing after that world was really a fundamental quality of the Indian soul. It was felt that man's original home was in that world. He is transplanted out of it into this one,which offers only outer sense-observation and the intelligence connected with it.

The supersensible world was felt to be the _real_ world,and the sense-world to be a deception of the human power of observation,an illusion (Maya). By every possible means these people strove to open up a view of the real world. They could take no interest in the illusory sense-world,or at any rate only so far as it proved to be a veil for the supersensible. The power going out from the Seven Great Teachers to such
people as these,was a mighty one. What they were able to reveal entered deeply into the Indian soul, and since the possession of the transmitted etheric and astral bodies invested the teachers with lofty powers,they were also able to work magically on their disciples. They did not really teach; they worked as though by magic power from one personality to another. Thus there arose a civilization completely saturated with supersensible wisdom. The contents of the books of wisdom of the Hindus, the Vedas,do not give the original form of the lofty wisdom imparted by the great teachers of most ancient times,only a feeble echo of it. Only the seer's eye,looking backward is able to find unwritten primeval wisdom behind the written words.

A particularly prominent feature of this ancient wisdom is the harmonious accord of the various wisdom oracles of the Atlantean time. For each of the Great Teachers was able to unveil the wisdom of one of these oracles, and these different aspects were in complete harmony,because behind them
all was the fundamental wisdom of the Christ Initiation. It is true the teacher who was the successor of the Christ Initiate did not impart to his disciples what the Christ Initiate himself was able to reveal. The latter had remained in the background during this period of evolution. At first he was unable to entrust his high office to any post-Atlantean. The

difference between him and the Christ Initiate of the Seven Great Indian Teachers was that the former was able to work his vision of the Christ Mystery completely into the form of human ideas,whereas the Indian Christ
Initiate could only offer a reflection of the Mystery in signs and symbols; for his humanly cultivated power of conception did not suffice for such a Mystery. However,from the union of the Seven Teachers there resulted a knowledge of the supersensible world,presented in one great wisdom-panorama,of which only separate portions could be imparted in the
ancient Atlantean oracles. The great Regents of the cosmos were revealed,
and the One great Sun-spirit,the Hidden One,ruling over those who were manifested through the seven teachers,was delicately indicated.

What is here meant by "ancient Indians" is not the same as what is usually
understood by that term. No outer documents exist of the period in question. The people usually known as "Indians" belong to a stage of historical evolution which was developed long after the time spoken of here. We have to distinguish a first post-Atlantean period of the earth, in which the Indian civilization now described was the predominant one; then came a second post-Atlantean period in which the prevailing civilization was that which later in this work is called the "ancient Persian," and still later was developed the Egypto-Chaldean civilization, also to be described. During the evolution of these second and third post-Atlantean epochs,"ancient" India also went through a second and third epoch,and to this third epoch belongs what is usually related of ancient India. What is described here must therefore not be applied to the "ancient India" mentioned elsewhere.

Another feature of this ancient Indian civilization is that which afterward led to the division of the race into castes. The inhabitants of India were descendants of Atlanteans who belonged to the various types of
Saturn and Jupiter humanities,etc. By means of supersensible teachings it was seen that it is not by chance that a soul is incarnated in a particular caste,but that the soul itself has determined its lot. Such an understanding of supersensible teachings was made much easier,because it
was possible to revive in many people the inner remembrance of their ancestors which has been described above; this,of course,might also easily lead to an erroneous idea of reincarnation. Just as,in the Atlantean age,it was only through the Initiates that the true idea of reincarnation could be realized,so in India,in most ancient times,it was possible only through direct contact with the great teachers. It is true that the erroneous idea of reincarnation mentioned above found the widest acceptance imaginable among the bands of people who were dispersed
over Europe,Asia and Africa in consequence of the Atlantean catastrophe. And because the Initiates who had gone astray during the Atlantean evolution had imparted the mystery of reincarnation to immature souls, mankind began to confuse more and more the true with the false ideas. Many
of these people indeed retained a kind of dim clairvoyance,as a heritage from the Atlantean period. Just as the Atlanteans had entered the spiritual world during sleep,their descendants had experience of it in abnormal states,intermediate between sleeping and waking. Then there arose in these people the images of the ancient times of their forefathers. They believed themselves to be reincarnations of people who had lived in those times. Teachings about reincarnation,which were at variance with the true ideas of the Initiates,were widely spread over the earth.

As a result of the long-continued migrations which had taken place from west to east since the beginning of the Atlantean catastrophe,a group of people settled in western Asia whose posterity is known to history as the Persian race and the tribes related thereto. Here we look back to a much earlier period than the historical times of these peoples. Next after the Indian period,we have first to do with the very early ancestors of the later Persians,among whom arose the second great civilization of post-Atlantean evolution. The peoples of this second era had a different mission from that of the Indians. Their longings and inclinations were not fixed on the supersensible world alone; they were also directed toward the physical sense-world,and the earth became dear to them. They valued what. man is able to acquire on it,and what he is able to win by means of its forces. Their achievements as a warlike people,and the methods which they discovered of acquiring the earth's treasures,are connected with this peculiarity of their nature. There was no danger of their turning their backs upon the "illusion" of the physical senses in their yearning after the supersensible,but rather of their entirely severing the connection of their souls with the supersensible world,through their appreciation for the physical world.

The oracle-sanctuaries,which had been transferred hither from the ancient Atlantean territory,also reflected,in their own way,the general character of the people. In them forces were present which it had formerly been possible to acquire through experiences in the supersensible world, and which could still be controlled in certain lower forms; these forces were used in the sanctuaries to direct the phenomena of nature in such a way as to make them subservient to man's personal interests. This ancient people still had a great mastery over those forces of nature which subsequently withdrew from the influence of the human will. The guardians of the oracles mastered certain inner forces connected with fire and other elements. They can be called magicians. What supersensible knowledge and force they had retained as a heritage from ancient times was certainly slight in comparison with man's powers in the remote past. But it nevertheless took all kinds of forms,from the noble arts,the only object of which was the welfare of humanity,--down to the most reprehensible transactions.

The Luciferian influence held sway over these people in a peculiar manner. It had brought them into connection with everything which diverts mankind from the purposes of those exalted beings who alone would have guided human evolution,had not the Luciferian influence interposed. Even those members of this race who were still gifted with some remnant of the old clairvoyant condition,described above as a state intermediate between sleeping and waking,felt themselves powerfully attracted by the lower beings of the spiritual world. In order to counteract these characteristic qualities it was necessary that a spiritual impulse should be given to this people. A leadership was established among them by the guardian of the Mysteries of the Sun oracle,from the same source from which the spiritual life of ancient India proceeded.

The leader of ancient Persian civilization,who was sent by the guardian of the Sun oracle to the people now under consideration,may be designated by the same name as the historical Zarathustra,or Zoroaster. Only the fact must be emphasized that the personality indicated belongs to a much earlier period than the historical possessor of the name. In this connection it is not a question of outer historical research,but of spiritual knowledge. And any one who instinctively thinks of a later time in connection with the bearer of the name Zarathustra may reconcile this idea with occult science on learning that the historical character represents himself as a successor of the first great Zarathustra,whose name he took,and in the spirit of whose teaching he worked.

The impulse which Zarathustra had to give to his people was to show them
that the physical world of sense is not merely the lifeless material, devoid of spirit,which it appears to a man who gives himself up exclusively to the influence of the Luciferian being. To this being man owes his personal independence and sense of freedom; but it should work within him in harmony with the opposite spiritual being. With the pre-historic Persians it was a question of keeping alive the sense of this last-named spiritual-being. Through their inclination toward the physical sense world they ran the risk of complete amalgamation with the Luciferian
beings. Now Zarathustra,through the guardian of the Sun oracle,had received an Initiation that enabled him to receive the revelations of the great Sun-spirits. In particular states of consciousness,brought about by his training,he was able to see the Regent of the Sun-spirits,who,as described above,had taken under His protection the human etheric body.

Zarathustra knew that This Spirit directs the course of human evolution, but that He must first,at a certain time,descend to earth out of cosmic space. For this purpose it was necessary that He should be able to live in a human astral body,just as in man. He had worked in the etheric body since the entrance of the Luciferic nature. It was therefore necessary that a man should appear who had retransformed the astral body to the same
level that it would have reached in the middle of the Atlantean evolution, had there been no Luciferian influence. Had Lucifer not appeared,mankind would certainly have attained this level before,but without personal independence or the possibility of freedom. Now,however,in spite of those qualities he should again arise to this height. Zarathustra,endowed with prophetic vision,could see that in the future it would be possible, within human evolution for a personality to exist,who would have a suitable astral body for that purpose. But he also knew that the great Sun-spirit could not appear on earth before that time,though He could be perceived by a seer in the spiritual part of the Sun. When as a seer he turned his attention to the Sun,Zarathustra was able to see This Spirit, whom he proclaimed to his people. He announced that the Sun-spirit was at
first to be found only in the spiritual world,but that later He would descend to earth. This was the great Sun-spirit,or Spirit of Light (the Aura of the Sun,Ahura-mazdao,or Ormuzd). He was revealed to Zarathustra
and his followers as the Spirit who,for the time being,was turning the light of His countenance on man from the spiritual world,and that it was He Who might be expected to appear in a human body amongst men in the
future. It was the Christ,before his appearance on earth,whom Zarathustra proclaimed as the Spirit of Light. On the other hand he represented Ahriman (Angra mainju) as a power working injuriously on the life of the human soul,when it engrosses that soul completely. This power is none other than the one previously described,which had acquired special dominion over the earth since the betrayal of the Vulcan Mysteries. Together with the message concerning the Light God, Zarathustra
proclaimed teachings about those spiritual beings who were revealed to the
seer's purified perception as associates of the Spirit of Light. These were in strong contrast to the tempters who appeared to that unpurified clairvoyance which was left over from the Atlantean period. It had to be

made clear to the ancient Persians that in man's soul,so far as it is engaged in work and endeavor in the physical sense world,a conflict is going on between the power of the Light God and his adversary. It had also to be shown them how man must act so as not to be engulfed by Ahriman,and
how to turn his influence to good through the power of the Light God.

The third era of post-Atlantean civilization began among the peoples who finally gathered together in western Asia and northern Africa after the migrations. This civilization was developed among the Chaldeans, Babylonians,and Assyrians on the one hand,and among the Egyptians on the
other. In these peoples the taste for the physical world of sense developed in a different form from that which it had taken among the Persians. The former had acquired the quality of mind lying at the root of the faculty of thought which has arisen since Atlantean times,that is, the gift of reason. Indeed,it was the mission of post-Atlantean humanity to develop within itself those faculties of the soul which it was possible to acquire through the newly awakened powers of thought and feeling. These
powers cannot be directly stimulated from the spiritual world,but result from man's observing the sense-world,becoming familiar with it,and working upon it. The conquest of the physical world of sense by these human faculties must be regarded as the mission of post-Atlantean humanity. Step by step that conquest proceeded. It is true that even in ancient India,man,through the condition of his soul,was already turned toward that world; but he still looked upon it as illusion,and his spirit turned to the supersensible world. In the Persian race,on the contrary, there sprang up the endeavour to conquer the physical world of sense,but the attempt was still largely made with those powers of the soul which had
been left over as an inheritance from the time when man could still reach the spiritual world directly. Among the peoples of the third epoch of civilization,the soul had for the most part lost the supersensible faculties. It was obliged to seek manifestations of the spiritual in the surrounding world of sense,and to continue its development by discovering the means of civilization existing in that world. Men sought to investigate,through the physical world,the spiritual laws underlying it, and in this way human sciences arose. Human technical skill,artistic work,and their tools and means came about through the recognition and use
of the forces of the physical world. To a man of the Chaldaic-Babylonian race the sense-world was no longer an illusion but a manifestation,in its different kingdoms,in mountains and seas,in air and water,of the spiritual activity of powers existing behind it,whose laws man was striving to learn.

To the Egyptian,the earth was a field of work,given to him in a condition which he must,by his own powers of intelligence,so transform that it should bear the impress of human power. From Atlantis, oracle-sanctuaries,originating chiefly from the Mercury oracle,had been transplanted to Egypt. Yet there were others as well,--for example,Venus oracles.

In that which was fostered,in their oracle-sanctuaries,among the Egyptian peoples,the germ of a new culture was planted. This germ proceeded from a great leader who had received his training in the Persian Zarathustra Mysteries,who was the reincarnated individuality of a disciple of the great Zarathustra himself. Let us call him "Hermes." Through acceptance of the Zarathustra Mysteries he was able to find the right way to guide the Egyptian people. This people had so turned its attention to the physical sense-world,during earthly life between birth and death that it was able only to a limited extent to directly behold the spiritual world behind the physical phenomena,although it recognized the spiritual laws of the world. Thus it could not think of the spiritual world as the one in which it could live while on earth,but on the other hand,it could be shown how man will live,in the disembodied state after death in the world of those spirits who,during earthly life,appear through their impressions upon the sense-world.

Hermes taught that man qualifies himself for union with spiritual forces after death,in proportion as he uses his powers on earth for furthering the purposes of those spiritual forces. Those especially,who had worked most zealously in this way between birth and death would be united with the lofty Sun-God Osiris. On the Chaldaic-Babylonian side of this stream of civilization the direction of the human mind toward the physical sense-world was more conspicuous than on the Egyptian side. The laws of that world were being investigated and from its reflection in the sense-world these people looked up to the corresponding spiritual prototypes. Yet in many respects the nation remained wedded to physical things. Instead of the star-spirit,the star was put first,and instead of other spiritual beings their earthly counterparts were made prominent. Only the leaders attained to really deep knowledge concerning the laws of the supersensible world and its connection with the physical. The contrast between the knowledge of the Initiates and the perverted beliefs of the people became more apparent in these nations than anywhere else.

Very different conditions existed in those parts of Southern Europe and western Asia where the fourth epoch of post-Atlantean civilization was unfolded. In occult science,it is called the Greco-Roman period. Descendants of peoples inhabiting widely distant parts of the older world had met together in these countries. Here were oracle-sanctuaries which conformed to the various Atlantean oracles; here were people with the heritage of ancient clairvoyance as a natural gift,and others who were able to acquire it,with comparative ease,by training. The traditions of the ancient Initiates were not only preserved in special places,but worthy successors to them arose,who attracted disciples capable of rising
to lofty levels of spiritual vision. Moreover,these races had within them the impulse to create a domain within the sense-world which expresses the
spiritual in perfect form through the physical.

Greek art is,among other things,a result of this impulse. It is only necessary to gaze with the eye of the spirit upon a Greek temple,in order to see that in this marvel of art,material substance is so worked upon by man that it appears in every detail as the expression of spirit. The Greek temple is the "House of the Spirit." One sees in its form what otherwise only The Spiritual eye of the seer perceives. The temple of Zeus-(or Jupiter) is so constructed as to present to the physical eye a fitting shrine for what the guardian of the Zeus-(or Jupiter) Initiation saw with spiritual vision. And it is the same with all Greek art. The wisdom of the Initiates flowed in mysterious ways into poets,artists,and thinkers. The Mysteries of the Initiates are found again,in the form of conceptions and ideas,in the systems of thought by which ancient Greek philosophers interpreted the universe. The influences of the spiritual life,the Mysteries of the Asiatic and African sanctuaries of Initiation,flowed into these nations and to their leaders. The great Indian teachers,the associates of Zarathustra,and the followers of Hermes had attracted disciples. These,or their successors,thereupon founded sanctuaries for Initiation,in which the ancient wisdom was revived in a new form. These were the Mysteries of antiquity. Here disciples were prepared to be brought into the condition of consciousness through which they might attain vision of the spiritual world.(23) From these sanctuaries of Initiation the Mysteries flowed forth to those who cultivated Spiritual Mysteries in Asia Minor,Greece,and Italy. (Important centres of Initiation were formed in the Greek world in the Orphic and Eleusinian Mysteries. In the Pythagorean School of wisdom,lingered the effects of the great wisdom-teachings and methods of past ages. On his distant travels,Pythagoras had been initiated into the secrets of the most varied kinds of Mysteries.)

But human life between birth and death in the post-Atlantean period had also an influence on the disembodied state after death. The more man's interests were fixed on the physical sense-world,the greater was the possibility of Ahriman gaining a hold upon the soul during earthly life and retaining his power of it after death. This danger was least among the peoples of ancient India,for during earthly life they had felt the physical sense-world to be an illusion,and thus had eluded the power of Ahriman after death. The danger for the primitive Persian peoples,who between birth and death had fixed their attention,with great interest, upon the physical sense-world was much greater. They would have largely fallen a prey to Ahriman's wiles had not Zarathustra pointed out, emphatically through his teaching concerning the Light of God,that behind the physical sense-world there exists the world of the Spirits of Light. In proportion to the ability of the people of this civilization to receive something into their souls out of the world of thought thus created,were they able to escape Ahriman's clutches during earthly life,and thereby elude him in the life after death,during which they were to be prepared for a new earth-life. The power of Ahriman in earthly life tends to make the physical sense-existence appear to be the only one,and thus to bar the way to any vista of a spiritual world. His power in the spiritual world leads man to complete isolation,and to the concentration of all his interest upon himself. Those who,at the time of death,are in Ahriman's power,are born again as egoists.

It is now possible for occult science to describe life between death and a new birth as it is,provided the Ahrimanic influence has,to a certain degree,been overcome. It is in this sense that it has been described by the author in the first chapter of this book as well as in other writings. And it must be described in this way if that which can be experienced by man during this form of existence is to be visualized and if he has attained to purely spiritual perception for that which really exists. The degree to which the individual experiences this,depends upon the extent to which he has overcome the Ahrimanic influence.

Man is approaching nearer and nearer to what it is possible for him to become in the spiritual world. How this progress is thwarted by other influences must however be clearly brought out in our consideration of the course of human evolution.

During the Egyptian period Hermes taught the people to prepare themselves during earth-life,for communion with the Spirit of Light. But because at that time human interests,between birth and death,were already so constituted that it was only possible to a slight degree to see through the veil of the physical sense-world,therefore the spiritual vision of the soul after death was also clouded and the perception of the world of light remained dim.

The obscuration of the spiritual world after death reached a climax in the souls who passed into the disembodied state out of a body belonging to the Greco-Roman civilization. During their earthly life they had brought to perfection the cultivation of physical sense-existence,and had thus condemned themselves to a shadowy existence after death. Hence the Greek felt life after death to be a shadowy existence,and it is not mere rhetoric but the realization of truth when the hero of that time,who is given up to the life of the senses,says,"Better a beggar on earth than a king in the realm of shades." All this was still more marked in those Asiatic peoples who had fixed their attention with veneration and worship

on material images instead of on their spiritual archetypes. A large proportion of mankind was in this condition at the time of the Greco-Roman
era of civilization. It can be seen how man's mission in post-Atlantean times,which consisted in the conquest of the physical sense-world,must necessarily lead to estrangement from the spiritual world. Thus greatness in one respect necessarily involves deterioration in another.

Man's connection with the spiritual world was kept alive in the Mysteries. Through these the Initiates,in special states of the soul,were able to receive revelations from that world. They were more or less the successors
of the guardians of the Atlantean oracles. To them was revealed what had been hidden through the influence of Lucifer and Ahriman. Lucifer concealed from man what had flowed from the spiritual world into the human
astral body,without his co-operation,up to the middle of the Atlantean period. Had the etheric body not been partially separated from the physical body,man would have been able to experience within himself this part of the spiritual world as an inner revelation to his soul. As a result of Lucifer's encroachment,this could be done only in special states of the soul. At those times a spiritual world appeared to man in the guise of the astral. The corresponding spiritual beings manifested themselves in forms which embodied only the higher principles of the human
being,and in those principles the symbols of their particular spiritual forces were astrally visible. Superhuman forms were manifested in this way.

After the encroachment of Ahriman,still another kind of Initiation was added to this one. Ahriman concealed from man everything out of the spiritual world which would have appeared behind physical sense-perception,had he not interfered in human affairs from the middle of the Atlantean period onward. The Initiates of the Mysteries owed the revelation of what he had thus kept hidden,to the fact that they had developed within their souls all those faculties which man had attained since that time,beyond the degree necessary for physical sense-impressions. Thus there were revealed to them the spiritual powers
lying behind the forces of nature. They could speak of the spiritual beings behind nature. The creative might of those forces acting in nature below man,was revealed to them. That which had been active since Saturn, Sun and the old Moon and had shaped man's physical,etheric and astral body as well as the mineral,plant and animal kingdoms,formed the contents of a certain kind of mystery-secrets,--namely those over which Ahriman held his hand. That which had formed the sentient-,rational-and consciousness-souls and which had been concealed from man by Lucifer, was
revealed in a second kind of Mystery-secrets.

But what the Mysteries could only prophesy was,that in time a man would appear possessing an astral body which,despite Lucifer,could become conscious of the light-world of the Sun-spirit through the etheric body, apart from any special condition of the soul. And the physical body of that human being must be of such a nature,that everything in the spiritual world would be revealed to him,which Ahriman is able to conceal from man up to the time of physical death. Physical death could bring no change into the life of such a being,that is to say,could have no power over it. The "Ego" so manifests in such a human being that the entire spiritual life is at the same time contained in his physical life. Such a being is the vehicle of the Spirit of Light,to whom the Initiate ascends from two directions,being led,under special conditions of the soul, either to the Superhuman Spirit or to the Being of the forces of nature. When the Initiates of the Mysteries foretold the appearance in the course of time,of such a human being,they were prophets of the Christ.

A personality arose,as the special prophet of this coming manifestation, within a nation which possessed through natural inheritance the qualities of the peoples of western Asia,and through education the learning of the Egyptians--the Hebrew nation. This prophet was Moses. The influences of Initiation had entered so deeply into his soul that in certain states of consciousness the being who had undertaken in the regular course of the earth evolution to shape human consciousness from the Moon,was revealed
to him. In thunder and lightning Moses realized not merely physical phenomena,but manifestations of this Spirit. At the same time the other kind of Mysteries had influenced his soul,so that he was able to distinguish,in astral vision,how the superhuman becomes human by means of the ego. Thus,from two directions,He Who was to come,was revealed to
Moses as the highest form of the Ego.

And in Christ the lofty Sun-spirit appeared in human form as the great ideal for human life on earth. At His coming,all mystery-wisdom had in some respects to take a new form. Up to that time this wisdom had existed
exclusively for the purpose of enabling man to put himself into such a condition of soul in which he would be able to view the kingdom of the Sun-spirit as something _outside_ of earthly evolution. Henceforth it was the mission of Mystery-wisdom to make man capable of recognizing in the incarnated Christ the Primordial Being. From this Primordial Being man was
enabled to understand the natural and spiritual worlds.(24)

At the point in His life at which the astral body of Christ Jesus contained everything which it is possible for the Luciferian influence to conceal,He came forward as the Teacher of humanity. From that moment, the
faculty was implanted in human earthly evolution for assimilating that wisdom whereby the physical goal of the earth may gradually be reached. At
the moment when the Event of Golgotha was accomplished,human nature was
endowed with another faculty,that by which Ahriman's influence may be turned into good. Henceforth man was able to take with him through the gate of death that which saves him from isolation in the spiritual world. What happened in Palestine was the central point,not only of human physical evolution but also of the other worlds to which man belongs; and when the "Mystery of Golgotha" had been accomplished,when the "death on
the cross" had been suffered,Christ appeared in that world where souls sojourn after death,and set limits to the power of Ahriman. From that moment the region which the Greeks had called the "realm of shades" was
illuminated by that flash of the Spirit indicating to its dwellers that light was to return. What had been gained for the physical world by the "Mystery of Golgotha" cast light also into the spiritual world.

Up to this event post-Atlantean human evolution had been a time of ascent
in the physical sense-world,but of descent as far as the spiritual world was concerned. Everything which flowed into the sense-world proceeded from
what had been in the spiritual world from remote ages. Since the coming of
Christ,those who attain to the Mystery of Christ are able to take with them into the spiritual world what they have won in the physical. And from the spiritual world it then flows back again into the earthly sense-world,

since reincarnated souls,on re-entering earth-life,bring with them what the Christ-impulse between death and a new birth,has bestowed.

What flowed into human evolution with the appearance of the Christ,acted in it like a seed. Only slowly can this seed mature. Only the smallest part of these profound new wisdom teachings,up to the present time,has reached down into physical existence. Christian evolution has just barely begun. During the successive periods of time following the appearance of the Christ,this Christian Evolution was able to reveal only so much of its inner essential nature as the humanity,the peoples of that time,were capable of receiving; only as much as they could grasp with their faculties of comprehension. The first form into which this essence of Christianity could be poured may be described as a comprehensive ideal of life. As such it was opposed to those forms of life which had been developed in post-Atlantean humanity. The conditions operating in human evolution since the repopulation of the earth in the Lemurian period have been described above. Accordingly,humanity can be traced back to different beings who,coming from other worlds,incarnated in the bodily descendants of the ancient Lemurians. The various races of man are a consequence of this,and the most diverse vital interests appeared in these reincarnated souls,as a result of their Karma. As long as all this was being worked out,there could be no ideal of "universal humanity." Human nature originated in unity,but earthly evolution up to the present time has led to division. In the figure of the Christ,we see an ideal which opposes all division,for in the man who bears the name of Christ there lives the lofty Sun-being from Whom every human ego is descended. The Hebrew nation still felt itself to be a nation,and each individual a member of that nation. When once the idea was grasped that in Christ-Jesus
there lives the ideal Man who stands above all that tends to divide humanity,Christianity became the Ideal of an all-Embracing brotherhood. Above all individual interests and relations,the feeling arose in some that the innermost ego of all human beings is of the same origin. (In addition to all the earthly forefathers,the great common Father of all humanity appears. "I and the Father are one.")

In the fourth,fifth,and sixth centuries after Christ,the era in which we are still living was being prepared in Europe. It was gradually to replace the fourth,or Greco-Roman civilization. It is the fifth post-Atlantean period. The races which,after many wanderings and varied fortunes,became the vehicles of this new civilization were descendants of those Atlanteans who had remained less affected than others by what had
been going on meanwhile during the four preceding periods of civilization. They had not penetrated into the countries in which those respective civilizations took root. On the contrary,they had,in their way,handed on Atlantean forms of civilization. There were many among them who had retained in a high degree the inheritance of the ancient dim clairvoyance, the state described above as intermediate between sleeping and waking. Such people knew the spiritual world from their own experience,and could reveal to their fellow-men what takes place there. Thus there sprang up a great number of narratives of spiritual beings and events,and the national treasures of legends and sagas had their origin in spiritual experiences of this kind. For the dim clairvoyance lasted on,in many people,into times not far removed from the present. There were other people who,although they had lost clairvoyance,nevertheless developed the faculties they acquired for use in the physical sense-world in accordance with feelings and emotions which corresponded to clairvoyant experiences. And even the Atlantean oracles had their successors in the new civilization.

There were everywhere Mysteries,but in them that Mystery of Initiation was most cultivated,which leads to the unveiling of that part of the spirit-world which Ahriman keeps hidden. The spiritual powers existing

behind the forces of nature were here revealed. In the mythologies of European nations are contained the remnants of what the Initiates of these
Mysteries were able to disclose to men. It is true that these mythologies also contain the other kind of mystery,although in a more imperfect form than that possessed by the Southern and Eastern Mysteries. Superhuman beings were also known in Europe,but they were seen to be in perpetual conflict with the associates of Lucifer. And the Light-God too was proclaimed,but in such a form that it was doubtful whether he would overcome Lucifer. On the other hand,these Mysteries were illuminated by the figure of the coming Christ. It was announced of Him that His kingdom would replace that of the other Light-God.(25)

From such influences as these,there came about a cleavage in the soul of the people of the fifth epoch of civilization which still continues,and is manifest in most diverse phenomena. The soul had not retained,from ancient times a sufficiently strong attraction for spiritual things to enable it to hold fast the connection between the worlds of spirit and sense. The attraction existed only as a training of feeling and emotion, not as direct vision of the spiritual world. On the other hand,man's attention was more and more directed toward the world of the senses and
its conquest; and the intellectual powers which had been awakened in the latter part of the Atlantean period,all those human powers of which the physical brain is the instrument,were concentrated upon the sense-world, and upon gaining knowledge of and mastery over it. Two worlds,so to speak,were developed within man: the one directed toward the life of physical sense; the other susceptible to the revelation of the spirit in such a way as to permeate with feeling and emotion even though lacking clairvoyant vision. The tendency to this cleavage of soul already existed when the teaching concerning the Christ was introduced into Europe.

This message from the spiritual world was received into men's hearts,and permeated feeling and emotion; but it was not possible to bridge the gulf between this state of devotion and what human intelligence,concentrated on the sense-world,was learning in the sphere of physical existence. What is now known as the contradiction between external science and spiritual knowledge is simply a consequence of this fact. The Christian mysticism (of Eckhart,Tauler and others) is the result of Christianity becoming permeated with feeling and emotion. Science,occupied as it is exclusively with the world of sense and its results in life,is the consequence of the other tendency of the soul,and all achievements in the sphere of outer material civilization are entirely due to this divergence of tendencies. Since those human faculties,of which the brain is the instrument,were concentrated exclusively on physical life,they were able to reach that pitch of perfection which makes contemporary science,technical skill,and other forms of mental activity possible. Such a material civilization could originate only among the nations of Europe,for they are those descendants of Atlantean ancestors who converted their natural inclination
toward the physical sense-world into faculties only when it had reached a certain degree of maturity. Previously they had allowed it to lie dormant, and had lived on what remained in them of the Atlantean clairvoyance and on the communications of their Initiates. While mental culture was outwardly almost entirely given up to these influences,in them ripened slowly the desire for the material conquest of the world.

Now,however,the dawn of the sixth post-Atlantean era of civilization is already at hand. What is to arise at a certain time in human evolution has ripened slowly in the preceding age. The first beginnings of that which can even now be developed,is to be discovered in the thread which binds together the two tendencies of the human breast,material civilization and life in the spiritual world. To this end it is necessary,on the one hand, that the results of spiritual vision should be understood; and on the other;that in the observations and experiences of of the sense-world the revelations of the Spirit be recognized. The sixth civilization-epoch will bring to full development the harmony between the two.

Herewith the studies in this book have reached a point where we may turn from the perspectives of the past to those of the future. But it will be better to precede the latter by a study of the Knowledge of Higher Worlds
and of Initiation. Then,after this study and in connection with it,we shall be able to indicate in brief the outlook for the future,in so far as that can be done within the framework of this book.

CHAPTER V. KNOWLEDGE OF THE HIGHER WORLDS

At the present stage of evolution there are three possible conditions of soul in which man ordinarily lives his life between birth and death: waking,sleeping and,between the two,dreaming. The last-mentioned will be briefly dealt with in a later part of this book; for the moment we shall consider life simply as it alternates between its two main conditions--waking and sleeping. Before he can "know" for himself in higher worlds,man has to add to these two a third condition of soul.

During waking life the soul is given up to the impressions of the senses, and to the thoughts and pictures that these evoke in it. During sleep the senses cease to make any impression,and the soul loses consciousness. The
whole of the day's experience sinks down into the sea of unconsciousness. Let us now consider how it would be if man were able to become conscious
during sleep,notwithstanding that all impressions of the senses were completely obliterated,as they are in deep sleep. Now would any memory remain to him of what had happened while he was awake. Would his soul find
itself in a state of vacuity? Would it be incapable of having any experiences? This is a question that can only be answered if conditions like or similar to those under discussion can actually be brought about. If the soul is capable of experiencing anything,even when sense-activities and recollection of such activities are lacking,then that soul would,so far as the external world is concerned,be "asleep"; and yet the soul would not be sleeping but awake to a world of reality.

Now such a condition of consciousness can be attained if man makes these
psychic experiences possible toward which occult science guides him. And everything that occult science tells us about those worlds beyond the sensible,has been found through such a condition of consciousness.

In the foregoing parts of this book certain communications have been made
concerning the higher worlds; and in the following pages,as far as is possible in a book of this kind,methods will be discussed whereby the state of consciousness requisite for such investigations may be acquired. This state of consciousness resembles that of sleep,in only one respect, namely: that through it,all outward sense activity ceases,and also all thoughts that might be aroused by the action of the senses,are obliterated. But although the soul has no power to experience anything consciously in sleep,yet it receives this power through this very state of consciousness. And through it a capacity for experiencing is awakened in the soul which in every day life can be awakened only through sense

impressions. The awakening of the soul to this higher state of consciousness is called _Initiation_.

The methods of initiation lead man away from the state of ordinary day-consciousness into such a soul activity as enables him to use his spiritual organs of perception. Like germs these organs lie dormant in the soul and must be developed. Now it may be that a person,at some particular moment of his earthly life,makes the discovery that these higher organs have developed within his soul without previous preparation. It is a kind of involuntary self-awakening. Such a person will become conscious of a change affecting his entire being; his soul's experiences will have been enriched beyond measure and he will find that no experiences of the sense-world can bring him such spiritual happiness, such soul satisfaction and inner warmth as that which now opens up to him,
which no physical eye can see and no hand can touch. From the spiritual world strength and a sense of security in all situations in life,will flow into his will. There are instances of such self-initiation; but they should not give rise to the idea that the only right course is to wait for the coming of such self-initiation,and to do nothing toward bringing about initiation through regular training. We need not here give further space to the subject of self-initiation,since it may take place without regard to rules of any kind whatsoever.

What we have to consider is how by training,one may develop those organs
of perception,lying dormant in the Soul. Those who do not feel themselves especially impelled toward doing something for their own development may easily say that man stands under the guidance of spiritual powers,that such guidance should therefore not be interfered with,and that the moment,deemed by those powers to be the right one for revealing another
world to the soul,should be awaited in patience. Indeed,persons who are of this opinion are inclined to consider it a kind of presumption,or unjustifiable desire for any one to interfere with the wisdom of such spiritual guidance.

Those who think in this way will only change their opinion if some other mode of presenting the case makes a sufficiently strong impression upon them. If they were to say to themselves,"This wise guidance has endowed me with certain faculties,and it has done so,not that I should let them lie idle,but rather that I should use them. Indeed,the very wisdom of such guidance lies in the fact of its having placed in me the rudiments of those organs necessary for a higher state of consciousness. I can, therefore,rightly comprehend this guidance only when I regard it as my duty to do everything in my power that may serve to bring such rudimentary
growths to their proper development." Should such thoughts make a sufficiently strong impression on the mind,scruples against training for the attainment of higher consciousness will disappear.

There is,it is true,another scruple which may arise in the mind with regard to such schooling. A person may say to himself: "This development of the inner faculties of the soul means an invasion of man's most hidden sanctuary. It involves a certain change of the entire human being; the method for such a change cannot be worked out by any ordinary procedure of
thought,for the manner in which the higher worlds are attained can be known only to those to whom the path has become visible by reason of experience. If,therefore,I turn to such an one,I am allowing him to exercise his influence over the innermost sanctuary of my soul." Any one given to this attitude of mind will hardly find it reassuring if the methods for bringing about a higher state of consciousness are imparted to

him in book form. For it is not a question of receiving communications either verbally or from some person who,having the knowledge,has set the same down in a book to which we have access. Now there are people possessing knowledge of the rules for developing the spiritual organs of perception who are of the opinion that these rules ought not to be entrusted to a book. These people,for the most part,consider the communication of certain truths relating to the spiritual world as forbidden. But this view must be characterized as in a certain sense out of date in view of the present stage of human evolution. It is true that the communication of the rules referred to can be made only up to a certain point. Yet what is imparted leads so far that one who applies it to his soul-life makes such progress in knowledge that he is able to go on by himself. This way then leads onward in a manner of which a true idea can be gained only through what has been previously experienced. From all these facts,scruples may arise concerning the path of spiritual knowledge.

These scruples however disappear when one clearly understands the essential nature of that course of development which is adapted to our age. Of this latter method of developing we shall speak here and other methods will be only briefly referred to.

The method of training to be here discussed furnishes to him who has the will for a higher development,the means for accomplishing the transformation of his soul. Any questionable encroachment on the personality of the student would only then be possible,should the teacher proceed to carry out the change by methods of which the pupil was not conscious. But no true teacher of occult science in our day would make use
of any such method,by which indeed,the pupil would be reduced to a blind tool. The teacher gives his pupil instructions as to the rules of conduct he is to pursue,and the pupil carries them out. At the same time,should the case seem to demand it,the teacher does not withhold the reasons justifying these rules of conduct.

The acceptance of the rules,and their application by a person seeking spiritual development,need not be a matter of blind belief. Such a belief ought to be quite out of the question in this sphere. One who studies the nature of the human soul as far as it can be followed by ordinary self-observation,without occult training may,after accepting the rules recommended for spiritual training,ask himself,"How do these rules act upon the life of the soul?" This question may be satisfactorily answered previous to any schooling by an unbiased use of common sense. Before these
rules are adopted,true conceptions may be gained as to the way in which they operate. The effect can be _experienced_ only during training,but even then the experience will always be accompanied by an understanding of
the experience,if each step that is to be taken is tested by sound judgment. And in this age any true spiritual science will only suggest such rules for training as can be vindicated by sound judgment. For him who is willing to simply trust himself to such schooling and does not permit prejudice to drive him into _blind_ faith,all scruples will vanish and objections against a regular training for higher states of consciousness will no longer disturb him.

Even such people as may have arrived at a state of inward maturity,--which
sooner or later would lead to the self-awakening of these spiritual organs of perception--even for these,training is by no means superfluous. On the contrary it is especially adapted to them. For there are but few cases in which personal initiation does not have to travel along tortuous and devious ways,and training spares them the traversing of such by-paths, leading them forward in a straight line. In cases where such

self-initiation comes to a soul,the reason is that the required degree of ripeness had already been attained in the course of previous incarnations.

It may easily happen that such a soul possesses a certain dim intuition of its ripeness,and by reason of this very feeling may assume an attitude of disinclination toward training. A feeling of this kind may produce a certain degree of pride,which refuses to place confidence in a teacher. Now it can happen that a certain degree of soul development may remain hidden up to a certain age and only then reveal itself. But such schooling may be just the very means needed to call it forth. Should the person hold aloof from such training,it may happen that the power will remain dormant during that particular Life,and will only reappear in a later incarnation.

The rising to a supersensible state of consciousness can only proceed from
ordinary waking day-consciousness. It is in this consciousness that the soul lives prior to its ascent,and schooling will furnish the means to lead it out of this consciousness. The first steps which the schooling here under consideration prescribes,are such as can still be characterized as actions of the ordinary day-consciousness. It is just those quiet acts of the soul which are the most effective steps. This requires that the soul should give itself up to definite perceptions and these perceptions are such as are able by their very nature to exercise an awakening influence upon certain hidden faculties of the inner nature of man.

They thereby differ from those perceptions of waking day-life,whose purpose is to portray external objects. The more faithfully they present these things,the truer they are. It is,indeed,in accordance with their nature that they should be true in this sense,but this is not the mission of those perceptions which the soul is to consider,when in pursuit of spiritual training; and they are therefore so formed as not to present anything external,having rather within themselves the power to act upon the soul. The best percepts for the purpose are the emblematic or symbolic
ones. Yet other percepts may be used. For it does not depend at all on what the percepts contain,but solely on the fact that the soul puts forth all its powers in order not to have anything in the consciousness except the one percept in question. Whereas,in ordinary life,its forces are divided among many things and perceptions change rapidly,the important point in spiritual training is the concentration of the whole inner life upon one single perception. And this perception must be voluntarily brought to the centre of one's consciousness. Symbolic perceptions are better than those which reflect outer objects or events,because the latter are related to the outer world,and the soul has to depend less on itself than in the case of symbolic perceptions,formed by its own inner energy. The chief object at which to aim is the _intensity_ of the force to be exercised by the soul. It is not what is before the soul that is essential,but the greatness of the effort and the length of time spent concentrating upon one perception. Strength ascends from unknown depths of
the soul,from which it is drawn up by concentration on one perception. Occult science contains many such perceptions,all of which have been proven to possess the power alluded to above.

One gains a comprehension of this immersion or sinking down into a percept
by calling the Memory-Concept before the soul. Say,for instance,that we allow the eye to rest on a tree,and then turn away from the object so that it is no longer presented to our sight; we shall,nevertheless,be able to retain the image of the tree in the soul. Now this image or perception of the tree which we have when it is no longer in sight,is a recollection of the tree. Then assume that this recollection is retained

in the soul,and the soul reposes,as it were,in this recollection, taking care to exclude all other perceptions from the memory. The soul then dwells in that memory-concept of the tree,and we then have to do with the immersion of the soul into a concept. Yet this concept is the image of an actual thing perceived through the senses. If howeverof our own free will,we take such images into our consciousness,gradually the effect desired will be attained.

One example of meditation based upon a symbolical concept will now be placed before the reader. Such a concept must first be built up in the soul,and this may be done in the following manner. Let us think of a plant,calling to mind how it is rooted in the ground,the way in which leaf after leaf shoots forth,until finally the blossom unfolds. And then let us imagine a human being placed beside this plant,and let us call up in our soul the thought that he has qualities and characteristics which, when compared with those of the plant,will be found to be more perfect. We dwell on the fact that this being is able to move here and there, according to his will and his desires,while the plant remains stationary, rooted in the soil.

But now let us also consider: Yes,man is certainly more perfect than the plant; but, on the other hand,I find in him qualities which I cannot perceive in the plant and, through the lack of which,the plant appears more perfect than man in certain respects. Man is filled with passions and desires and these govern his conduct. With him we can speak of sin committed by reason of his impulses and passions,whereas in the plant,we see that it follows the pure laws of growth from leaf to leaf,and that the blossom without passion opens to the chaste rays of the Sun. So we can
see that man possesses a certain perfection beyond the plant,but that on the other hand he has paid for this perfection by admitting into his being inclinations,desires and passions in addition to the pure forces of the plant. And then we call to mind the green sap flowing through the plant, and think of it as the expression of the pure and passionless laws of growth. And then again,we call to mind the red blood as it courses through the veins of man,and we recognize in it an expression of man's instincts,his passions and desires. Let a vivid picture of all this arise in our souls. We then think of man's faculties of development; how he can purify and cleanse his inclinations and passions through his higher soul faculties. We think how through this process something that is low is destroyed in these inclinations and passions which thereby are born upon a
higher plane. Then we may be able to think of the blood as the expression of these purified and cleansed inclinations and passions.

Now we gaze in spirit on the rose and say to ourselves: "In the red sap of the rose is the erstwhile green sap of the plant--now changed to crimson--and the red rose follows the same pure,passionless laws of growth
as does the green leaf." Thus the red of the rose may offer us a symbol of a kind of blood which is the expression of cleansed impulses and passions, purged of all lower elements,and resembling in their purity the forces working in the red rose. Let us now try not only to assimilate such thoughts within our reason,but also let them come to life within our feelings. We can experience a blissful sensation when contemplating the purity and passionless nature of the growing plant. We can awaken the feeling within us how certain higher perfections must be paid for through the acquisition of passions and desires. This,then,can change the blissful sensation previously experienced into a serious mood: and then only can it stir within us the feeling of liberating happiness,if we abandon ourselves to the thought of the red blood that can become the carrier of inner pure experiences,like the red sap of the rose. The important point is that we should not look coldly and without feeling upon these thoughts which serve to build up such a symbolical concept. After

dwelling for a time upon the above mentioned thoughts and feelings,let us try to transmute them into the following symbolical concept. Let us imagine a black cross. Let this be the symbol for the destroyed lower element of our desires and passions and there where the beams of the cross
intersect,let us imagine seven red radiating roses arranged in a circle. Let these roses be the symbol for a blood that is the expression of cleansed and purified passions and desires.(26)

Now we must call up this symbolical concept before our soul just as has been described in the case of a memory-concept. Such a concept has an awakening power if one abandons oneself to it in inner meditation. One must try during this meditation to exclude all other concepts. Only the described symbol must float before the soul as vividly as possible.

It is not without significance that this symbol has been introduced,not merely as an awakening percept,but because it has been constructed out of
certain perceptions concerning plants and man. For the effect of such a symbol depends upon the fact of its being put together in this definite manner,before employing it as an instrument for meditation. Should it be called up without a previous process of construction such as has here been
delineated,the picture must remain cold and will be far less effective than if it had by previous preparation gathered force with which to give warmth to the soul. During meditation,however,one should not call up in the soul all the preparatory thoughts,but merely allow the life-like image to float before one's mind and at the same time permit those feelings which are the result of these preparatory thoughts to vibrate with it. Thus the symbol becomes a sign,co-existent with the inner experience. And it is the dwelling of the soul in this experience that is the active principle. The longer one can do this,without admitting disturbing impressions,the more effective will be the whole process.

It is well,however,in addition to the time used in meditation itself,to repeat the building up of the image through the feelings,as described above,so that the corresponding sensation may not pale.

The greater the patience brought to bear in performing these acts of repetition,the more effective becomes this image for the soul.(27)

Such a symbol as has just been described represents no external object or
being evolved by nature,but for this very reason it possesses an awakening power for certain inner faculties. It is true,someone may raise the objection: certainly the "whole" as a symbol,does not exist in nature; yet all its details are borrowed from nature,the black color,the roses,etc. It can all be observed through the senses. He who is troubled by such objections,ought to consider that it is not the images of these sense perceptions that awaken the higher faculties of the soul,but that this result is produced purely by the manner in which these details are combined. And this combination does not then picture something that exists
in the sense-world.

A symbol was chosen as an example to show the process of effective meditation of the soul. Many symbols of this kind are used in occult training and are built up according to varying methods. Certain sentences, formulæ,and single words can also be given as subjects for meditations, and in every case the means used will have the same object,namely: to detach the soul from sense-impressions and to stimulate it to an activity in which the impressions of the physical senses play no longer any part and in which the unfoldment of inner latent soul capacities becomes the essential.

There are,however,also meditations based exclusively upon feelings, sensations,etc.,and these are especially effectual. Let us,for instance,take the feeling of joy. In the normal course of life the soul experiences pleasure when there exists an outer stimulus to pleasure. If a healthily constituted soul perceives some act performed by a person, indicative of the doer's goodness of heart,then the soul will assuredly feel pleasure and joy at such an act. But the soul is able to reflect upon such an act,and can say to itself that an act done from sheer kindness of heart is one in which the doer is following the interests of his fellow-creatures rather than his own,and such an act may be called ethically good. But the soul can lift itself above the perception of any particular case in the outer world which has given it joy or pleasure,and instead may arrive at a general concept of kindness. It can for instance, think of kindness coming into existence through one soul making the interests of others his own. And the soul can then experience joy over the ethical idea of kindness. Therefore,the joy is then not over this or that event of the sense-world,but it is the joy over the idea as such. If the student now tries for some time to let this joy come to life within his soul,then this is a meditation on a feeling,on a sensation. It is then not the idea which is the active principle in the awakening of the inner soul faculties,but the sustained dwelling upon that feeling within the soul which has not been caused by merely a single external impression.

Occult science being in a position to penetrate far deeper into the being of things than can be done by ordinary perception,the teacher will be able to indicate to the pupil feelings and sentiments which are still more powerful as awakening agents for the unfolding of the soul's faculties when used as subjects of meditation. Yet,necessary as this will be for the higher degrees of training,it should be remembered that energetic meditating upon subjects,such as kindness of heart may carry the student very far on his way.

Since the natures of human beings differ,special methods of training are effective for particular individuals. As to the duration of time to be devoted to meditation,we may remind the student that the greater the length of time during which he can meditate uninterruptedly,the stronger will be the effect. But every excess in these matters should be avoided. There is,however,a certain inner discretion,resulting from these exercises themselves which teaches the pupil to keep within due bounds in this regard. Those who pursue their studies in occult science under the personal guidance of a teacher will receive from him precise instruction and advice in these particulars. Nevertheless,it must be emphatically understood that only experienced occultists are in a position to impart such advice.

Such exercises in meditation will generally require practice for some time before the student can become aware of any result. What is essential to occult science is patience and perseverance. He who is unable to awaken these two qualities within himself and who cannot continually practice his exercises in quietude,so that patience and perseverance are always the predominant note in his soul-life,cannot attain very great progress. From what has been said above,the reader will have gathered that meditation is a means of acquiring knowledge of the higher worlds,but he will also see that not just any percept whatsoever,taken at random,is productive of this result,but only those of the kind before-mentioned.

The path here indicated leads in the first place to what is called imaginative knowledge,and this is the first step toward the higher knowledge. Knowledge,dependent upon sense-perceptions and upon the working up of such perceptions by reason,which is sense-bound,is,to use the occult term,known as "objective cognition." Beyond this are higher degrees of knowledge,the imaginative stage being,as we have said,the first. Now the term "imaginative" can cause confusion in the minds of some,to whom "imagination" stands only for "imaginings"--that is concepts that lack reality. In occult science,however,"imaginative" cognition must be understood to be that kind of cognition which results from a supersensible state of consciousness of the soul. The things perceived in this state of consciousness are spiritual facts,and spiritual beings,to which the senses have no access,and--since this condition of the soul is caused by meditating upon symbols,or "imaginations"--the sphere to which this condition of higher consciousness belongs may be termed the imaginative world,and the knowledge relating to it,imaginative knowledge. "Imaginative" stands,therefore,in this sense,for that which is "actual" in a higher sense than are the facts and beings of physical sense-perception.

A very natural objection to the use of the symbolic pictures here characterized is that they arise from a dreamy thinking and an arbitrary imagination,and might therefore have doubtful consequences. But any such doubts are unjustified in regard to the symbols given by true occult schools. For these symbols are chosen in such a way that they can be looked at quite apart from their connection with outer sense reality,and their value is to be found exclusively in the power with which they work upon the soul when it turns its attention wholly away from the outer world,when it suppresses all sense-impressions and shuts out every thought to which it might be stimulated from without. The process of meditations is best demonstrated by comparison with sleep. In one respect
it is like the state of sleep; in another,the exact opposite of it. It is a sleep which when compared to the day-consciousness,represents a higher
state of being. The point is that by concentration on the given conception or image,the soul is obliged to call up much stronger forces out of its own depths than it uses in ordinary life or knowledge. Its inner activity is thereby enhanced. It becomes detached from the body,as it does in sleep; but instead of passing,as in the latter case,into unconsciousness,it experiences a world it did not know before. Although as regards detachment from the body this condition may be compared with
sleep,yet it is such that,compared with ordinary waking consciousness, it may be characterized as a more intense waking state. By this means the
soul learns to know itself in its true,inner,independent being. But in ordinary life,owing to the weaker development of its forces,it is only with the help of the body that the soul arrives at self-consciousness. Therefore it does not experience itself but merely sees itself in that image which--like a kind of reflection--is traced,by the physical body (or, properly speaking,by its processes).

These symbols built up in the manner above described are not as yet related to anything real in the spiritual world,but they serve to detach the human soul from sense-observations and from that instrument,the brain,to which the reason is at first fettered. This detachment is not effected until man is able to feel: "I am now perceiving something by means of powers for which neither my senses nor my brain serve as the instruments"; and the first thing man thus experiences is a liberation from the organs of sense. He is then able to say to himself: "My consciousness does not vanish when I cease to take cognizance of sense-perceptions and ordinary reasoned thought; I can lift myself out of those conditions and then feel myself as a being alongside of that which I was before"--and this is the first purely spiritual experience; the perception of a psycho-spiritual Ego-being. This has arisen as a new self out of that self which is linked to the physical senses and physical reason only.

Had this detachment from the world of the senses and from the reason been effected without meditation,the person would have lapsed into the nothingness of the unconscious state. This psycho-spiritual being was our possession prior to meditation also,but it then lacked the organs for perception of the spirit-world; and it might,indeed,have been compared to the physical body without the eye to see--the ear to hear. The strength thus employed in meditation has,in fact,been the creative means by which these psycho-spiritual organs have been formed out of a previously unorganized psycho-spiritual being. But this which man thus creates for himself is also the first thing to be perceived by him. The first experience is therefore in a certain sense,a kind of "self-perception." It belongs to the nature of spiritual training that the soul,through the self training which it gives itself at this point of its development, becomes fully conscious that the first thing it perceives in the world of imaginative forms,which appear as a result of the exercises described,is itself. It is true that these images make their appearance as a new world, but the soul must recognize that they are,however,at first nothing but the reflection of its own being,which has been strengthened by exercises. And it must not only recognize this by correct reasoning,but must have arrived at such a cultivation of the will that it is able at any time to put away and obliterate the images from the consciousness.

The soul must be able to act with complete independence within these images. This is part of true spiritual training at this stage. If it could not do this,it would be in the same position,in the sphere of spiritual experiences,as a soul in the physical world which,on looking at an object,has its attention so arrested by it that it cannot look away. An exception to this possibility of obliteration is formed by a group of inner imaginative experiences which should _not_ be extinguished at this stage of spiritual training. They correspond to the inmost kernel of the soul's being,and the occult student recognizes in those images that which forms the very essence of his being which passes through the various repeated earth lives. At this point the knowledge of repeated earth lives becomes an actual experience. In relation to everything else the before-mentioned independence of experience must prevail. And only after acquiring the faculty of obliterating experiences,is the spiritual outer world really approached. What is obliterated returns in another form,and is experienced as a spiritual outer reality. One feels that out of something indefinite one grows psychically into something definite. From this self-perception,one must then proceed to the observation of a psycho-spiritual outer world. This comes to pass when we can order our inner experience after the manner to be indicated in the following pages.

At first,the soul of the occult student is feeble in all that appertains to a perception of the psycho-spiritual world; and he will therefore need all the inner energy he can summon in order,while meditating,to hold firm the symbols or other concepts which he has built up from the impulses
of the sense-world. Should he,however,desire to attain to an actual observation of the higher world,he will not alone have to maintain his hold on these,he must also,after having done this,be able to remain in a condition in which not only no influences of the outer sense-world can affect the soul,but in which also the images above characterized shall have been effaced from his consciousness. Only now can that which has been
previously formed by means of meditation enter the plane of his consciousness. The important point is that there should be at this stage sufficient soul force to spiritually perceive that which has thus been formed through meditation,so that it may not elude the observer's attention,as is always the case if this inner energy is still insufficiently developed.

That which is here evolved as a psycho-spiritual organism and which should
be comprehended through self-perception,is delicate and subtle. The

disturbing influences of the outer sense-world,however one may try to exclude them,are nevertheless great. It is not merely a question of those disturbances to which we are able to pay heed,but far more of those which
in ordinary life are ever eluding our notice. But it is just through the very nature of man that a transitory condition in this respect becomes possible. What the soul,in its waking state,was powerless to effect, owing to the disturbances of the physical world,it is capable of achieving during sleep. One who gives himself up to serious meditation will,with the proper attention,become aware of a certain change in his sleep. He will feel that while sleeping,he is yet not quite asleep,but that his soul has times when,although asleep,still it is,in a certain way,active. During these conditions,nature wards off the influences of the outer world which the waking soul is not yet able to keep away of its own strength. When,however,the meditation exercises have taken effect, the soul,during sleep,detaches itself from unconsciousness,and becomes aware of the psycho-spiritual world. This can happen in two ways: the person may,while asleep,become aware that is is in another world,or he may,after awakening,remember that he has been in another world. But the former of these two feelings requires the greater degree of inner energy, for which reason the second is the more common among beginners in occult
training. But it may gradually come to pass that the student will become aware of having been during the entire time of sleep in this other world, only emerging therefrom when he awakes. And his memory of beings and facts
connected with this other world will become ever more and more distinct, thus showing that in one form or another he has now entered upon what one
may call continuity of consciousness. (The continuation of consciousness during sleep.)

Still,for this to be so,it is not necessary that man's consciousness should _always_ continue during sleep. Much will already have been attained in the matter of the continuity of consciousness should the person,whose sleep is in general like that of the ordinary individual, have certain periods during his sleeping hours when he is aware of being in the psycho-spiritual world; or if,on awakening,he is able to remember such a condition of consciousness. It should,however,be borne in mind that what is here described is to be understood only as a transition state. It is well to pass through this state as a part of training; yet it should not be imagined that any conclusive views concerning the psycho-spiritual world may be gained from this transition state,for in this condition the soul is uncertain,and unable as yet to rely upon its own perceptions. But through such experiences the soul gathers ever more
strength enabling it also during waking hours to ward off the disturbing influences of the physical outer and inner world and thus to attain psycho-spiritual observation. Then impressions through the senses no longer reach the soul; brain-fettered reason is silent and even the image of the meditation,through which one has only prepared oneself for spiritual vision,has been dropped from consciousness. Whatever is given out through occult science in this or that form should never originate in any psycho-spiritual observation other than that which is made with fully waking consciousness. The first experience is one in which the student can
say to himself: Even should I now disregard everything that can come to me
through impressions from the outer physical world,still I look upon my inner being not as upon one in which all activity has ceased,but I look upon a being which is self-conscious in a world of which I know nothing as long as I permit myself to be governed only by the impressions of ordinary reason and of the senses. The soul at this moment has the sensation that in the manner described above,it has given birth to a new being as its

own essential soul-kernel. And the being possesses totally different qualities from those which were previously present in the soul.

The second experience of the soul is one in which man has his former being,like a second independent one,alongside of himself. That which had up to this time been imprisoned,evolves now into something we are able to confront; we feel,in fact,at certain times outside of what we have been accustomed to regard as our own being,as our own ego. It is as though one
now lived in two egos,--one,which we have hitherto known; the other,a newly born being,superior to the first,--and we become aware that the former ego acquires a certain independence in its relationship to the second,just as the physical body has a certain measure of freedom in its relation to that first ego.

This is an event of great importance,for through it man comes to know what it means to live in that world which he has been endeavoring to reach
by means of training. It is this second,this new-born,ego which can be led to cognizance of the spiritual world,and in it can be developed that which has as much significance for the spiritual world as our sense organs have for the physical world of the senses. Should this development have attained to the requisite degree,the student will not only be aware of himself as a new-born ego,but he will recognize the spiritual facts and entities around him,just as he perceives the physical world through the action of his physical senses; and this is a third important experience.

To meet properly this stage of spiritual training one must take into account that with the strengthening of the forces of the soul a degree of self love and egoism appears with such intensity as is quite unknown in the ordinary life of the soul. It would be a mistake for anyone to think that it is only a case of ordinary self-love at this point. Self-love becomes so strong at this stage of development that it acquires the strength of a nature-force within the soul,and a vigorous training of the will is necessary in order to conquer this powerful egoism. This training of the will must go hand in hand with the rest of the spiritual training. A strong inclination exists to feel absolutely happy in a world which we have gradually created for ourselves. And we must be able to obliterate, in the manner above described,that to which we have previously devoted ourselves with all our powers. We must efface _ourselves_ in the imaginative world we have reached. But this effacement is opposed by the strongest impulses of egoism.

The idea might easily arise that the exercises in spiritual training are something merely external which have no connection with the moral development of the soul. In this connection it must be said that the moral force necessary for the conquest of egoism,as described,cannot be gained unless the moral condition of the soul is brought to a corresponding stage. Progress in spiritual training is unthinkable unless moral progress takes place at the same time. The conquest of egoism is impossible without
moral force. All talk of spiritual training not being at the same time moral training is certainly contrary to fact.

Only he who passes through such an experience might advance the following
objections: how can one be sure to be dealing with actualities,and not with mere fancies,visions or hallucinations,when he thinks he is having spiritual perceptions? Now the matter lies thus: every person,who has been systematically trained and who has arrived at the stage already characterized,will be in a position to note the difference between his own percept and a spiritual reality,just as well as a man endowed with sound sense knows the difference between the percept of a bar of hot iron

and the actual presence of such a bar that he touches with his hand. The difference is determined by experience and by nothing else; and in the spiritual world,too,life is the touchstone. Just as we know that in the world of the senses an imagined bar of iron,however hot,will burn no one's fingers,so does the trained occultist know whether he is passing through a spiritual experience merely in his imagination or whether his awakened spiritual organs of perceptions are impressed by actual facts or beings. The precautions to be taken during schooling,in order that the student may not fall a victim to such delusions will be dealt with in the following pages.

It is of the greatest importance that the student should have attained to a certain very definite condition of the soul when the consciousness of the new-born ego commences.. For through his ego,man is the ruler of his sensations,feelings,and conceptions,his impulses,desires,and passions. Observations and percepts cannot be left in the soul to follow their own devices; they must be regulated according to the laws of thought. And it is the ego,as it were,that controls these thought-laws, and by means of them brings order into the life of perception and thought.

It is similar with regard to desires and passions,inclinations and impulses. The fundamental ethical laws become the guides of these forces of the soul,and by reason of the moral judgment,the ego becomes the soul's guide within this domain. Now if a person detaches a higher ego from his ordinary ego,the latter becomes to a certain extent independent. That much life-power is now taken away from it as is needed for the use of
that higher ego. But let us consider the case of a person who has not,as yet,developed certain ability and firmness in exercising the laws of thought and in the power of judgment,but who nevertheless desires to bring about the birth of his higher ego. He will be able to leave to his ordinary ego only as much thought capacity as he has previously developed.
If the amount of well-ordered thinking is insufficient,then the ordinary ego which has now become independent,will certainly fall victim to confused,disordered,fantastic thoughts and judgment,and moreover,since in such a case the new-born ego must inevitably be weak also,the disordered lower ego will gain the upper hand,and the person will lose his ability for balanced judgment. Had he developed sufficient capability and firmness in logical thinking,he might have calmly left his ordinary ego to go its own way.

In the ethical sphere it is precisely the same. Should a person not have attained firmness in the matter of his moral judgment,should he not have become sufficiently master over his inclinations,impulses,and passions, he will then render his ordinary ego independent while in a condition in which it will be overwhelmed by all these soul forces. It may then happen that the person will become worse through the birth of his higher ego than he was before. Had he waited to bring about this birth until he had sufficiently developed his ordinary self,attaining firmness in the matter of ethical judgment,stability of character,and depth of conscience,he would then have been in a position to have all these virtues left within that first ego when the birth of the second came about. Neglecting to do so,however,lays him open to the danger of losing his moral balance, which under the right course of training cannot happen.

Two things must here be borne in mind. First,that the facts above related should be taken as seriously as possible; secondly,that,on the other hand,they should in no way deter one from entering upon such training.

Anyone who has the firm intention of doing all in his power that may give confidence to the first ego in the execution of what it has to fulfil, need never be dismayed when the second ego becomes detached as the result of such spiritual training. Yet he must remember that the power of self-delusion in man is very great with regard to the belief that he has now reached the stage of "ripeness" for any special thing.

During the spiritual training here described the student develops his thought-life to such an extent that he is not exposed to dangers which are often thought to be connected with training. This cultivation of thought brings about all the inner experiences that are necessary,but causes them to be so enacted that the soul lives through them without any injurious shocks. Without an adequate development of thought,these experiences may produce a feeling of great uncertainty in the soul. The method here emphasized calls forth experiences in such a way that they may produce all their effect and yet not cause serious shocks. By developing the life of thought the student becomes more of a _spectator_ of the experiences of his inner life,whereas without such thought-development he is in the very midst of the experience and is shaken by all the shocks incidental to it.

Systematic training points out certain qualities which the student must acquire by means of exercises,in order to find the way to the higher worlds and especial stress is laid on the following,--control of the soul over its thoughts,its will,and its feelings. The manner in which this control is acquired through exercise has a dual aim. On the one hand,the soul by this practice acquires a firmness,reliance,and balance,which will not forsake it even after the birth of the second ego; and on the other hand,this latter ego is provided with strength and inner fortitude for its journey.

What is required is that man's thinking power shall in all domains conform to facts. In the physical world of the senses,life is the great teacher of the human ego with regard to reality. Were the soul to allow its thoughts to roam aimlessly hither and thither,it would soon be corrected by life,unless it were willing to enter into combat with it; the soul must conform its thoughts to the facts of life. Now,when man leads his thoughts away from the world of the physical senses,he misses the corrective influence of this latter. If his thought is not able to be its own mentor,it will be as unsteady as a will-o'-the-wisp. Consequently, the student's thought must be exercised in such a way that its course and object are self-determined. Inner firmness and a capacity to concentrate strictly on one object: this is what such thinking must of itself engender. And for this reason the thought exercises should not be concerned with complicated objects or those foreign to life,but should, on the contrary,deal with those that are simple and familiar. Any one who succeeds in fixing his mind,over a period of several months and for a space of at least five minutes a day,on such ordinary objects as a pin or a lead pencil,excluding for the time being all other thoughts not concerned with the object under contemplation,will have accomplished much in the right direction. (A new article may be chosen each day,or the same one adhered to for the space of several days.)

Even those who feel themselves to be "thinkers" need not despise this method of preparing themselves for occult training,because by fixing the attention for a time upon a really familiar object one may be sure that he will be thinking in accordance with facts,and one who asks himself the questions: "What are the constituent parts of a pencil?" "How are these materials prepared?" "How are they afterwards put together?" "When were pencils invented,etc.?" will surely be adapting his perceptions to realities more than he who meditates on the descent of man,or asks himself what life is.

Simple thought exercises prepare us better for an adequate concept of the
world in its Saturn,Sun,and Moon stages of development than those based on learned and complicated ideas. For the important thing is not at all just to think,but to think in conformity with facts by means of an inner force. Once one has been trained to accuracy by means of an obvious, physical sense process,the desire to think in conformity with facts will have become habitual,even if thought does not feel itself under the control of the physical sense-world and its laws; we then lose the tendency to let our thoughts drift about aimlessly.

And as in the world of thought,so in the realm of the will,the soul must become the ruler. In the physical sense-world it is life that rules. It urges upon man this or that as a necessity,and the will feels itself constrained to satisfy these same wants. In following higher training,man must accustom himself to obey his own commands strictly,and those who acquire this habit will feel less and less inclined to desire what is of no moment. All that is unsatisfying and unstable in the life of the will comes from the desire for things of the possession of which we have formed
no distinct concept. Discontent such as this may,when the higher ego is desirous of emerging from the soul,throw that person's whole inner life into disorder; and it is a good exercise to give oneself for the space of several months some command to be carried out at a specified time of day:
"To-day,at this or that particular hour,you will do this or that thing." Thus we gradually become able to command the time at which a thing is to
be done and the manner in which it is to be performed,so as to admit of its being accomplished with utmost exactitude. Thus we lift ourselves above the bad habit of saying,"I should like this," and "I want the other," while exercising no thought of the possibility of its accomplishment.

In the second part of _Faust_,Goethe puts the following words into the mouth of a seeress: "Him I love who craves the impossible," and Goethe himself,in his "Prose Proverbs," says: "To live in the idea means treating the impossible as though 't were possible."

Such sentiments must not be put forward as objections against what has here been stated,for the demands made by Goethe and his seeress (Manto)
can be fulfilled only by those who have first educated themselves through desire for that which is possible,and have in so doing,arrived at being able,by means of their strong "will," to treat the "impossible" in such a manner that through their willing it becomes transformed into the possible.

A certain equanimity should pervade the soul of the occult student concerning the world of feeling. And to attain this result,it is necessary that the soul should have mastery over the expressions of joy and sorrow,pleasure and pain. But it is just concerning the acquisition of this faculty that some prejudice might arise: one might be afraid of becoming dull and indifferent if he does not "rejoice with them that do rejoice,and weep with them that weep." Yet this is not what is meant. What is pleasurable _should_ rejoice the soul,and sorrow _should_ give it pain,but what the soul is to learn to achieve is control over the expression of joy and sorrow. If that is his aim,the student will become aware that,far from becoming "dull and unsympathetic," he will be growing all the more receptive to the joy and sorrow around him. But it is true that the student will here find that he needs to watch himself carefully for a considerable time to be able to acquire the faculty indicated. He must be careful to see that he partakes of pain and pleasure to the full, yet without so giving himself up to either that he gives involuntary expression to it. It is not justified sorrow that should be suppressed, but the involuntary weeping; not the revulsion against a mean act,but the blind raging in anger; not the precaution against danger,but the senseless "being afraid," etc.

It is only by means of such exercises that the occult student can gain the inner calmness of soul necessary in order that,at the birth of the higher ego,the soul may not find itself as a kind of double,leading a second and unhealthy life alongside of the higher self. It is especially in these matters that we should not yield to self-deception. Some people may be of the opinion that they already possess in everyday life a certain degree of equanimity,and that they therefore stand in no need of such exercises; yet it is especially those who doubly need them. For it is quite possible to remain equable when surveying the things of this life,and then when ascending into the higher world to show evidences of a want of equanimity all the greater because it had only been held in check. For it should be emphatically understood that in the matter of occult training it is not so much a question of what we may already seem to possess,but of carefully and regularly practicing what we need. Contradictory as this phrase may appear,it is nevertheless true that though life may have trained us to this or to that,the qualities to serve us in occult training are those that we have acquired for ourselves. Should life have rendered us excitable,we must train ourselves to conquering this trait; yet if life has engendered in us equanimity,we should so rouse ourselves by our own efforts that the soul may be capable of responding to the impressions it receives. The man who cannot laugh at anything,has just as little control over his laughter as one who is perpetually giving way to uncontrolled laughter.

Thought and feeling may be cultivated by yet another means,namely,by the acquirement of the characteristic known as positiveness. There is a beautiful legend in which it is related of Christ Jesus,that He,with others,passed the dead body of a dog. The others turned aside from the hideous sight,but Christ Jesus spoke admiringly of the creature's beautiful teeth. One can,through practice,attain to the condition of mind in regard to the world,which is indicated in this legend. Error, vice,and ugliness should not deter the soul from seeing truth,goodness, and beauty,wherever they are to be found. Nor is this positiveness to be mistaken for want of judgment,or for deliberately closing the eyes to what is bad,false,and inferior. He who can admire the beautiful teeth of a decaying animal can also see that decaying corpse--yet the corpse does not hinder his observing the beauty of the teeth. Thus,though what is bad cannot be deemed good,nor error acclaimed as truth,we can yet train ourselves so that what is bad need not prevent us from recognizing what is
good,nor need errors render us insensible to that which is true.

Thought,combined with will,attains to a certain maturity if we strive never to allow what we have already experienced or learned to rob us of our unbiased receptiveness for new experiences. Such a thought as: "I have
never heard that before; I don't believe it!" should lose all significance where the occult student is concerned; indeed,he should endeavour,for a fixed period of time,to allow every thing and every creature to convey something new to his mind. Every breath of air,every leaf on the tree, the prattling of a child,--each and all will teach him something,provided he be willing to bring a different point of view to bear upon it from the one he has hitherto held.

It may,of course,be possible to go too far in this particular,and we must not at any time lose sight of the experiences we have previously had. Indeed,what we experience in the present should be judged in accordance with the sum of our past experiences. These must be laid on one side of the scale,while on the other the occult student should place an inclination for ever gathering new knowledge. Above all,a belief in the possibility that new experiences may contradict the old.

Thus we have enumerated those five qualities of the soul which the occult student in regular training,should acquire; control of the trend of his thoughts; control of the impulses of his will; equanimity in sorrow and joy; positiveness in his judgment of the world; and impartiality in his view of life. After giving consecutive periods of time to the acquiring of these qualities through continued practice,the student must go still further,and bring all these qualities into a harmonious whole within the soul,to achieve which,he will have to practice the exercises in twos and twos together,or three and one,simultaneously,so as to bring about the harmony desired.

The exercises indicated above are thus given out by occult teaching because if faithfully carried out,they not only produce in the occult student what we have called above direct results,but they lead indirectly to much else that is needed on the path to the higher worlds. He who practices these exercises sufficiently will,while doing so,become aware of many a lack and many a failing in his own soul-life,and he will at the same time find in them the very means necessary to give strength and security to the intellect,to the emotional tendencies and to the character as well. He will assuredly need many additional exercises, according to his capacities,temperament,and character; these,however, will present themselves if the above be frequently carried out. Indeed, one will notice that the already indicated exercises,indirectly, gradually yield that which at first does not seem to be in them. A person endowed with but little self-confidence,for instance,finds in the course of time,that by persistent practice the needed confidence in himself has come about. And it is the same with many other soul qualities.(28)

It is a matter of significance that the occult student is capable of raising these capabilities to ever higher degrees; and he must succeed in so controlling his thoughts and feelings that the soul will have power to maintain complete inner quietude for certain periods of time--periods during which he can keep out of his mind and heart all those things that in any way concern the outer everyday life,its joys and sorrows,its pleasures and cares,even its tasks and demands. At such a time nothing should be allowed entrance into the soul except what the soul itself admits. An abjection may easily be made to this. One might imagine that alienation must result if the student withdraws in heart and spirit from life and its duties for a certain part of the day. Yet in reality,this is by no means the case. For those who,in the above manner,give themselves up to periods of inner quietude and peace will find that out of these there grows such a fund of energy for fulfilling the outer duties of life that they are not only not less efficiently performed,but assuredly more so.

It is of great benefit at such times to detach oneself entirely from thoughts of personal affairs,and to be able to raise oneself to that which affects not oneself alone,but all mankind. If he is then able to fill his soul with messages from a higher spiritual world,and if they have the power of enthralling his soul to as intense a degree as any personal concern or care,then indeed will his soul have gathered fruit of especial value.

Those who thus exert themselves to regulate their soul-life will arrive at the possibility of a degree of self-observation that will permit them to review their personal affairs with the same tranquillity as those of others. Seeing one's own experiences and one's own joys and sorrows in the
light in which those of another appear,is a good preparation for occult

training. We bring this exercise gradually to the necessary stage,if, after the day's work is over,we allow the pictures of the day's occurrences to pass before the mind's eye. We would then see ourselves within our own experiences as in a picture; in other words,we would look at ourselves in our daily life,as an outside observer.

A certain practice in self-observation having been gained by concentrating the attention upon short divisions of the day's experience,the student will become more and more expert in this kind of retrospect,continued practice enabling him to review the events of the whole day completely and
quickly. It will become ever more and more the ideal of the occult student to assume such an attitude with regard to the events of life which confront him that he will be able to await their approach with absolute calm and inner confidence,no longer judging them by the state of his own soul but according to their own inner meaning and inner worth. And it is by looking to this ideal that he will create a condition of soul that will enable him to meditate profoundly,as described above,upon symbolical and other thoughts and feelings.

The conditions here described must be fulfilled,because supersensible experience is built upon the foundation on which the student stands in his ordinary soul-life,before he enters the supersensible world. In a two-fold way,all supersensible experience is dependent upon the soul's point of departure before entering that world. One who is not intent,from the outset,on making sound powers of judgment the foundation of his spiritual training will develop supersensible capacities which perceive the spiritual world inaccurately and incorrectly. To a certain extent his spiritual organs of perception will develop in the wrong way. And just as a man with a defective or diseased eye cannot see correctly in the sense-world,so it is not possible to have true perceptions with spiritual organs which are not built upon the foundation of sound powers of judgment. One who starts from an immoral state of soul rises into the spiritual worlds with his spiritual vision stupified and clouded. In regard to supersensible worlds he is like a person in the sense-world who makes observations in a state of lethargy. The latter,however,will not be able to make any statements of consequence,whereas the spiritual observer,even in his stupefaction,is more awake than a person in the ordinary state of consciousness,and the results of his observations will therefore be erroneous in regard to the spiritual world.

The highest possibilities of imaginative cognition can be realized by supporting the aforesaid meditations by that which one might call "sense-free" thinking. Now when we formulate an idea based upon observations made in the physical sense-world,our thought is not free from sense-impressions. Yet it is not as though man could formulate only such ideas: human thought need not become void and meaningless simply because it is not filled with observations derived through the channels of the senses. The most direct and the safest way for the occult student to acquire this "sense-free" thinking,is to make the facts of the higher worlds presented by occult science,the subject of his thoughts. These facts cannot be observed by means of the physical senses; nevertheless, the student will find that he will be able to grasp them--if only he has enough patience and perseverance. No one can explore higher worlds,or make his own observations therein,without having been trained. But it is quite possible without training to understand everything which investigators communicate about those regions. Should anyone ask,"How can
I accept on trust what the occultist tells me,being myself as yet unable to see it?"--such an objection would be groundless,for it is perfectly possible to arrive through mere reflective thinking at the sure conviction that the matters thus communicated are true.

If a man is unable,through reflecting,to arrive at such a conviction, the reason is not that he cannot possibly "believe" something he cannot see,but simply because he has not as yet applied his powers of reflective thinking in a sufficiently unbiased,comprehensive and profound manner.

In order to be clear on this point,it must be borne in mind that human thought,if it arouses itself to energetic activity,can understand more than it usually imagines possible. For in thought there is an inner essence which is in connection with the supersensible world. The soul is not usually conscious of this connection,because it is wont to train its faculty of thought only through the world of sense. On this account it thinks incomprehensible what is imparted to it from the supersensible world. What is thus communicated is,however,not only intelligible to thought which has been spiritually trained,but to any thinking which is fully conscious of its power and is willing to make use of it.

By the persevering assimilation of what occult teachers are able to impart to us we habituate ourselves to a line of thought that is not derived from sense-observation,and we learn to recognize how,within the soul,one thought is allied to another,and how one thought calls forth another, even when the connection of ideas is not occasioned by any power of sense-observation. The essential point is that by this method we become aware of the fact that the world of thought possesses an inner life,and that while we are engaged in thought we are,indeed,in the realm of a supersensible living power. Thus we may say to ourselves: "There is something within me that develops an organism of thought; nevertheless,I am one with this something." And thus in yielding to this sense-free thinking,we experience something like a being,which flows into our inner life,just as the qualities of the things of the senses flow into us through our physical organs when used for sense-observation.

"Out there in space," says the observer of the sense-world,"is a rose: it is not unfamiliar to me,for both scent and colour proclaim its presence." And in like manner,when sense-free thought is working within us,we need only be sufficiently unbiased in order to be able to say: "Something real proclaims its presence to me,linking thought to thought and constituting a thought-organism"--only there is a difference to be noted between the communication coming to the observer from the outer world of the senses,
and that which actually reaches the sense-free thinker. The former feels that he is standing without--in front of the rose--whereas he who has given
himself up to thinking which is untrammelled by the senses will feel _within himself_ whatever thus proclaims its presence to him; he will feel himself one with it.

Those who,more or less,unconsciously consider as beings only that which they can perceive as external objects,will,it is true,be unable to entertain the feeling that whatever has the nature of a being,can also manifest itself within man by his becoming one with it. In order to judge correctly one must be able to have the following inner experiences: one must learn to distinguish between the thought combinations created through
one's own volition,and those experienced without any voluntary exercise of the will. In the latter case,we may then say: I remain quite still within myself; I produce no trains of thought; I yield to that which "thinks within me." Then we are fully justified in saying: Within me a being is acting,just as we are justified in saying that the rose acts upon us when we see a certain red,when we perceive a certain odor.

Nor is there any contradiction in having derived the contents of our ideas from communications made by the occult seer. The ideas are,it is true already there when we devote ourselves to them; yet they cannot be

"thought",without in each case being created anew within the soul. The important point is that the occult teacher seeks to awaken in his hearers and readers the kind of thoughts which they must first call forth from within themselves,whereas he who describes some physical object indicates
something that the listener or reader may observe within the sense-world.

(The path which leads to sense-free thinking by means of the communications made by occult science is thoroughly safe. But there is also another method even safer and above all things more exact,yet for this very reason more difficult for the majority. This method is set forth in my two books,"_Goethe's Conception of the World_" and "_The Philosophy of Spiritual Activity_." These writings set forth what human thought can achieve for itself,if the thinking is not under the influence of the physical sense impressions but relies merely upon itself. Then pure thinking works within man like a living being. At the same time nothing in the above-mentioned writings is derived from communications due to occult
science itself,and yet it is shown that pure,self-reliant thinking can obtain information about the world,life and man.

These writings therefore occupy a very important intermediate position between the actual cognition of the sense-world and that of the spiritual world. They present that which thinking can gain when it raises itself above sense-observation and yet does not enter into occult research. Anyone who allows these books to work upon his whole soul,already stands
within the spiritual world,but it appears to him as a world of thought. Those who are in a position to allow this intermediate condition to act upon them,will be following a safe and sane path and can thus win for themselves a feeling concerning the higher worlds,which will for all future time ensure for them most abundant results.)

The object of meditating upon the above described symbolical concepts and
feelings is,strictly speaking,the development of the higher organs of cognition within man's astral body. They are in the first place created from the substance of the astral body. These new organs of observation establish a connection with a new world wherein man learns to know himself
as a new ego.

These new organs of perception are first of all to be distinguished from those of the physical sense-world by being _active_ organs. Whereas the eye and ear are passive,allowing light and sound to work upon them,it may be said of these perceptive organs of the soul and spirit that,while functioning they are in a perpetual state of activity,and that they seize hold of their objects and facts,as it were,in full consciousness. This gives rise to the feeling that psycho-spiritual cognition is a union with,--a "dwelling within,"--the corresponding facts.

These separately evolving psycho-spiritual organs may be compared to "lotus flowers" corresponding to the appearance which they present to the
clairvoyant consciousness,as they are formed from the substance of the astral body.(29)

Very definite kinds of meditation act upon the astral body in such manner that certain psycho-spiritual organs,the so-called "lotus flowers," are developed. Any proper meditation undertaken with the view of attaining to imaginative cognition has its effect upon one or another of these organs.(30)

A regular course of training arranges and orders the separate exercises to be practised by the occult student,so that these organs may either simultaneously or consecutively attain their suitable development,and on this process the student will have to bring much patience and perseverance to bear. Those,indeed,who are possessed of no more than the average amount of patience with which man,under ordinary conditions of life is endowed,will not reach very far. For it takes a long--often a very long time indeed--before these organs have reached a point at which the occult student is able to use them for observing things in the higher worlds. At this point comes what is known as "illumination," in contradistinction to the "preparation," or "purification," which consists in the practices undertaken for the formation of these organs. (The term "purification" is used because in order to reach certain phases of inner life,the pupil cleanses himself through the corresponding exercises,of that which belongs to the world of sense observation.)

It is,however,quite possible that before actual illumination,the student may get repeated "flashes of light" from a higher world. These he should receive gratefully. Even these can make him a witness of the spiritual realms. Yet he must not falter should this never be vouchsafed him during his entire period of preparation,and should its consequent duration seem all too long to him. Indeed,those who yield to impatience "because they can as yet see nothing," have not yet acquired the right attitude toward the higher worlds. Those alone will be in a position to grasp this who can view the exercises they undertake as an object in themselves. For this practice is in truth a working on something psycho-spiritual,namely,on their own astral body; even though they do not "see," they can "feel" that they are working on the psycho-spiritual plane. Only when we have a preconceived idea of what we "wish to see," are we unable to experience this feeling. In that case we may consider as nothing what is,in reality,of immeasurable importance. But one should observe minutely everything which one experiences while practicing,--experiences which are so fundamentally different from those of the sense-world. We shall then become aware that we cannot work upon our astral body as though it were some indifferent substance; but that in it there lives a totally different world of which the life of our senses does not inform us.

Higher entities act upon the astral body in the same way in which the world of the physical senses acts upon the physical body,and we "come upon" that higher life in our own astral body,provided only we do not shut ourselves out from it. If we are perpetually saying: "I am aware of nothing," then it is generally the case that we imagined that these experiences should appear thus and so; and because we do not see what we imagined we should see,we say,"I can see nothing."

However,he who is able to acquire the right attitude of mind with regard to his practice during training,will find more and more that he has something which he loves for its own sake and which,as an immeasurably important vital function,he can no longer do without. He will then know that through these very practices he is standing in the psycho-spiritual world and will await with patience and resignation what may further transpire. This attitude of mind of the student may best be expressed in such words as these: "I _will_ do all the exercises which have been assigned to me; for I know that in the fullness of time as much will come to me as I should receive; I do not ask for it impatiently,but I prepare myself to receive it." On the other hand one should not raise the objection: The occult student,then,is expected perhaps for a long time to feel around in the dark,because he cannot know that he is on the right path with his exercises,before he obtains results. It is not true, however,that he must wait until the results prove to him the correctness of the exercises. If the attitude of the student is right,then the satisfaction which he experiences in the practice of these exercises,in itself carries the conviction that he is doing the right thing,and he does not need to wait for results to prove it. The correct practice of exercises in occult training brings with it a satisfaction that is not merely satisfaction,but conviction--the conviction that I am doing something which shows me that it is leading me forward in the right direction. Every occult student may have this conviction at any moment if he pays careful attention to his experiences. Should he not exercise such attention,he will simply pass by these experiences just as a wayfarer in profound thought does not notice the trees alongside of the road,though he would surely see them if he would but direct his attention to them.

It is by no means desirable that results,other than those which are always due to such practice,should in any way be hastened. For such results might easily be only an infinitesimal part of what should really take place. Indeed,in the matter of occult development,partial results are,more often than not,the cause of considerable delay in complete development. Contact with such forms of spiritual life corresponding to partial development,tends to dull the perceptive faculties to the influences of those powers which would lead on to higher stages of development; while the benefit derived from such a "glimpse" of the spiritual world,is after all only a seeming one,because this glimpse cannot divulge the truth,but only deceptive illusions.

The psycho-spiritual organs,the "lotus flowers," shape themselves in such a manner that to clairvoyant consciousness they appear in the vicinity of particular physical organs of the body of the person undergoing training. From among these psycho-spiritual organs the following should be enumerated: that which is to be perceived between the eye-brows is the so-called two-petalled lotus flower; that in the region of the larynx is the sixteen-petalled lotus; in the region of the heart is to be found the twelve-petalled lotus flower and the fourth is near the navel. Others appear in close conjunction with other parts of the physical body.(31)

The lotus flowers are formed in the astral body,and by the time one or the other has developed,we become conscious of them. We then feel that we
can make use of them,and that by doing so we really enter a higher world. The impressions received of that world still resemble in many respects those of the physical senses; and one with imaginative cognition will be able to designate the new higher world as impressions of heat or cold, perceptions of sound or words,effects of light or color--because it is in this way that he perceives them. He is,however,conscious of the fact that these perceptions express something different in the imaginative world from what they do in the actual sense-world; and he recognizes that behind them lie causes which are not physical,but psycho-spiritual ones.

Should he receive an impression of heat he will not,for instance, attribute this to a piece of hot iron,but will regard it as the emanation of some soul-process,which he has hitherto experienced only with his soul's inner life. He knows that behind imaginative experiences exist psycho-spiritual things and processes just as behind physical perceptions we have physical entities and material facts.

And yet this similarity,apparent between the world of imagination and the physical world,is modified by one important difference. There is something present in the physical world which,when met in the imaginative world,bears quite another appearance. In the former we are aware of a perpetual ebb and flow,an alternation between birth and death. But in the imaginative world there appears,in place of this phenomenon,a continual metamorphosis of the one into the other. In the physical world we see,for instance,how a plant fades away,but in the imaginative world there emerges,in proportion as the plant fades,another form,not physically discernible,into which the withering plant is gradually transformed. When once the plant has faded away completely,this form will have become fully developed in its place. Birth and death are conceptions which lose their value in the imaginative world,making way for a comprehension of the transmutation of the one into the other.

This being the case,those truths concerning which we have already made certain communications in an earlier chapter of this book (see Chapter II, "The Nature of Man") become accessible to the imaginative perception. Physical sense-perception is able to perceive only what takes place in the physical body,processes which are enacted within the "domain of birth and death." The other principles of man's being,namely,the etheric or vital body,the sentient body,and the ego,are subject to the law of transmutation,and the perception of them is unlocked by imaginative cognition. Any one who has advanced this far will observe that that which lives on under other conditions of being after death,detaches itself from the physical body.

But development does not come to a standstill within the imaginative world. Anyone who would like to remain stationary in it,would,it is true,be able to note the entities in process of transmutation,but he would be unable to interpret the meaning of these processes of change. He
would not be in a position to find his way about in this newly attained world. For the imaginative world is a realm of unrest--there is naught in it but movement and change; nowhere are there stationary points. Such points of rest are reached only by the person who,having transcended the stage of imaginative knowledge,has attained to that grade of development known to occult science as "understanding through inspiration."

It is not necessary for one seeking knowledge of the supersensible world to develop his capacities so that the imaginative cognition should have been acquired in full measure,before moving on to the stage of "inspiration." His exercises may,indeed,be so regulated that two processes may go on simultaneously,one leading to imagination and the other to inspiration. The student will then in due time enter a higher world,in which he not only perceives,but where he can also find his way about,as it were,and which he becomes able to interpret. Progress,as a rule,consists in the occult student perceiving some apparitions of the imaginative world and becoming conscious,after a while,that he is beginning to get his bearings.

Yet the world of inspiration is something quite new compared with the purely imaginative realm. By means of the latter we learn to know the transformation of one process into another; while through the former we come to recognize the inner qualities of ever changing beings. Imagination shows us the soul-expression of such beings; through inspiration we penetrate into their spiritual core. Above all,we become aware of a multiplicity of spiritual beings and of their relation to one another. In the physical sense-world we have also,of course,to do with a multiplicity of different beings,yet in the world of inspiration this multiplicity is of a different character. In that world each being sustains quite definite relations to all the other beings,not,however, as in the physical world through outer influence upon them,but through their essential inner nature.

When we become aware of a being in the world of inspiration,no external impression made upon another is apparent,such as might be compared with the influence of one physical being upon another; a relation nevertheless exists which is purely the result of the inner constitution of the two beings. This relationship may be compared with that in which the separate sounds or letters of a word stand to one another in the physical world. If we take the word "man," the impression made is due to a consonance of the letters,m-a-n. There is no impact nor other outer influence passing from the "m" to the "a," but both letters sound together within "a whole," owing to their very nature. This is why observations made in the world of inspirations can only be compared to reading and the observer sees the beings of this world like written characters which he must learn and whose inner relations must reveal themselves to him like a supersensible writing. Therefore occult science can call cognition through inspiration, figuratively,the "reading of the secret script." How one may read by this "secret script" and how one can communicate what has thus been read will now be made clear by reference to previous chapters in this book. Man's being was first described as composed of different principles. It was then further shown how the cosmos in which man is developing,passes through various conditions; those of Saturn,Sun,Moon,and Earth. The perception by means of which we are able on the one hand to discern the principles of the human being,and,on the other,the successive states of the Earth and its previous transformations,is revealed to the imaginative cognition. But it is now further necessary that the relations existing between the Saturn state and man's physical body; between the Sun state and the etheric body,etc.,be understood. It must be shown that even during the Saturn state the germ of man's physical body came into existence,and that it has then further developed to its present form during the Sun,Moon, and Earth periods.

It had to be shown for example,what changes took place in the human being owing to the separation of the sun from the earth,and also that something similar again took place in connection with the moon. We had,moreover,to make plain what contributed to the bringing about of such changes in mankind as those which took place in the Atlantean era,how they were manifested in the successive Indian,ancient Persian,Egyptian,and other periods. The description of this sequence of events is not the result of imaginative perception,but of inspirational cognition derived from the reading of the secret script. For such reading,the imaginative perceptions are like letters,or sounds,although such reading is not alone necessary for interpretations like the above. It would be impossible to comprehend the whole life-process of man by means of imaginative cognition alone. One might possibly be in a position to note how,in the process of dying,the psycho-spiritual principles detach themselves from what remains in the physical world,but it would be impossible to understand the connection between what happens to man after death and the preceding and following stages,were we unable to find our way through the facts obtained by imaginative cognition. Without inspirational knowledge the entire imaginative world would remain mere writing,at which we gaze but which we are unable to read.

As the student proceeds from imagination to inspiration he will soon see how wrong it would be to neglect this understanding of the facts of the universe and limit himself only to those facts which,so to speak,touch his close personal interests. Indeed,those who are not initiated into these matters may be inclined to say: "The only thing that seems of any importance to me is that I should ascertain the fate of the human soul after death. If anyone can give me information upon that subject,it will suffice; but of what use is it for occult science to present to me such remote subjects as the Saturn and Sun states,or the separation of the moon and the sun,etc.?"

Those,however,who have been properly instructed in these things will recognize that a true understanding of what they desire to learn could not be obtained without knowledge of these matters,which appear so unnecessary to them. A delineation of man's states after death would remain utterly incomprehensible and valueless to one who is unable to connect it with ideas derived from those very far-off events. Even the most elementary observations of a clairvoyant necessitate his acquaintance with such things.

When,for example,a plant passes from the blossom to a state of fruition, the clairvoyant observes a change in the astral being,which,while the plant is in blossom,has covered and surrounded the blossoming plant from above like a cloud. Had fructification not taken place,this astral being would have been changed into quite a different form from the one it now assumes in consequence of this fertilization. Now we understand the entire process thus clairvoyantly observed,if we have learned to comprehend our own nature through a knowledge of that great cosmic process,in which the earth and all its inhabitants were involved at the time of the separation from the sun. Before fertilization,the plant is in the same condition as was the whole earth before the sun separated from it. After the fertilization of the blossom,however,the condition of the plant is that of the earth after the separation of the Sun had taken place,while the moon-forces were still active in it.

Those who have thoroughly assimilated the idea to be gained by a comprehension of this separation of the sun,will now be able to interpret correctly the significance of the process of plant fertilization,when it is said that "the plant previous to fructification is in a 'sun state,' and afterward in the 'moon state.' " Indeed,it may be said of even the smallest occurrence in the world that it can be fully understood only when the reflection of great cosmic events is recognized in it. Otherwise its inner nature remains just as unintelligible as Raphael's Sistine Madonna would be for one who could see only a small blue speck,while the rest of it remained covered.

Everything that happens to man is a reflection of all those great cosmic events that have to do with his existence. Those who wish to understand the observations made by clairvoyant consciousness of the phenomena taking place between birth and death,and again between death and a new birth, will be able to do so if they first acquire the faculty of interpreting imaginative observations by means of conceptions gained by reflecting upon great cosmic events. These contemplations,indeed,furnish the key to a comprehension of human life. Therefore the study of Saturn,Sun,and Moon are,from the standpoint of occult science,at the same time a study of man.

Through inspiration one arrives at a knowledge of the relationships between the beings of the higher world,and a further stage of cognition makes it then possible to recognize the inner essential nature of these beings themselves. This stage of cognition is known to occult science as that of intuitive cognition.(32)

Cognition of a sense-being implies standing outside of it,and judging it according to outer impressions. Intuitive cognition of a spiritual being implies being at one with it; uniting oneself with the inner nature of that being. Step by step,the occult student ascends toward such cognition. Imagination leads him no longer to consider phenomena as the external qualities of beings,but to recognize them as psycho-spiritual emanations; inspiration leads him further into the inner nature of these beings. Here we can again illustrate by means of the foregoing chapters what is the meaning of intuition. In those earlier chapters it has not only been stated how the progress of the Saturn,Sun and Moon evolutions proceeded; but also that beings took part,in widely different ways,in that progress,and mention was made of the Thrones or Spirits of Will,the Spirits of Wisdom,the Spirits of Motion,and so on. In connection with the earth's development,reference was made to the Luciferian spirits and spirits of Ahriman. The structure of the world was traced back to those beings who took part in it. All knowledge pertaining to these beings is derived from intuitive cognition,which is also necessary,if we wish to understand man's life.

That which is released from the human physical body at death passes on through various states in the future. The more immediate conditions after death might,to some extent,be described by referring to imaginative cognition,but that which takes place when man has proceeded farther into that time lying between death and a new birth would be entirely incomprehensible to the imagination,did not inspiration come to its aid. For inspiration alone can disclose what can be revealed about man's life after its purification in the "land of spirits." We come to a point where inspiration is no longer adequate--where it reaches the limit of its possibilities. For there is a period in human development,between death and a new birth,in which the human being is accessible only to intuition.

Yet this part of the human being is _always_ within man,and if we wish to understand it in its true inner nature we must also seek it,between birth and death,by means of intuition. Anyone attempting to fathom man by means
of imagination and inspiration alone would miss the very innermost being, that which continues from incarnation to incarnation. It is therefore by intuitive cognition alone that adequate research concerning reincarnation and Karma becomes possible,and all genuine knowledge of these processes
is derived from research undertaken by means of intuition. If a man wishes to know his own inner self,he can only do so by intuition; by its aid he becomes aware of what it is that moves onward within him from incarnation
to incarnation; and should it fall to anyone's lot to know something about his earlier incarnations,this can only take place through intuitive cognition.

Cognition through inspiration and intuition is attainable only by means of psycho-spiritual exercises,and they resemble those meditations practiced for the attainment of imagination which have already been described. While,however,in exercises for the development of the imagination,a connection is set up with impressions belonging to the world of the physical senses,such connections gradually cease in the case of exercises for inspiration. In order to understand more clearly what must be done, let us recall once more the symbol of the "rosy cross." When we meditate
on this we have before us a picture,of which the component parts have been taken from the world of the senses; there is the black colour of the cross,the roses,etc.,and yet the combination of those various parts into the "rosy cross" is not derived from the world of the senses. If the student now endeavours to banish from his consciousness both the black cross and the red roses,as pictures of sense-realities,only retaining in his soul that spiritual activity which has been used in putting these

parts togetherhe will then have a means for a meditation that will gradually lead him on to inspiration. He should put the question to himself somewhat in the following manner: "What have I done inwardly to construct that symbol from cross and rose? What I did (an act of my own
soul),I will retain within my hold; but the picture itself I will allow to fade away out of my consciousness. I shall then be able to feel within me all that my soul did in order to produce the picture,though I no longer recall the picture itself. I will now live wholly within my own activity that created the picture. I will not meditate upon a picture,but upon the powers of my own soul which are capable of creating pictures."

Such meditations must now be practised with various other symbols. This leads then to cognition through Inspiration. Here is another example,that of meditating upon the growth and subsequent withering of a plant. Let the
picture of a slowly growing plant arise in the soul,as it sprouts from the seed,unfolds leaf after leaf,then blossoms and fruits; then again as it begins to wither on to its complete dissolution. By the help of meditations on such a symbol as this,the student gradually attains a feeling concerning growth and decay of which the plant is but a symbol. If the exercises be persevered in continuously,the image of the transformation which underlies physical growth and decay can be evolved from this feeling.

But if one wishes to attain the corresponding stage of inspiration,this exercise must be practised quite differently. Here one's own activity of soul must be called to mind,--that which had obtained the conception of growth and decay from the image of the plant. The plant must now be allowed to vanish altogether from the consciousness,and the attention be concentrated entirely upon the student's own inner activity. It is only such exercises as these that help us to rise to inspiration. At first the occult student will find it difficult to fully grasp how to set about such an exercise. This is because man is used to permitting his inner life to be governed by outward impressions,and thus falls immediately into uncertainty and wavering when now he must unfold in addition a soul life which has freed itself from all connections with outward impressions.

Here the student must clearly understand that he should only undertake these exercises if along with them he cultivates everything that may lead to firmness and stability in his judgment,emotional life,and character; these precautions are even more necessary than when seeking to acquire the
faculty of imagination. Should he take these precautions,he will be doubly successful,for,in the first place,he will not risk losing the balance of his personality through the exercises; and secondly,he will acquire the capacity of being really able to carry out what is demanded in these exercises. They will be deemed difficult only as long as one has not yet attained a particular attitude of soul,and certain feelings and sentiments. He who patiently and perseveringly cultivates within his soul such qualities as are favourable to the growth of supersensible cognition, will not be long in acquiring both the understanding and the faculty for these practices.

Any one who can acquire the habit of frequently entering into the quiet of his own soul,and who,instead of brooding over himself,transforms and orders those experiences he has had in life,will gain much. For he will perceive that his thoughts and feelings become richer,if through memory he establishes a relationship between the different experiences of life. He will become aware that he gains stores of new knowledge not only through new impressions and new experiences,but also by letting the old ones be active within him.

He who allows his experiences and his opinions free play,keeping himself with his sympathies and antipathies,personal interests and feelings entirely in the background,will prepare an especially fertile soil for supersensible cognition. He will in very truth be developing what may be called a rich inner life. But what is of primary importance is the balance and equilibrium of the qualities of the soul. People are very apt to become one-sided when indulging in certain activities of the soul. Thus, when a person has come to know the advantages of contemplation,and of dwelling upon pictures derived from his own thought-world,he is apt to develop a tendency to withdraw himself from the impressions of the outer world. Yet such a step only leads to parching and withering the inner life; and he will go farthest who manages to retain an unchecked receptivity for all impressions of the outer world,while possessing the power to withdraw within his own inner self. It is by no means necessary to think only of the so-called important events of life: every one,in every sphere of life,be his four walls ever so humble,will be possessed of experience enough,provided only his mind is truly receptive. Experiences need not be sought--they abound on every hand.

Of particular importance is the way in which experience may be utilized by the human soul. For instance,one may make the discovery that someone whom
he or another greatly reveres,has some quality that must be regarded as a
flaw in his character. An experience of this kind may lead the person to whom it comes to thoughts which will tend toward one of two different directions. He may simply feel that he can never again regard the person in question with the same degree of veneration; or on the other hand,he may say to himself: "How has it been possible for this revered person to be burdened with such a failing? How can I present the matter to my mind so as to see in this failing not merely a fault,but something that is the outcome of his life,possibly even caused by his noble qualities?" Whoever can place the question thus before his own mind may,perhaps,arrive at the conclusion that his veneration for his friend need not suffer the least diminution,in spite of the failing that has come to light.

Experiences of this nature will,each time they are met with,add something to our understanding of life. Yet it would certainly be a bad thing for one to allow himself to be tempted through this generous view of life,to excuse everything in those whom he happens to like,or to drop into the habit of ignoring every blamable action,in order thereby to seek some benefit to his own inner development. Blaming or excusing the mistakes of others merely as a result of an inner impulse,does not further our development. This can only happen if our action is governed by the particular case itself,regardless of what we may thereby gain or lose. It is absolutely true that we cannot learn by condemning a fault, but only by understanding it; but,at the same time,if,owing to understanding it,we exclude all disapproval of it,we likewise would not progress very far.

Here,again,the important thing is to avoid one-sidedness,either in one direction or the other,and to establish harmony and balance of all qualities in the soul; and this is especially to be kept in mind in regard to one quality which is pre-eminently important to man's development: the feeling of devotion. Those who can cultivate this feeling,or on whom nature herself has bestowed so inestimable a gift,have a good foundation for the powers of supersensible cognition. Those who in childhood and youth have been able to look up to certain persons with feelings of devoted admiration,beholding in them some high ideal,will already possess in the depths of their souls the soil in which supersensible cognition may flourish abundantly. And those who,possessed of the maturer
judgment of later life,can direct their gaze upon the starry heavens and surrender themselves unreservedly to admiration of the revelations of the Higher Powers,are in a like manner ripening their senses for the

acquisition of knowledge with regard to the supersensible worlds. So is it also with those who can admire the powers ruling over human life itself. It is by no means of small importance for a fully matured man to be able to feel veneration to the highest degree for other people whose worth he senses or recognizes. For it is only where veneration such as this is present that a vista of the higher worlds can be revealed. Those who possess no sense of reverence will never go very far in their attainment of cognition; for from those who decline to appreciate anything in this world,the essence of all things will assuredly be withheld.

Nevertheless,any one who permits his feelings of reverence and devotion to kill his healthy self-consciousness and self-confidence,is guilty of sinning against the laws of balance and equilibrium. The occult student must work constantly in order to mature his own nature; then indeed he may
well have confidence in his own personality,and believe that its powers are increasing more and more. Any one arriving at the right feeling in this respect will say to himself: "There are within me hidden powers,and I am able to call them forth from within. If,therefore,I see something which fills me with reverence because it is above me,I need no longer merely venerate it,but I may confidently assume that,if I develop all that is in me,I may raise myself to the level of the object of my veneration."

The more capable a man is of fixing his attention upon these events of life with which he is not directly familiar,the greater will be the possibility of providing himself with a foundation for development in higher worlds. The following example will make this evident. Let us assume that some one is placed in a position in which it rests with him either to do,or leave undone,a certain thing. His judgment bids him "Do this," while at the same time there may be a certain indefinite something in his feelings which deters him from the deed. It may so happen that the person in question will pay no heed to this inexplicable something,carrying out the action in accordance with his judgment. But it may also be that the person so placed will yield to this inner impulse and not perform the act. Now,pursuing the matter further,he may find that mischief would have resulted from his following the dictates of his reason,and that a blessing awaited him through the omission of the act. An experience of this nature may lead a man's thoughts into quite a definite channel,and then he will put the matter to himself in this way: "There is something within me that is a surer guide than that measure of judgment of which I am at present possessed. I must therefore retain an open mind toward this
inner something,to the height of which my own capacity for judgment has not yet attained."

The soul derives much benefit when it directs its attention to occurrences in life such as these,for they demonstrate that man's healthy premonitions bear something in them which is of greater moment than he, with his present degree of judgment,is able to perceive. Attention in this direction has the effect of enlarging the life of the soul. Yet here again certain peculiarities may arise which are of themselves dangerous. One who accustoms himself to a perpetual disregarding of his judgment, owing to this or that "premonition," would easily become a shuttle-cock tossed at the mercy of every kind of undefined impulse; indeed,it is not a far cry from such habitual indecision to a state of absolute superstition.

Every superstition is disastrous to the student of occult science. The possibility of gaining admission,by legitimate means,to the realms of the spiritual life must depend upon a careful exclusion of all superstition,phantasy,and dreaming. One who is pleased at having had a certain experience which cannot be grasped by human reason will not approach the spiritual world in the right manner. No partiality for the "inexplicable" will ever make one qualified for discipleship of the Spirit. Indeed the pupil should utterly discard the notion that a true mystic is one who is always ready to surmise the presence of what cannot be explained or explored. The right way is to be prepared to recognize on all hands hidden forces and hidden beings,yet at the same time to assume that what is "unexplored" today will be able to be explored when the requisite ability has been developed.

There is a certain mood of soul which it is important for the pupil to maintain at every stage of his development. He should not let his urge for higher knowledge lead him to keep on aiming to get answers to particular questions. Rather should he continually be asking: How am I to develop the needed faculties within myself? For when by dint of patient inner work some faculty develops in him,he will receive the answer to some of his questions. Genuine pupils of the Spirit will always take pains to cultivate this attitude of soul. They will thereby be encouraged to work upon themselves,that they may become ever more and more mature in spirit, and they will abjure the desire to extort answers to particular questions. They will _wait_ until such time as the answers come.

Here again,however,there is the possibility of a one-sidedness,which may prevent the pupil from going forward in the way he should. For at some moment he may quite rightly feel that _according to the measure of his powers_ he can answer for himself even questions of the highest order. Thus at every turn moderation and balance play an essential part in the life of the soul.

Many more qualities of soul could be cited that may with advantage be fostered and developed,if the pupil is seriously wanting to work through a training for Inspiration; and in connection with every one of them we should find that emphasis is laid on the supreme importance of moderation and balance. These attributes of soul help the pupil to understand the exercises that are given for the attainment of Inspiration,and also make him capable of carrying them out.

The exercises for Intuition demand from the pupil that he let disappear from consciousness not only the pictures to which he gave himself up in contemplation in order to arrive at Imaginative cognition,but also that meditating upon his own activity of soul,which he practiced for the attainment of Inspiration. This means that he is now to have in his soul literally nothing of what he has experienced hitherto,whether outwardly or inwardly. If,after discarding all outward and inward experience, nothing whatever is left in his consciousness _that is to say,if consciousness simply slips away from him and he sinks into unconsciousness_ then that will tell him that he is not yet ripe to undertake the exercises for Intuition and must continue working with those for Imagination and Inspiration. A time will come however when an effect will linger in the consciousness which can just as well be made the object of meditation,as were before those outer and inner impressions. This something is,however,of a very special nature,and in comparison with all previous experiences,it is something absolutely new. When it occurs, we recognize it as something we have never known before. It is a perception,just as an actual sound is a perception,that strikes upon the ear; yet it can enter the consciousness only through intuition,just as the sound can only enter the consciousness by way of the ear. Thus with intuition,the last remnants of the physical and sentient are stripped from man's impressions,while the spiritual world begins to expand before the understanding in a form that has nothing in common with the characteristics of the world of the physical senses.

Imaginative cognition is attained by developing the lotus flowers within the astral body. Through those exercises undertaken for the attainment of inspiration and intuition,particular movements,formations and currents which were previously absent,now appear in the human etheric or vital body. These are the very organs which enable man to "read the secret script," and bring that which lies beyond it within his reach. For to the clairvoyant,the changes which occur in the etheric body of a person attaining to inspiration and intuition appear in the following manner. Near the physical heart a new center is forming in the etheric body,which develops into an etheric organ. From this organ,movements and currents flow toward different parts of the human body,in the most varied manner. The most important of these currents approach the lotus flowers,pass through them and their separate petals,and thence direct their course outward,pouring themselves into outer space in the form of rays. The more developed a person is,the greater will be the circumference around him in which these rays become discernible. This centre near the heart is not, however,formed at the very beginning,under correct training. It is first prepared. A temporary center is first formed in the head: this then moves down to the region of the larynx and is finally transferred into the region of the heart. Under an irregular course of development it would be possible for the organ in question to develop near the heart at the outset. In that case the student,instead of arriving in due course at adequate,tranquil clairvoyance by regular means,would run the risk of turning into a visionary and dreamer.

Subsequent development enables the occult student to render these currents and organized parts of this etheric body independent of his physical body and to use them independently. The lotus flowers then serve him as instruments by which to move his etheric body. Yet,before this can take place,certain currents and radiations must come into action around his entire etheric body,surrounding this,as it were,with a fine network, thus encasing it as though it were a separate entity. When this has taken place,the movements and currents of the etheric body can without hindrance touch the outer psycho-spiritual world and unite with it so that outer psycho-spiritual occurrences and inner ones (those within the human etheric body) blend into one another. When this comes to pass,the moment has arrived when man can consciously experience the world of inspiration. This cognition takes place in a manner different from cognition of the physical sense-world. In this latter,we become aware of the world by means of our senses and form our ideas and concepts from these perceptions. But in the case of cognition through inspiration,this is not so.

What is thus perceived is instantaneous; there is no thinking after the perception has taken place. That which in the case of physical sense-cognition is only afterward gained through the concept,is,in the case of inspiration,simultaneous with the perception. One would therefore become merged with the surrounding psycho-spiritual world,and be unable to differentiate oneself from it had not the fine network above alluded to been previously formed in the etheric body.

When exercises for intuition are practiced,they not only affect the etheric body but extend their influence to the supersensible forces of the physical body. But it must not,of course,be imagined that effects are brought about in the physical body which are discernible to ordinary sense-observation,for these effects the clairvoyant alone is able to judge,and they have nothing to do with external powers of perception.

They come as the result of a ripened consciousness,when this latter is able to have intuitional experiences,even though it has divested itself of all previous inner and outer experiences. The experiences of intuition are,however,subtle,delicate and intimate,in comparison with which the physical body,at its present stage of development,is coarse. For this reason,it offers a positive hindrance to the success of any exercises for attaining intuition. Nevertheless,should these be pursued with energy and perseverance,and with the requisite inner calm,they will ultimately overcome those powerful hindrances of the physical body. The occult student will become aware of this when he notices how,by degrees, particular actions of his physical body which hitherto had taken place without his own volition,now come under his control. He will also become aware that for a brief time he will feel the need,for instance,of so regulating his breathing (or some similar act) as to bring it into a kind of harmonious accord with whatever is being enacted within his soul,be it exercises or other forms of inner concentration.

The ideal development would be that no exercises should be done by means
of the physical body but that everything which has to take place within it should result only as a consequence of exercises for intuition. As, however,the physical body offers such powerful impediments,the training may permit of some alleviations. These consist in exercises which affect the physical body; yet everything in this domain that has not been directly imparted by the teacher,or those having knowledge and experience of these things,is fraught with danger. Such exercises,for instance, include a certain regulated process of breathing to be carried out for a very short space of time. These regulations of the breathing correspond in quite a definite way to particular laws of the psycho-spiritual world. Breathing is a physical process,and when this act is so carried out as to be the expression of a psycho-spiritual law,physical existence receives the direct stamp,as it were,of spirituality,and the physical matter is transformed.

For this reason occult science is able to call the change due to such direct spiritual influence,a transmutation of the physical body,and this process represents what is called "working with the philosopher's stone" by him who has a knowledge of these matters. He who knows these things,
frees himself indeed from those concepts which have been limited by superstition,humbug and charlatanry. The significance of the phenomena does not become less to him who knows,just because,as a spiritual investigator,all superstition is foreign to him. When he has acquired a concept of a significant fact,he may be allowed to call it by its _correct name_ although that name has been fixed upon it as a result of misunderstanding,error and nonsense.

Every true intuition is in fact a "working with the philosopher's stone," because each genuine intuition calls directly upon those powers which act from out the supersensible world,into the world of the senses.

As the occult student climbs the path leading to cognition of the higher worlds,he becomes aware at a particular point that the cohesion of the powers of his own personality is assuming a different form from that which
it possesses in the world of the physical senses. In the latter the ego brings about a uniform co-operation of the powers of the soul--primarily of thought,feeling and will. These three soul powers are actually,under normal conditions of human life,in perpetual relation one with another. For instance,we see a particular object in the external world,and it is pleasing or is displeasing to the soul; that is to say,the perception of the thing will be followed by a sense of either pleasure or displeasure.

Possibly we may desire the object,or may have the impulse to alter it in some way or other; that is to say,desire and will associate themselves with perception and feeling. Now this association is due to the fact that the ego co-ordinates presentment (thinking),feeling,and willing,and in this way introduces order among the forces of the personality. This healthy arrangement would be interrupted should the ego prove itself powerless in this respect: if,for instance,the will went a different way from the feeling or thinking. No man would be in a healthy condition of mind who,while thinking this or that to be right,nevertheless wished to do something which he did not consider right.

The same would hold good if a person desired,not the thing that pleased him,but that which displeased him. Now the person progressing toward higher cognition becomes aware that feeling,thinking,and willing do actually assume a certain independence; that,for example,a particular thought no longer urges him,as though of itself,to a certain condition of feeling and willing. The matter resolves itself thus: We may comprehend something correctly by means of thinking,but in order to arrive at a feeling or impulse of the will on the subject,we need a further independent impetus,coming from within ourselves. Thinking,feeling and willing no longer remain three forces,radiating from the ego as their common centre,but become,as it were,independent entities,just as though they were three separate personalities. For this reason,therefore, a person's own ego must be strengthened,for not only must it introduce order among three powers,but the leadership and guidance of three entities have devolved upon it.

And this is what is known to occult science as the cleavage of the personality. Here is once more clearly revealed how important it is to add to the exercises for higher training others for giving fixity and firmness to the judgment,and to the life of feeling and will. For if certainty and firmness are not brought into the higher world,it will at once be seen how weak the ego proves to be,and how it can be no fitting ruler over the powers of thought,feeling and will. In the presence of this weakness,the soul would be dragged by three different personalities in as many directions,and its inner individual separateness would cease. But should the development of the occult student proceed on the right lines,this multiplication of himself,so to speak,will prove to be a real step forward,and he will nevertheless continue,as a new ego,to be the strong ruler over the independent entities which now make up his soul.

In the subsequent course of development this division or cleavage is carried further; thought,now functioning independently,arouses the activities of a fourth distinct psycho-spiritual being; one that may be described as a direct influx into the individual,of currents which bear a resemblance to thoughts. The entire world then appears as thought-structure,confronting man just like the plant and animal worlds in the realm of the physical senses. In the same manner feeling and will, which have become independent,stimulate two other powers within the soul
to work in it as separate entities. And yet a seventh power and entity must be added,which resembles the ego itself. Thus man,on reaching a particular stage of development,finds himself to be composed of seven entities,all of which he has to guide and control.

The whole of this experience becomes associated with a further one. Before
entering the supersensible world,thinking,feeling,and willing were known to man merely as inner soul-experiences. But as soon as he enters the supersensible world he becomes aware of things which do not express
physical sense realities,but psycho-spiritual realities. Behind the characteristics of the new world of which he has become aware,he now perceives spiritual beings. These now present themselves to him as an

external world,just as stones,plants and animals in the physical sense world,have impressed his senses. Now the occult student is able to observe an important difference between the spiritual world unfolding itself before him and the world he has hitherto been accustomed to recognize by means of his physical senses. A plant of the sense-world remains what it is,whatever man's soul may think or feel about it. This is not the case,however,with the images of the psycho-spiritual world, for these change according to man's own thoughts and feelings. Man stamps
upon them an impression which is the result of his own being.

Let us imagine a particular picture presenting itself to man in the imaginative world. As long as he maintains indifference toward it,it will continue to show a particular form. As soon,however,as he is moved by feelings of like or dislike with regard to it,its form will change. Pictures,therefore,at first present not only something independent and external to man,but they reflect also what man himself is. These pictures are permeated through and through with man's own being. This falls like a veil over the other beings. In this case man,even if confronted by a real being,does not see this,but sees what he himself has created. Thus he may have something true before him,and yet see what is false. Indeed, this is not only the case in respect to what man has observed concerning his own being,but everything that is in him impresses itself upon the spiritual world.

If,for example,a person has secret inclinations,which owing to education and character are precluded from revealing themselves in life, those inclinations will,nevertheless,take effect in the psycho-spiritual world,which is thus colored in a peculiar way,due to that person's being,quite irrespective of how much he may or may not know of his own being. And in order to be able to advance beyond this stage of development,it becomes necessary that man should learn to distinguish between himself and the spiritual world around him. It is necessary that he should learn to eliminate all the effects produced by his own nature upon the surrounding psycho-spiritual world. This can be done only by acquiring a knowledge of what we ourselves take with us into this new world. It is therefore primarily a question of self-knowledge,in order that we may become able to perceive clearly the surrounding psycho-spiritual world. It is true that certain facts of human development entail such self-knowledge as must naturally be acquired when one enters higher worlds. In the ordinary world of the physical senses man develops his ego,his self-consciousness,and this ego then acts as a point of attraction for all that appertains to man. All personal propensities, sympathies,antipathies,passions,opinions,etc.,possessed by a person, group themselves,as it were,around this ego,and it is this ego likewise to which human Karma is attached. Were we able to see this ego unveiled, it would also be possible to see just what blows of fate it must yet endure in this and future incarnations,as a result of its life in previous incarnations and the qualities acquired. Encumbered as it is with all this,the ego must be the first picture that presents itself to the human soul,when ascending into the psycho-spiritual world. This double of the human being,in accordance with a law of the spiritual world,is bound to be his first impression in that world. It is easy to explain this fundamental law to ourselves,if we consider the following. In the life of the physical senses man is cognizant of himself only so far as he is inwardly conscious of himself in his thinking,feeling,and willing. This cognition is an inner one; it does not present itself to him externally, as do stones,plants and animals; but even through inner experiences,man learns to know himself only partially,for he has within him something that prevents deep self-knowledge,namely,the impulse to immediately transform this quality,when through self-cognition he is forced to admit its presence and concerning which he is unwilling to deceive himself.

If he did not yield to this impulse,but simply turned his attention away

from himself--remaining as he is--he would naturally deprive himself of even
the possibility of knowing himself in regard to that particular matter. Yet should he "explore" himself,facing his characteristics without self-deception,he would either be able to improve them,or in his present condition of life he would be unable to do so. In the latter case a feeling would steal over his soul which we must designate a feeling of shame. Indeed,this is the way in which man's sound nature acts; it experiences through self-knowledge various feelings of shame. Even in ordinary life this feeling has a certain definite effect. A healthy-minded person will take care that that which fills him with this feeling does not express itself outwardly or manifest itself in deeds. Thus the sense of shame is a force urging man to conceal something within himself,not allowing it to be outwardly apparent.

If we consider this well,we shall find it possible to understand why occult science should ascribe more far-reaching effects to another inner experience of the soul,very closely allied to this feeling of shame. Occult science finds that within the hidden depths of the soul a kind of secret feeling of shame exists,of which man in his life of the physical senses is unaware. Yet this secret feeling acts much in the same way as the conscious feeling of shame of ordinary life to which we have alluded; it prevents man's inmost being from confronting him in a recognizable image,or double. Were this feeling not present,man would see himself as he is in very truth; not only would he experience his thoughts,ideas, feelings and decisions inwardly,but he would perceive these as he now perceives stones,animals and plants.

This feeling,therefore,is that which veils man from himself,and at the same time hides from him the entire spiritual world. For owing to this veiling of man's inner self,he becomes unable to perceive those things by means of which he is to develop organs for penetrating into the psycho-spiritual world; he becomes unable to so transform his own being as
to render it capable of obtaining spiritual organs of perception.

If man aims however to form these organs of perception through correct training,that which he himself really is appears before him as the first impression. He perceives his double. This self-recognition is inseparable from perception of the rest of the psycho-spiritual world. In the everyday life of the physical world the feeling of shame here described acts in such a manner as to be perpetually closing the door which leads into the psycho-spiritual world. If man would take but a single step in order to penetrate into that world,this instantly appearing but unconscious feeling of shame,conceals that portion of the psycho-spiritual world which would reveal itself. The exercises here described do,however, unlock this world: and it so happens that the above-mentioned hidden feeling acts as a great benefactor to man,for all that we may have gained,apart from occult training,in the matter of judgment,feeling and character,is insufficient to support us when confronted by our own being in its true form; its apparition would rob us of all feeling of selfhood, self-reliance and self-consciousness. And that this may not happen, provision must be made for cultivating sound judgment,good feeling and character,along with the exercises given for the attainment of higher knowledge.

A correct method of tuition teaches the student as much of occult science
as will,in combination with the many means provided for self-knowledge and self-observation,enable him to meet his double with assured strength. It will then appear to the student that he sees,in another form,a picture of the imaginative world with which he has already become acquainted in the physical world. Anyone who has first learned in the physical world,by means of his understanding,to apprehend rightly the

law of Karma,is not likely to be greatly frightened when he sees his fate traced upon the image of his double. Anyone who,by means of his own powers of judgment,has made himself acquainted with the evolution of the universe,and the development of the human race,and who is aware that at a particular epoch of this development the powers of Lucifer penetrated into the human soul,will have little difficulty in enduring the sight of the image of his own individuality when he knows that it includes those Luciferian powers and all their accumulated effects.

This will suffice to show how necessary it is that no one should demand admission into the spiritual world before having learned to understand certain truths concerning it; learning them by means of his own judgment, as developed in this world of the physical senses. All that has been said in this book previous to the chapter concerning "Perception of the higher worlds," should have been assimilated by the student in the course of his regular development,by means of his ordinary judgment,before he has any desire to seek entrance himself into the supersensible worlds.

Where the training has been such as to pay little heed to firmness and surety of judgment,and to the life of feeling and character,it may happen that the student will approach the higher world before being possessed of the necessary inner capacities. The meeting with his double would in this case overwhelm him. But what might also happen is that the person introduced into the supersensible world then would be totally unable to recognize this world in its true form,for it would be impossible for him to differentiate between what he sees in the things, and what they really are. For this distinction becomes possible only when a person himself has beheld the image of his own being and becomes able to separate from his surroundings everything which proceeds from his inner being.

In respect to life in the world of physical sense,man's double becomes at once visible through the already mentioned feeling of shame when man nears the psycho-spiritual world,and in so doing,it also conceals the whole of that world. The double stands before the entrance as a "guardian," denying admission to all who are as yet unfit,and it is therefore designated in occult science as the "guardian of the threshold of the psycho-spiritual world." However,we may call it the "lesser guardian," for there is another,of whom we shall speak later.

And besides this meeting with his double on entering the supersensible world as here described,man encounters the Guardian of the Threshold when he passes the portals of physical death,and it gradually reveals itself during that psycho-spiritual development which takes place between death and a new birth. However,the encounter can in no wise crush us,for we then know of other worlds of which we are ignorant during the life between birth and death. A person entering the psycho-spiritual world without having encountered the Guardian of the Threshold would be liable to fall a prey to one delusion after another. For he would never be able to distinguish between that which he himself brings into that world and what really belongs to it. But correct training should lead the student into the domain of truth,not of error,and with such training the meeting must,at one time or another,inevitably take place,for it is the one indispensable precaution against the possibilities of deception and phantasm in the observation of supersensible worlds. It is one of the most indispensable precautions to be taken by every occult student,to work carefully upon himself in order not to become a visionary,subject to every possible deception and self-deception,suggestion and auto-suggestion. Wherever correct occult training is followed,the causes of such deceptions are destroyed at their source. It would of course be impossible to speak here exhaustively of the many details to be included in such precautions,and we can only indicate in general the underlying principles. The illusions to be taken into account arise from two sources. In part they proceed from the fact that our own soul-being colors reality. In the ordinary life of the physical sense-world,the danger arising from this source of deception is comparatively small,because here the outer world always obtrudes itself upon the observer in its own sharp outline, no matter how much the observer is inclined to color it according to his wishes and interests. As soon,however,as we enter the imaginative world, the images are changed by such wishes and interests,and we then have actually before us that which we ourselves have formed or,at any rate, helped to form. Now,since through this meeting with the Guardian of the Threshold the occult student becomes aware of everything within him,of that which he can take with him into the psycho-spiritual world,this source of delusion is removed,and the preparation which the occult student undergoes prior to his entering that world is in itself calculated to accustom him to exclude himself--even in matters appertaining to the physical world--when making his observations,thus allowing things and occurrences to speak for themselves. Any one who has sufficiently practiced these preparatory exercises may await this meeting with the Guardian of the Threshold in all tranquillity; by this meeting he will be definitely tested whether he is now really capable of putting aside his own being even when confronting the psycho-spiritual world.

In addition to this there is another source of delusion. This becomes apparent when we place the wrong interpretation upon an impression we receive. We may illustrate it by means of a very simple example taken from
the world of the physical senses. It is the delusion we may encounter when
sitting in a railway carriage; we _think_ the trees are moving in the reverse direction to the train,whereas in fact we ourselves are moving with the train. Although there are many cases in which such illusions occurring in the physical world are more difficult to correct than the simple one we have mentioned,yet it is easy to see that,even within that world,means may be found for getting rid of those delusions if a person of sound judgment brings everything to bear upon the matter which may help
to clear it up.

But as soon as we penetrate into the psycho-spiritual world such elucidations become less easy. In the world of sense,facts are not altered by human delusions about them; it is therefore possible to correct a delusion by unprejudiced observation of facts. But in the supersensible world this is not immediately possible. If we desire to study a supersensible occurrence and approach it with the wrong judgment,we then
carry that wrong judgment over into the thing itself,and it becomes so interwoven with the thing,that the two cannot be easily distinguished. The error then is not in the person and the correct fact external to him, but the error will have become a component part of the external fact. It cannot therefore be cleared up simply by unprejudiced observation of the fact. This is enough to indicate an extremely fertile source of illusion and deception for one who would venture to approach the supersensible world without adequate preparation.

As the occult student has now acquired the faculty to exclude those illusions originating from the coloring of the supersensible
world-phenomena with his own being,so must he now acquire the faculty of
making ineffective the second source of illusions mentioned above.

Only after the meeting with his double,can he eliminate what comes from himself and thus he will be able to remove the second source of delusion when he has acquired the faculty for judging by the very nature of a fact seen in the supersensible world,whether it is a reality or an illusion. Now if the illusions were of precisely the same appearance as the realities,differentiation would be impossible. But this is not the case. Illusions of the supersensible world have in themselves qualities which distinguish them definitely from the realities,and the important thing is for the occult student to know by what qualities he may be able to recognize those realities.

Nothing seems more natural than that those ignorant of occult training should say: "How,then,is it at all possible to guard against delusions, since their sources are so numerous?" And further: "Can an occult student
ever be safe from the possibility that all his so-called higher experiences may not turn out to be based on mere deception and self-deception (suggestion and auto-suggestion)?" Any one advancing these
objections ignores the fact that all true occult training proceeds in such a manner as to remove those sources of delusion. In the first place,the occult student during his preparation,will have become possessed of enough knowledge about all that which may lead to delusion and self-delusion,that he will be in a position to protect himself against them. He has,in this respect,an opportunity,like that of no other human being,to render himself sober and capable of sound judgment for the journey of life. Everything he learns teaches him not to rely upon vague presentiments and premonitions. Training makes him as cautious as possible,and,in addition to this,all true training leads in the first place to concepts of the great cosmic events,to matters,therefore,which necessitate the exertion of the judgment,a process by which this faculty is at the same time rendered keener and more refined. But those who decline to occupy themselves with these remote subjects,and prefer keeping the revelations nearer at hand,might miss the strengthening of that sound power of judgment which gives certainty in distinguishing between illusion and reality. Yet even this is not the most important thing,but the exercises themselves,carried out through a systematic course of occult training. These must be so arranged that the consciousness of the student is enabled during meditation to scan minutely
all that passes within his soul. In order to bring about imagination,the first thing to be done is to form a symbol. In this there are still elements taken from external observation; it is not only man who participates in their content,he himself does not produce them. Therefore he may deceive himself concerning them and assign their origin to wrong sources. But when the occult student proceeds to the exercises for inspiration,he drops this content from his consciousness and immerses himself only in the soul-activity which formed the symbol. Even here error is still possible: education and study etc.,have induced a particular kind of soul-activity in man. He is unable to know everything about the origin of this activity. Now,however,the occult student removes this, his own soul-activity,from his consciousness; if then something remains, nothing adheres to it that cannot easily be reviewed; nothing can intrude itself in respect to its entire content that cannot easily be judged.

In his intuition,therefore,the occult student possesses something which shows him the pure,clear reality of the psycho-spiritual world. And if he applies this recognized test to all that meets his observation in the realm of psycho-spiritual realities,he will be well able to distinguish appearance from reality. He may also feel sure that the application of this law provides just as effectually against delusions in the spiritual world as does the knowledge in the physical world that an _imaginary_ piece of red-hot iron cannot burn him.

It is obvious that this test applies only to our own experiences in the

supersensible world,and not to communications made to us which we have to
apprehend by means of our physical understanding and our healthy sense of
truth. The occult student should exert himself to draw a distinct line of demarcation between the knowledge he acquires by the one means,and by the
other. He should be ready on one the hand to accept communications made to
him regarding the higher worlds,and should seek to understand them by using his powers of judgment. When,however,he is confronted by an "experience," which he may so name because it is due to personal observation,he will first carefully test the same to ascertain whether it possesses exactly those characteristics which he has learned to recognize
by means of infallible intuition.

The meeting with the Guardian of the Threshold being over,the occult student will have to face other new experiences,and the first thing that he will become aware of is the inner connection which exists between this Guardian of the Threshold and that soul-power we have already characterized,when describing the cleavage of personality,as being the seventh power to resolve itself into an independent entity. This seventh entity is,indeed,in certain respects no other than the double,or Guardian of the Threshold itself,and it lays a particular task upon the student. Namely,that which he is in his lower self and which now appears to him in the image,he must guide and lead by means of the new-born higher self. This will result in a sort of battle with this double,which will continually strive for the upper hand. Now to establish the right relationship to it,to allow it to do nothing except what takes place under the influence of the new-born ego,this is what strengthens and fortifies man's forces.

This matter of self-cognition is,in certain respects,different in the higher worlds from what it is in the physical sense-world. For whereas in the latter,self-cognition is only an inner experience,the newly born self immediately presents itself as an outward psycho-spiritual apparition. We see our new-born self before us like another being,yet we cannot perceive it in its entirety,for,whatever the stage to which we may have climbed on our journey to the supersensible worlds,there will always be still higher stages which will enable us to perceive more and more of our "higher self." It can therefore only partially reveal itself to the student at any particular stage. Having once caught a glimpse of this higher self,man feels a tremendous temptation to look upon it in the same manner in which he is accustomed to regard the things of the physical
sense-world. And yet this temptation is salutary; it is indeed necessary, if man's development is to proceed in the right manner. The student must here note what it is that appears as his double,as the Guardian of the Threshold,and place it by the side of the higher self,in order that he may rightly observe the disparity between what he is and what he is to become. But while thus engaged in observation he will find that the Guardian of the Threshold will assume quite a different aspect,for it will now reveal itself as a picture of all the _obstacles_ which oppose the development of the higher ego,and he then becomes aware of what a load he drags about with him in his ordinary ego. And should the student's preparation not have rendered him strong enough to be able to say: "I will not remain at this point,but will persistently work my way upward toward the higher ego," he will grow weak and will shrink back dismayed before the labor that lies before him. He has plunged into the psycho-spiritual world,but gives up working his way farther,and becomes a captive to that image which,as Guardian of the Threshold,now confronts the soul. And the

remarkable thing here is that the person so situated will have no feeling of being a captive. He will,on the contrary,think he is going through quite a different experience,for the image called forth by the Guardian of the Threshold may be such as to awaken in the soul of the observer the
impression that in the pictures which appear at this stage of development he has before him the whole universe in its entirety--the impression of having attained to the summit of all knowledge,and of there being, therefore,nothing left to strive after. Therefore,instead of feeling himself a captive,the student would believe himself rich beyond all measure,and in possession of all the secrets of the universe. Nor need this experience fill one with surprise,though it be the reverse of the facts,for we must remember that by the time these experiences are felt, we are already standing within the psycho-spiritual world,and that the special peculiarity of this world is that it reverses events--a fact which has already been alluded to in our consideration of life after death.

The image seen by the occult student at this stage of development shows him a different aspect from that in which the Guardian of the Threshold first revealed itself. In the double first mentioned,were to be seen all those qualities which,as the result of the influence of Lucifer,are possessed by man's ordinary ego. But in the course of human development, another power has,in consequence of Lucifer's influence,also been drawn into the human soul; this is known as the force of Ahriman. It is this force that,during his physical existence,prevents man from becoming aware of those psycho-spiritual beings which lie behind the surface of the external world. All that man's soul has become under the influence of this force,may be discerned in the image revealing itself during the experience just described. Those who have been sufficiently prepared for this experience will,when thus confronted,be able to assign to it its true meaning,and then another form will soon become visible--one we may describe as the "greater Guardian of the Threshold." This one will tell the student not to rest content with the stage to which he has attained, but to work on energetically. It will call forth in him the consciousness that the world he has conquered will only become a truth,and not an illusion,if the work thus begun be continued in a corresponding manner. Those,however,who have gone through incorrect occult training and would approach this meeting unprepared,would then experience something in their
souls when they come to the "greater Guardian of the Threshold," which can
only be described as a "feeling of inexpressible fright",of "boundless fear."

Just as the meeting with the "lesser Guardian" gives the occult student the opportunity of judging whether or not he is proof against delusions such as might arise through interweaving his own personality with the supersensible world,so too must he be able to prove from the experiences which finally lead to the "greater Guardian," whether he is able to withstand those illusions which are to be traced to the second source mentioned farther back in this chapter. Should he be proof against the powerful illusion by which the world of images to which he has attained, is falsely displayed to him as a rich possession,when actually he is only a captive,then he is guarded also against the danger of mistaking appearance for reality during the further course of his development.

To a certain degree the Guardian of the Threshold will assume a different form in the case of each individual. The meeting with him corresponds exactly to the way in which the personal element in supersensible observations is overcome,and therefore the possibility exists of entering a realm of experience which is free from any tinge of personality and is open to every human being.

When the occult student has passed through the above experiences,he will
be capable of distinguishing in the psycho-spiritual world between what he himself is and what is outside of him,and he will then recognize why an understanding of the cosmic occurrences narrated in this book,is necessary to man's understanding of humanity itself and its life process. In fact,we can understand the physical body only when we recognize the manner in which it has been built up through the developments undergone in
the Saturn,Sun,Moon,and Earth periods,and we understand the etheric body when we follow its evolution through the Sun,Moon,and Earth stages of evolution. We further comprehend what is bound up with our earth-development at present,if we can grasp how all things proceed by the process of gradual evolution. Occult training places us in a position to recognize the connection between everything that is within man and the
corresponding facts and beings existing in the world external to him. For it is a fact that each principle of man stands in some connection with the rest of the world. The outlines of these subjects could only be briefly sketched in this book. It must however be borne in mind that the physical body had,at the time of the Saturn development,for instance,no more than its rudimentary beginnings. Its organs--such as the heart,lungs,and brain--developed later during the Sun,Moon,and Earth periods,for which reason heart,lungs and brain are related to the evolutionary process of Sun,Moon and Earth.

It is the same with the members of the etheric body,the sentient body, and the sentient soul. Man is the outcome of the entire world surrounding him,and every part of his constitution corresponds to some event,to some being in the external world. At a certain stage of his development the occult student comes to a realization of this relation of his own being to the great cosmos,and this stage of development may in the occult sense be
termed a becoming aware of the relationship of the little world,the microcosm--that is,man himself--to the great world,the macrocosm. And when
the occult student has struggled through to such cognition,he may then go through a new experience; he begins to feel himself united,as it were, with the entire cosmic structure,although he remains fully conscious of his own independence. This sensation is a merging into the whole world,a becoming "at one" with it,yet _ without _ losing one's own individual identity. Occult science describes this stage as the "becoming one with the macrocosm." It is important that this union should not be imagined as one in which separate consciousness ceases and in which the human being
flowers forth into the universe,for such a thought would only be the expression of an opinion resulting from untutored reasoning.

Following this stage of development something takes place that in occult science is described as "beatitude." It is neither possible nor necessary that this stage be more closely described,for no human words have the power to picture this experience and it may rightly be said that any conception of this state could be acquired only by means of such thought-power as would no longer be dependent upon the instrument of the
human brain. The separate stages of higher knowledge,according to the methods of initiation that have been here described,may be enumerated as follows:

1. The study of occult science,in the course of which we first of all make use of the reasoning powers we have acquired in the world of the physical senses.

2. Attainment of imaginative cognition.

3. Reading the secret script (which corresponds to inspiration).

4. Working with the philosopher's stone (corresponding to intuition).

5. Cognition of the relationship between the microcosm and the macrocosm.

6. Being one with the macrocosm.

7. Beatitude.

These stages however need not necessarily be thought of as following one another consecutively,for in the course of training,the occult student, according to his individuality,may have attained a preceding stage only to a certain degree when he has already begun to practice exercises, corresponding to the next higher stage. For instance,it may be that when he has gained only a few reliable imaginative pictures,he will already be doing exercises which lead him on to draw inspiration,intuition,or cognition of the relationship between microcosm and macrocosm into the sphere of his own experiences.

When the occult student has experienced intuition he comes to know not only the forms of the psycho-spiritual world,not only can he recognize their inter-relationship through the "secret script," but he attains a cognition of these beings themselves through whose co-operation the world,
to which he belongs,comes into being. Thus he learns to know himself in the true form which he possesses as a spiritual being in the psycho-spiritual world. He has struggled through to the higher ego,and has learned how he must continue the work in order that he may master his
double,the Guardian of the Threshold. But he has also met the "greater guardian of the Threshold" who stands before him perpetually urging him to
further labors, It is this greater Guardian of the Threshold who now becomes the ideal he must strive to resemble,and when the student has acquired this feeling he will have risen to that important stage of development in which he will be in a position to recognize who it is that is really standing before him as that "greater Guardian." For henceforth, in the student's consciousness,the Guardian is gradually transformed into the figure of the Christ,whose Being and intervention in the evolution of the earth have been dealt with in a foregoing chapter.

Thus the student,through his intuition,will have become initiated into that sublime Mystery which is linked with the name of Christ. The Christ reveals himself to him as the "Great Ideal of humanity on earth."

When in this manner through intuition,the Christ has been recognized in the spiritual world,then we can also understand those events that took place historically upon earth during the fourth post-Atlantean period (the Greco-Roman time),and how at that time the great Sun-Spirit,the Christ-Being,intervened in the world's development,and how He still continues to guide its evolution. These are matters the student will then know by personal experience. Therefore it is through intuition that the meaning and significance of the earth's evolution are disclosed to the occult student.

The path leading to cognition of the supersensible worlds as above indicated,is one which all men may travel,whatever their position under the present conditions of life may be. And in speaking of such a path it must be borne in mind that,while the goal of cognition and truth is the same at all times of the earth's development,yet the starting-point for man has varied considerably at different periods. For instance,the man of the present day who wishes to find his way into supersensible worlds, cannot start from the same point as the Egyptian candidate for initiation of old. This is why it is impossible for modern humanity to apply,without modification,the exercises given to the candidate for initiation in ancient Egypt. For since those times men's souls have passed through different incarnations,and this passing onward from incarnation to incarnation is not without significance and importance. The capacities and qualities of souls change from one incarnation to another. Those who have studied human history only superficially can note that since the twelfth and thirteenth centuries all life conditions have changed and that opinions,feelings and even human capabilities have become different from what they were before that time. The path here described for the acquirement of higher knowledge is one which is suitable for souls incarnating in the immediate present. It fixes the starting-point of spiritual development just where the man of the present day stands,in whatever conditions of life he may be placed.

From epoch to epoch,progressive evolution leads humanity,in respect to the path of higher cognition,to ever changing modes,just as outer life likewise changes its form. For at all times it is necessary that perfect harmony should reign between external life and initiation. It will be pointed out in the next chapter of this book what changes initiation, which in the ancient mysteries lead into the higher worlds,must undergo, in order to become modern "initiation" for the attainment of supersensible cognition in its present form.

CHAPTER VI. THE PRESENT AND FUTURE EVOLUTION OF THE WORLD AND OF HUMANITY

It is impossible to know anything in the occult sense of the present and future of human or planetary evolution without understanding that evolution in the past. Forthat which presents itself to the occult student's observation when he watches the hidden events of the past, contains at the same time everything that he can learn of the present and future. In this book we have spoken of the Saturn,Sun,Moon and Earth evolutions. We cannot follow the evolution of the earth,as the occultist understands it,unless we observe the events of preceding evolutionary periods. For what meets us today,within the bounds of our earthly globe, comprises in a certain sense the facts of the evolution of the Moon,Sun and Saturn. The beings and things that took part in the evolution of the Moon have gone on developing,and all that now belongs to the earth,is the outcome of that development.

But not all that has evolved from the Moon to the Earth is perceptible to physical sense-consciousness. A part of what came over to us from the Moon.
evolution is revealed only at a certain stage of clairvoyant consciousness,at which knowledge of supersensible worlds is reached. When
this knowledge is gained,the fact that our earthly planet is united to a supersensible world is recognized. The latter includes that part of lunar existence which is not sufficiently densified to be observed by the physical senses. In the first place it does not include it as it was at the time of the evolution of the original Moon. If this clairvoyant consciousness occupies itself with the perception of these things,which it can have at present,this latter gradually separates into two images.

One presents the shape borne by the earth during the lunar evolution,the other shows itself in such a way,that we recognize as its content a form as yet in the germinal stage which will become a reality--in the sense in which the earth is now a reality--but only in the future.

On further observation it is seen that the results,in a certain sense,of that which is taking place on the earth are continually streaming into that future form,so that in it we have before us that which our earth will ultimately become. The effects of earthly existence will unite with the events in the world described,and out of this the new cosmos will arise,into which the Earth will be transformed as the Moon was transformed into the Earth. This future form is called in occult science the Jupiter condition. The clairvoyant observer of this Jupiter state sees the revelation of certain events which _must_ take place in the future. The reason for this is that in the supersensible part of the Earth which had its origin in the Moon,beings and things are present which will assume definite form when certain events have actually happened in the physical world. Therefore there will be something in the Jupiter condition which was already predetermined by the Moon evolution and it will contain new factors,which can come into the whole evolution only in consequence of terrestrial events. In this way clairvoyant consciousness is able to learn something of what will happen during the Jupiter state.

The beings and facts observed in this field of consciousness have not the nature of sense-images; they do not even appear as fine air-structures from which effects might proceed which resemble sense-impressions. They
give purely spiritual impressions of sound,light and heat. These are _not_ expressed through any material embodiments. They can be apprehended
only by clairvoyant consciousness. One may say,however,that these beings which at present manifest on the psycho-spiritual plane,possess a "body." This body,however,appears like a sum of _condensed memories_ which they
carry within their souls.

One can distinguish within their being what they are now experiencing and what they have experienced and now remember. This last is contained within
them like a bodily element. They are conscious of it in the same way that an earthly human being is conscious of his body.

At a stage of clairvoyant development higher than that just described as necessary for a knowledge of the Moon and Jupiter,the student is able to perceive supersensible beings and things which are,in fact,the more highly developed forms of those present during the Sun condition,but which have now reached stages of existence so lofty as to be quite imperceptible to a consciousness capable of observing the Moon forms only.
During meditation the picture of this world also divides in two. The one leads to a knowledge of the Sun state of the past; the other represents a future form of the earth existence--namely,that into which the earth will have been transformed when the fruits of all that takes place on it and Jupiter have merged into the forms of that future world. What can thus be
observed of this future world may be characterized in occult phraseology as the Venus condition.

In a similar manner,to a still more highly evolved clairvoyant consciousness,a future state of evolution is revealed,which we may call the Vulcan state. It stands in the same relationship to the Saturn state as the Venus condition does to that of the Sun,or the Jupiter state to the evolution of the Moon. Therefore,when we contemplate the past, present,and future of the earth's evolution,we may speak of the Saturn,

Sun,Moon,Earth,Jupiter,Venus,and Vulcan evolutions.

Just as these far-reaching conditions of the evolution of our earth lie disclosed to clairvoyant vision,the same vision is also able to cover the nearer future. There is a picture of the future corresponding to every picture of the past. In speaking of such things,however,one fact must be emphasized which should be taken into strict account: that in order to recognize facts of this kind,one must absolutely do away with the idea that they can be fathomed through mere philosophical reflection. These things cannot,and never should be investigated by that kind of thinking. Anyone would be labouring under a prodigious delusion who,after becoming acquainted with the teachings of occult science regarding the Moon state, thinks that he could discover the future conditions of Jupiter by comparing those of the Moon and Earth. These conditions must be investigated only when the requisite clairvoyant consciousness has been attained; but once communicated to others after such investigation,they can be understood without clairvoyant consciousness.

Now the occultist finds himself in quite a different position,with regard to observations concerning the future,from that in which he stands with regard to those of the past. It is impossible at first for man to contemplate future events as impartially as he does those of the past. Future events excite human will and feeling; while the past affects us in quite a different way. He who observes life knows how true this is of everyday existence; but how enormously this truth is enhanced,and what an intimate bearing it has upon the hidden facts of life,can only be realized by one who has some knowledge of the supersensible world. That is the reason why those who know such things are very definitely limited as to what they are allowed to give out. Certain things bearing on the future can,in fact,be imparted only to those who have themselves determined to follow the path leading to the supersensible worlds. Such people by their mental attitude have acquired something which gives them the disinterestedness necessary for the reception of these teachings. For this reason certain secret facts,even of the past and present,can be spoken of only to those who are prepared for them in this way. These are facts so closely connected with future evolution,that their effect on the human soul is similar to that produced by communications regarding the future itself.

This explains,also,why the information in this book concerning the present and the future is given in the merest outline as compared with the more detailed descriptions of the evolution of the world and of humanity in the past. What is said here is not intended to appeal to the love of sensation in the smallest degree; not even to awaken it. We shall only state where the answer can be found to vital questions which naturally present themselves to one who holds a certain definite attitude of mind.

Just as the great cosmic evolution can be portrayed in the successive states,from the Saturn to the Vulcan period,so also is this possible for shorter periods of time; for example,for those of the evolution of the earth. Since that mighty upheaval which terminated the ancient Atlantean life,successive periods of human evolution have followed one another which have been called in this work the ancient Indian,the ancient Persian,the Egypto-Chaldean,and the Greco-Roman. The fifth period is that in which humanity finds itself to-day,--it is the present time. This period gradually took its rise in the eleventh,twelfth,and thirteen centuries A.D.,after a period of preparation commencing in the fourth and fifth centuries. The Greco-Roman period preceding it began about the eighth century B.C. When one-third of this period had elapsed,the Christ-event took place.

During the transition from the Egypto-Chaldean to the Greco-Roman period,
the attitude of the human mind and,indeed,all human faculties,underwent a change. In the first of these two periods what we now know as logical thinking,as a mere intellectual concept of the world,was still wanting. The knowledge which a man now acquires through his intelligence,he then gained in a manner suited to that time,--directly through an inner,in a certain sense,clairvoyant cognition. He perceived the things around him, and while perceiving them there arose within his soul the percept,the image that was needed. Whenever knowledge is gained in this way,not only pictures of the physical sense-world come to light,but from the depths of consciousness a certain knowledge of facts and beings arises which are not
of the physical world. This was a remnant of the ancient dim clairvoyance, once the common property of the whole of humanity.

During the Greco-Roman period an ever-increasing number of individuals appeared without these capacities. Intelligent reflection concerning things took their place. Mankind was more and more shut off from the immediate perception of the psycho-spiritual world,and was more and more
restricted to forming a picture of it through intelligence and feeling. This condition lasted more or less during the whole of the fourth division of the post-Atlantean period. Only those individuals who had preserved the old mental state as an inheritance could still become directly conscious of the spiritual world. But these were stragglers from an earlier time. Their manner of gaining knowledge was no longer suitable for later conditions. For,as a consequence of the laws of evolution,old faculties of the soul lose something of their former significance when new faculties appear. Human life then adapts itself to these new faculties,and can no longer use the old ones properly.

There were individuals,however,who began in full consciousness to add to the powers of intelligence and feeling already gained,the development of other and higher powers,which made it possible for them once more to penetrate into the psycho-spiritual world. To this end they were obliged to set to work in a different way from that in which the pupils of the old Initiates had been trained. The latter had not been obliged to take into account those faculties of the soul which were developed only in the fourth period. The method of occult training which has been described in this work as that of the present age,began in its first rudiments in the fourth period. But it was then only in its beginning,it could not attain real maturity until the fifth period (from the twelfth and thirteenth centuries onward). Those who sought to rise into supersensible worlds in this manner could learn something of the higher regions of existence through the exercise of their own imagination,inspiration,and intuition. Those who went no further than the development of the faculties of reason
and feeling could learn only through tradition what had been known to ancient clairvoyance. This was handed on,either by word of mouth or in writing,from generation to generation.

Neither could those born later know anything of the real nature of the Christ-event save by such traditions,if they did not rise to the level of the supersensible worlds. Certainly there were such Initiates who still possessed the natural faculties of supersensible perception and yet who, through their development,had ascended into the higher worlds,in spite of their disregard of the new powers of intelligence and feeling. Through them a transition was effected from the old method of Initiation to the new. Such persons lived in later times as well. The essential characteristic of the fourth period is that,by the exclusion of the soul from direct communion with the psycho-spiritual world,the human faculties of intelligence and feeling were thereby strengthened and invigorated. The souls whose powers of intelligence and feeling had at that time developed to a great extent as the result of former incarnations,carried over with them the fruits of this development into their incarnations during the fifth period. As a compensation for this exclusion from the higher worlds, mighty traditions of Ancient Wisdom then existed,especially those of the Christ-event,which by the power of their content gave men confident knowledge of the higher worlds.

But there were still certain human beings existing who had evolved the higher powers of cognition in addition to the faculties of reason and feeling. It devolved upon them to learn the facts of the higher worlds, and especially of the Mystery of the Christ-event,by direct supersensible perception. From these individuals there always flowed into the souls of other men as much as was intelligible and good for them.

The first spreading of Christianity was to take place just at a time when the capacities for supersensible cognition were undeveloped in a great part of humanity. And this is why tradition at that time possessed such mighty power. The strongest possible force was necessary to lead mankind
to a faith in a supersensible world which they themselves could not perceive. How Christianity worked during that period has been shown in previous pages. There were always those,however,who were able to rise into higher worlds through imagination,inspiration,and intuition. These men were the post-Christian successors of the old Initiates,the teachers and members of the Mysteries. Their task was to recognize again,through their own faculties,what man had been able to perceive through ancient clairvoyance,and through the methods of ascent into higher worlds taught in the old Initiations; and in addition to this,to acquire the knowledge of the real nature of the Christ-event.

Thus there arose,among these "New Initiates," a knowledge embracing everything contained in the old form of Initiation; but the central point of this teaching was the higher knowledge concerning the Mysteries of the
coming of the Christ. Such teaching could only filter through into the general life of the world in scanty measure while the human souls of the fourth period were further developing the faculties of intellect and feeling; therefore,while this lasted,the doctrine was in truth secret. Then began the dawn of the new period designated as the fifth. Its essential characteristic lay in the progress made in the evolution of the intellectual faculties,which were then developed to a very high degree, and will unfold still further in the future. This process has been slowly going on from the twelfth and thirteenth centuries,becoming ever more rapid from the sixteenth century up to the present time.

Under these influences the evolution of the fifth period became an ever-increasing endeavour to foster the powers of intellect,while,on the contrary,the knowledge by faith of former times,and traditional wisdom, gradually lost its hold over the human soul. On the other hand,however, from the twelfth and thirteenth centuries on,there developed that which may be called an ever increasing flow of cognition born of modern clairvoyant consciousness. This "hidden knowledge" flows even though at first quite imperceptibly,into the human concepts of that period. It is only natural that even up to the present time the purely intellectual forces should have maintained an antagonistic attitude toward this knowledge. But that which must come to pass will do so in spite of all temporary antagonism. That "hidden knowledge" which is taking possession
of humanity more and more may be called symbolically,the "wisdom of the Holy Grail."

For he who learns to understand this symbol in its deeper meaning,as it is told in story and legend,will find that it symbolizes the nature of what has been called above,the knowledge of the new Initiation,with the Christ Mystery as its central point. Modern Initiates may therefore be called "the Initiates of the Grail." The preliminary stages of the path to the supersensible worlds described in this book,leads to the "Wisdom of the Grail." It is a peculiarity of this wisdom that its facts can be investigated only when the necessary means,as described in this book, have been acquired. Once investigated,however,these facts can be understood by means of those very soul-forces which are the result of the evolution of the fifth period. Indeed,it will become more and more evident that to an ever increasing extent those forces find satisfaction through this knowledge. We are now living at a time in which this knowledge must be absorbed by human consciousness in general to a much fuller extent than was formerly the case. And it is from this point of view that the teachings contained in this Christ-event will grow ever more powerful in proportion as human evolution assimilates the Wisdom of the Grail. The inner side of the development of Christianity will more and more keep pace with the exoteric side. That which may be learned through imagination,inspiration and intuition,concerning the higher worlds,in connection with the Christ Mystery,will penetrate ever more and more human thinking,feeling,and willing. The "hidden wisdom of the Grail" will be revealed,and as an inner force will more and more permeate the manifestations of human life.

Through the whole of the fifth period,knowledge concerning the supersensible world will flow into human consciousness; and when the sixth period begins,humanity will be able to regain on a higher level that clairvoyance which it possessed at an earlier epoch in a dim and indistinct manner. Yet the new acquisition will take a form quite different from the old. What the soul knew of higher worlds in ancient times,was not permeated by its own forces of intellect and feeling. Its knowledge was instinctive. In the future it will not only have instincts, but it will understand them,and feel them to be the essence of its own nature. When the soul learns a fact concerning some other being or thing, its intellect will find this fact verified through its own nature. Or when some fact regarding an ethical law or human conduct presents itself,the soul will say to itself: "My feeling is only justified when I carry out what is implied in this knowledge." Such a condition of soul will have to be developed by a large part of humanity in the sixth period.

In a certain manner,that which human evolution accomplished during the third period--the Egypto-Chaldean--is repeated in the fifth. At that time the soul could still perceive certain facts of the supersensible worlds, but this perception was disappearing. For the intellectual faculties were at that time beginning to develop and it was their mission to at first exclude man from the higher worlds. In the fifth period supersensible facts which in the third period were perceived in hazy clairvoyance,are again becoming manifest; but they are now interpenetrated by the intellectual and emotional life of the individual man. They are also imbued with what may be imparted to the soul by a knowledge of the Christ Mystery; therefore they assume a form totally different from that which they had previously.

Whereas in ancient times impressions from the higher worlds were felt as forces acting from out a spiritual world to which man did not properly belong,through development in later times these impressions are felt as those of a world into which man is growing,of which he more and more forms a part. Let no one suppose that a repetition of the Egypto-Chaldean civilization can take place in such a way that the soul would merely regain what then existed,and which has been handed on from that time. The Christ-impulse,rightly understood,impels the human soul which has experienced it,to feel and conduct itself as a member of a spiritual world,now recognizing it as a world to which it belongs,outside of which it previously existed.

In the same way that the third reappears in the fifth period,in order to become penetrated with those new qualities which the human soul gained during the fourth,so similarly the second period will revive within the sixth and the first,the ancient Indian,during the seventh. All the marvelous wisdom of ancient India which the great teachers of that day were able to proclaim,will reappear in the seventh period,as living truth in human souls.

Now the changes in the earthly environment of man take place in a manner which bears a certain relationship to his own evolution. When the seventh period has run its course,the earth will experience an upheaval which may be compared with the one which separated Atlantean from post-Atlantean times. And the transformed earth will again continue its evolution in seven divisions of time. The human souls which will then incarnate will experience,on a more exalted level,the kinship with the higher worlds which was possessed by the Atlanteans at a lower stage. But only those individuals will be able to cope with the new conditions of the earth who have built into their souls the qualities made possible by the influences of the Greco-Roman age,and of the periods following it,--the fifth,sixth, and seventh of the post-Atlantean evolution.

The inner nature of such souls will correspond to that which the earth has become by that time. All other souls must then remain behind,although up to that point they had been able to choose whether or not they would create for themselves the conditions necessary to advance with the others.
Those souls alone will be ripe for the conditions arising after the next great catastrophe,who at the point of transition from the fifth to the sixth post-Atlantean period have attained the capacity for penetrating supersensible cognition with the forces of intelligence and feeling. The fifth and sixth are in a way the decisive periods. Those souls which have attained the goal of the sixth period will continue to develop accordingly in the seventh; but the others will,under the altered conditions of their surroundings,find but little opportunity to proceed with their neglected task. Only in a distant future will conditions again appear which will permit of this being done.

Thus evolution proceeds from period to period. Clairvoyance observes not only those changes in the future in which the earth alone takes part,but those also which take place in conjunction with the heavenly bodies in its environment. A time will come in which the terrestrial and human evolution will be advanced so far that those forces and beings which were compelled to detach themselves from the earth during the Lemurian period,so as to afford to earth-beings the possibility of further progress,will be able once more to unite with the earth. Then the moon will again be united with the earth. This will happen because a sufficiently large number of human souls will then possess the inner powers which will enable them to render the Moon forces fruitful for further development. And this will occur at a time when,side by side with the high development of a certain number of human souls,another development,that of those who have chosen the path of evil,will parallel it. These straggler-souls will have accumulated in their Karma so much sin,ugliness and evil,that at first they will form a separate community,a perverse and erring section of humanity,keenly opposing what we understand as "good." The "good" humanity will acquire little by little the power of using the Moon forces,and will thereby so transform the evil section as to enable it to keep pace with the advance of evolution as a separate earth kingdom. Through these labours of the good part of humanity,the earth,then reunited with the moon,will be able,after a certain period of development,to again unite with the sun and also with the other planets.

After an intermediate state,which will be a sojourn in a higher world, the earth will be transformed into the Jupiter condition. That which we now call the mineral kingdom will not exist on Jupiter; the forces of this mineral kingdom will be transformed into plant forces and the plant kingdom,which will have quite a new form compared with its present one, will appear in the Jupiter state as the lowest of the kingdoms,while above it,we find the animal kingdom,likewise transformed. Next comes a human kingdom--the descendants of the evil earth humanity. And then will appear the descendants of the good earth humanity,as a human kingdom on a
higher level. A great part of the work of this last human kingdom consists in ennobling the souls which have sunk into the evil community,so that they may still gain admittance into the true human kingdom.

The Venus condition will be of such a nature that the plant kingdom will have disappeared also; the lowest kingdom will be the animal kingdom once more transformed,and above that there will be three successive human kingdoms of different degrees of perfection. The earth will remain united with the sun during the Venus period; while during that of Jupiter it will have happened that,at a certain point,the sun separates from Jupiter, the latter receiving its influence from outside. Then there is again a union between the sun and Jupiter,the transformation gradually passing into the Venus state. During that state another planet detaches itself from Venus,containing all kinds of beings which have opposed evolution, an "irredeemable moon," as it were,following a path of evolution which is of a character impossible to describe,because it is too unlike anything which man can experience on earth. But evolved humanity will pass on in a fully spiritualized state of existence to the Vulcan evolution,a description of which lies beyond the scope of this work.

We see that from the fruits of the "Wisdom of the Grail" springs the highest ideal of human evolution conceivable for man: spiritualization attained by him through his own efforts. For in the end this spiritualization appears as a product of the harmony which he wrought out in the fifth and sixth periods of the present evolution,between the faculties of reason and emotion which he had then attained and cognition of supersensible worlds. That which he thus achieves within his soul will finally become in itself the outer world. The human spirit rises to the mighty impressions of its outer world and at first divines,later recognizes spiritual beings behind these impressions; the human heart senses the unspeakable exaltedness of the Spirit. Man can,however,also recognize that his inner experiences of intellect,feeling and character are but the germs of a nascent spirit world.

He who thinks that human liberty is not compatible with a foreknowledge and predestination of future conditions,ought to consider that man's freedom of action in the future depends just as little on the arrangement of predestined things as does his liberty of action with regard to inhabiting a house a year hence,on the plans for which he is now settling. He will be as free as his innermost being will permit,within the house he has built; and he will be as free on Jupiter and on Venus as his inner life permits,even under the conditions which will arise there. Freedom will not depend on what has been predetermined by antecedent conditions,but on what the soul has made out of itself.

In the earth condition is contained that which has developed within the preceding Saturn,Sun and Moon states. Earth-man finds "wisdom" in the processes going on around him. This wisdom is there as the fruit of what has happened in the past. The Earth is the descendant of the "old Moon"; and the latter developed with all that belonged to it,into the "Cosmos of Wisdom." The Earth is now at the commencement of an evolution,which will introduce a new force into this wisdom. It will cause man to feel himself an independent member of a spiritual world. This will come to pass because his ego will have been formed within him during the Earth period by the Lords of Form,as was his physical body on Saturn by the Lords of Will, his vital body on the Sun by the Lords of Wisdom,and his astral body on the Moon by the Lords of Motion.

By means of the co-operation of the Lords of Will,Wisdom and Motion, that which manifests as wisdom is brought forth. Through the labours of these three classes of spirits,the beings and processes of earth can harmonize in wisdom with the other beings of their world. It is the Lords of Form who bestowed on man his independent ego. In the future this ego will harmonize with the beings of Earth,Jupiter,Venus,and of Vulcan,by means of the force added to the existing wisdom during the Earth period. It is the force of love. This force must begin to arise within earth-humanity and the Cosmos of Wisdom develop into a _Cosmos of Love_.
Everything which the ego is able to unfold within itself must give birth to love. The all-embracing archetype of love is set forth in the revelation of that lofty Sun-spirit indicated in the description of the Christ Mystery. Through Him the germ of love is planted in the innermost core of the human being; and from this starting-point it must flow through the whole of evolution. Just as the wisdom previously formed manifests in the forces of the earthly sense-world,in the "elementary forces" of to-day,so love itself will manifest in the future,in all phenomena,as the new "elementary force."

The secret of all future development is a recognition that everything achieved by man from a right comprehension of evolution is a sowing of seed which must ripen into love. And the greater the amount of love-force, so much the greater will be the creative force available for the future. In that which will grow from love,will lie the mighty forces leading to that culminating point of spiritualization described above. The greater the amount of spiritual knowledge that flows into human and terrestrial evolution,so much more living and fruitful seed will be stored up for the future. Spiritual knowledge is transmuted _through its own nature_ into love. The whole process which has been described,beginning with the Greco-Roman period and extending throughout the present time,shows how this transformation,for which the beginning has now been made for future times,is to take place and to what end. That which has been prepared as wisdom on Saturn,Sun and Moon,is active in the physical,etheric and astral bodies of man; it shows itself there as the "Wisdom of the World", but within the "ego" it becomes intensified. The wisdom of the outer world becomes inner wisdom in man from the Earth period onward and when it is concentrated in him,it becomes the germ of love. Wisdom is the necessary preliminary condition for love; love is the fruit of wisdom,reborn in the ego.

CHAPTER VII. DETAILS FROM THE DOMAIN OF OCCULT SCIENCE MAN'S ETHERIC BODY

When the higher principles of man are observed with clairvoyant vision, the mode of perception is never precisely the same as that which comes from the outer senses. If we touch an object,and experience a sensation of warmth,we must distinguish between that which comes from the object, that which,as it were,streams out from it,and our own psychic experience. The inner psychic experience of perceiving warmth is something
distinct from the heat which streams from the object. Now let us imagine this psychic experience quite by itself without the outer object. Let us call up the experience of a sensation of heat in our soul,without the presence of any external physical object to cause it. If such a sensation simply existed _without_ cause,it would be mere fancy. The student of occult science experiences such inner perceptions without any physical cause. But at a certain stage of development they present themselves in such a manner that he knows (it has been shown that by the very nature of
the experience he can know) that the inner perception is not fancy,but is caused by a psycho-spiritual being belonging to a supersensible world, just as the ordinary sensation of heat,for example,is caused by an external physical-sense object.

It is the same with the perception of colour in the supersensible world. Here we must distinguish between the colour associated with the outer object,and the inner colour-sensation in the soul. Let us call up the soul's inner sensation when it perceives a _red_ object in the physical, outer world of the senses. Let us imagine that we retain a very vivid recollection of the impression,but that we are looking away from the object. Let us imagine what we still retain as a memory-picture of the colour,to be an inner experience. We shall then distinguish between that which is an inner experience of the colour,and the external colour itself. These inner experiences differ entirely in their content from impressions of the outer senses. They bear much more the impress of what
is felt as joy and sorrow than that of normal physical sensation. Now let us imagine an inner experience of this kind arising in the soul,without any suggestion from an outer sense object. A clairvoyant may have an experience of this kind,and may know too,in that case,that it is no fancy,but the expression of a psycho-spiritual being. Now if this psycho-spiritual being excites the same impression as does a red object of
the physical-sense world,then that being is red. There will,however, always be the external impression first,and then the inner experience of colour,in the case of the physical-sense object; in that of the genuine clairvoyance of a man of to-day,it _must_ be the contrary,--first the inner experience,shadowy,like a mere recollection of colour,and then a picture,growing more and more vivid. The less heed we pay to this necessary sequence of events the less we are able to distinguish between actual,spiritual perception and the delusions of fancy (illusion, hallucination,etc.).

The vividness of the picture in a psycho-spiritual perception of this kind,whether it remains quite shadowy,like a dim concept,or whether it impresses us as intensively as an outer object,depends altogether upon the clairvoyant's stage of development. Now,the general impression obtained by the clairvoyant of the etheric body,may be thus described. When the clairvoyant has strengthened his will power to such a degree that,in spite of the fact that an individual stands before him in a physical body,he can abstract his attention from what the physical eye sees,--he is then able to see clairvoyantly into the space occupied by the man's physical body. Of course,a great increase of will power is

necessary,in order to withdraw the attention not only from something in the mind,but from something standing before one,in such a way that the physical impression is quite extinguished. But this increase of will is possible,and is brought about by exercises for the attainment of supersensible cognition. The clairvoyant can then first have a general impression of the etheric body. Within his soul there arises the same inner sensation which he has,let us say,at the sight of a peach blossom; then this becomes vivid,so that he is able to say that the etheric body has the colour of peach blossoms. He next perceives the separate organs and currents of the etheric body. A further description of the etheric body may be given by relating the psychic experiences which correspond to
sensations of heat or of sound-impressions,etc.,for this etheric body is not merely a colour phenomenon. The astral body and the other principles of the human being,may also be described in like manner. He who takes this into consideration will understand just how descriptions should be taken which are given by occult science.

The Astral World

As long as we observe the physical world only,the earth,as man's dwelling place,appears like a separate cosmic body. But when supersensible cognition rises to higher spheres,this separation ceases. Thus one can say that the imagination,when beholding the earth,at the same time also perceives the Moon condition as it has developed up to the
present time.

Now that world which is entered in this way is one to which not only the supersensible part of the Earth belongs,but is one in which also other cosmic bodies are imbedded,which in a physical sense are entirely separate from the earth. Therefore,the observer of supersensible worlds thus beholds not only the supersensible part of the earth,but also the supersensible part of other cosmic beings. If one should be impelled to ask why clairvoyants do not describe the appearance of Mars,etc.,he should bear in mind that it is primarily a question of observing supersensible conditions of other planetary bodies,whereas the questioner is thinking of physical sense conditions. Therefore in this work it was possible to speak of certain relations of the earth's evolution to the simultaneous evolution on Saturn,Jupiter,Mars,etc. Now when the human astral body has been drawn away by sleep,it belongs not only to the earth,but to worlds of which still other regions of the universe (stellar worlds) are a part. Indeed,these worlds extend their influence to man's astral body even when he is awake. For this reason the name "astral body" appears to be justified.

Of Man's Life After Death

Mention has been made,in the course of this book,of the time during which the astral body still remains joined to the etheric body of man after death. During this time there exists a slowly paleing recollection of the whole earth life just ended. The duration of this time varies in different individuals. It depends upon the strength with which the astral body clings to the etheric body,on the power which the former has over the latter. Supersensible cognition can gain an idea of this power by observing a person who,judging from his degree of fatigue,must of necessity fall asleep,but,by sheer inner force,keeps awake. It then appears that different people can keep awake for different lengths of time without being overpowered by sleep. The memory of the past life,in other words the connection with the etheric body,lasts about as long after death as the length of time a man can keep awake when,in the most extreme
case,he is compelled to.

When the etheric body is detached from the individual after death, something of it nevertheless remains for man's whole subsequent development; this may be described as an extract,or the essence of it. This extract contains the result of the past life,and is the vehicle of all that which,during man's spiritual development between death and a new birth,unfolds like a germ for the following life.

The duration of time between death and a new birth is determined by the fact that the ego,as a rule,returns to the physical sense-world only when that world has been so transformed that the ego can experience something new. During its sojourn in spiritual regions,its dwelling place on earth undergoes a change. But this change is connected with the great changes in the universe,with changes in the constellation of the earth, sun and so forth. These are changes in which certain repetitions take place,in connection with new conditions. They find an external expression in the fact,for example,that the point in the vault of heaven at which the sun rises at the beginning of spring makes a complete circuit in the course of about twenty-six thousand years. Hence this vernal point,in the course of the period mentioned,moves from one region of the heavens to another. In the course of the twelfth part of that time,that is to say, in about twenty-one hundred years,conditions on the earth have changed sufficiently for the human soul to experience something new upon it since its previous incarnation. However,since the experiences of an individual vary according to whether he is incarnated as a woman or as a man,there are,as a rule,two incarnations within the time stated,one as a man and one as a woman. But these things are also dependent upon the nature of the forces which man carries with him from his earthly existence through death. Therefore all the statements given here are to be taken only in a general sense,but can be subject to the greatest variations in special cases.

The Course Of Human Life

Man's life,as it manifests itself in the sequence of events between birth and death,can be fully understood only by taking into account both the physical body with its senses and the changes undergone by man's supersensible principles. Occult science views those changes in the following manner. Physical birth is seen to be the detachment of the human being from its maternal covering. Forces which before birth the embryo shared in common with its mother's body,are present independently in the child after birth. But in later life supersensible events,similar to those of the sense-world at physical birth,become perceptible to supersensible observation. That is,the etheric body of the human being up to the change of teeth (the sixth or seventh year) is still enveloped in an etheric sheath. The etheric sheath falls away at that period,and then the "birth" of the etheric body occurs. But man is still surrounded by an astral sheath,which falls away between its twelfth and sixteenth year (at the time of puberty). This is the "birth" of the astral body; and at a still later period the real ego is born.(33)

Now after the birth of the ego,man lives in such a way that he adapts himself to the conditions of the world and of life,and occupies himself within them,in accordance with the principles active through his ego,--the sentient,- the intellectual-, and the consciousness-soul. Then there comes a time in which the etheric body retraces the process of its development from the seventh year onward,in reverse order. At first the astral body has so developed itself that it unfolds that which was present within it at birth as a germ. After the birth of the ego,this astral body enriches itself by experiencing the outer world. Finally,at a definite time,it begins to nourish itself spiritually by consuming its own etheric body; it actually lives upon the etheric body. The decay of the physical body in old age is a consequence of this.

The course of human life therefore falls into three divisions: a time of unfoldment for the physical and etheric bodies,then one in which the astral body and the ego develop,and lastly that in which the etheric and physical bodies are changed back again. But the astral body plays a part in all the events that take place between birth and death. Since it is really born in a spiritual sense only between the twelfth and sixteenth years and must,during man's declining years,draw upon the forces of the etheric and physical bodies,that which it is able to perform by its own powers will develop more slowly than if it were not within a physical and an etheric body. After death,when the physical and etheric bodies have fallen away,evolution,during the time of purification,proceeds in such a manner that it occupies about one-third of the duration of life between birth and death.

The Higher Regions Of The Spiritual World

By imagination,inspiration,and intuition,supersensible cognition gradually ascends into those regions of the spiritual world within which it can reach the beings who have to do with human and cosmic evolution. And thus it also becomes possible to trace human evolution between death and a new birth in such a way that it becomes comprehensible. Now there are still higher regions of existence,which can only be briefly indicated here. When supersensible cognition has risen to intuition,it lives in a world of spiritual beings. These too,are evolving. That which concerns humanity of the present day extends upward,in a certain sense,as far as the world of intuition. True,man receives impulses from yet higher worlds in the course of his evolution between death and re-birth. But he does not experience these impulses directly; they are brought to him by beings belonging to the spiritual world. And if these are considered,everything that happens reveals itself to man. But the special conditions of these beings,that which they themselves require in order to guide human evolution,can only be observed by means of a cognition that transcends intuition. We thus have a glimpse of worlds which we must so picture that within them the most highly spiritual features of the earth are there among the lowest. Logical decisions,for example,count among the highest things within the earthly sphere; while the activities of the mineral kingdom are among the lowest. Now in those higher spheres,logical decisions correspond to about what the mineral activities are on earth. Above the domain of intuition,lies the region in which the cosmic plan is woven out of spiritual causes.

The Principles Of Man

When it is said that the ego works on the human principles,on the physical,etheric,and astral bodies,and transforms them in reverse order into Spirit-Self,Life-Spirit,and Spirit-Man,this statement relates to the work of the ego on the human being by means of the highest faculties, the development of which was begun only under earthly conditions. But this transformation is preceded at a lower level by another change,giving rise to the sentient-,the intellectual- or rational-,and the consciousness-soul. For while,in the course of human evolution,the sentient-soul is being formed,changes are taking place in the astral body; the growth of the intellectual-soul expresses itself in transformations in the etheric body; and that of the consciousness-soul in similar transformations in the physical body. Fuller information on this subject has been given in this book in the accounts of the evolution of the earth. Thus in a certain sense we may say that the sentient-soul itself is the result of a transformed astral body,the intellectual- or rational-soul of a transformed etheric body,and the consciousness-soul of a transformed physical body. But we may also say that these three divisions of the soul are parts of the astral body; for example,the consciousness-soul is only possible because it is an astral entity existing in a physical body suited to it. It lives an astral life within a physical body fashioned to be its dwelling place.

The Dream State

A description of the dream state has been given in another chapter of this book. On the one hand it is to be regarded as a relic of the old picture-consciousness peculiar to man during the Moon evolution,and also during a great part of the evolution of the Earth. Evolution goes forward in such a way that earlier conditions resolve themselves into later ones. And so,in the dream state,there now appears in man a relic of what was once his normal condition. But at the same time this condition from another aspect is different from the old picture-consciousness. For since its development,the ego also has taken part in those activities of the astral body which are carried on during sleep in the dream life. Thus through the presence of the ego there arises in dreams a transformed picture-consciousness. But since the ego does not consciously exercise its authority over the astral body during dream life,nothing belonging to the sphere of that life can be regarded as being really able to lead to a knowledge of higher worlds in an occult sense. Something similar holds good with regard to what is often called vision,premonition,or "second sight." These arise through silencing the ego and the consequent appearance of remnants of the old condition of consciousness. In spiritual science these are of no value. What may be observed in them cannot in any real sense be regarded as a result of it.

The Attainment Of Supersensible Knowledge

The path to the attainment of knowledge of the higher worlds,which has been more fully described in this book,may also be called the "direct path of knowledge." In addition to this path there is another,which we may designate as the "path of feeling." It would be quite a mistake, however,to believe that the former had nothing to do with the development of feeling. On the contrary,it leads to the greatest possible deepening of the life of feeling. But the "path of feeling" addresses itself directly and solely to the feelings,and seeks from this point to rise to knowledge. It rests on the fact that when the soul entirely surrenders itself to a feeling for a certain length of time,the latter is transformed into knowledge,into imaginative perception. When,for example,the soul is filled for weeks or months,or even longer,with the feeling of humility,the content of the feeling becomes transformed into a perception. Now a path leading to supersensible regions may be found by devoting oneself to such feelings one by one; but for the man of today, bound by the ordinary circumstances of life,this is not easily carried out. Solitude,retirement from the life of the present day,is almost indispensable. For the impressions of everyday life disturb the soul especially at the beginning of development,through absorption in certain feelings. On the other hand,the path of knowledge described in this book can be pursued in every situation of present-day life.

Observation Of Special Events And Beings In The Spiritual World

The question may be asked whether inner concentration and the other means described for the attainment of supersensible cognition permit us to observe only in a general way what happens between death and a new birth or other spiritual events; or whether they furnish the possibility of observing quite definite events and beings,as,for example,any given deceased person. To this we must answer that one who has acquired the ability to see in the spiritual world by the methods explained,can also perceive particular events which occur there; he acquires the power of putting himself in communication with individuals living in the spiritual world between death and a new birth. It must be observed,however,that in an occult sense this ought to take place only after the proper training required for supersensible cognition has been undergone. For not until then is it possible to distinguish between illusion and reality,in regard to certain events and beings. A man who tries to observe particular cases without due instruction,may fall a victim to innumerable deceptions. The training which leads to the observation in higher worlds of what has been described in this book,also leads to the ability to trace the post-mortem life of any special individual,and no less does it lead to the observation and comprehension of all psycho-spiritual beings who,from the hidden worlds,work upon the visible ones. Correct observation of individual cases is only possible,however,on the basis of a knowledge of the universal great facts of the spiritual world,--facts regarding the world and humanity which concern every human being. The desire for the one without the other,leads one into error.

FOOTNOTES

1 We may also say,it could only live the life of a plant in the physical body.

2 Explanations such as those given in this book regarding the faculty of memory may very easily be misunderstood. For one who observes external events only would not at first sight notice the difference between what happens in the animal,or even in the plant,when something appears in them resembling memory,and what is here characterized as actual recollection in man. Of course,when an animal has performed an action for a third or fourth time it may perform it in such a way that the outer process gives the impression that memory and the training associated with it are present. Nay,we may even extend our conception of memory or of recollection as far as some naturalists and their disciples,when they point out that the chicken begins to pick up grain as soon as it comes out of the shell; that it even knows the proper movements of head and body for gaining its end. It could not have learned this in the eggshell; hence it must have done so through the thousands and thousands of creatures from which it is descended (so says Hering,for example). We may call the phenomenon before us something resembling memory, but we shall never arrive at a real comprehension of human nature if we do not take into account that every distinctive element which shows itself in the human being as an inner process,as an actual perception of earlier experiences at a later date,is not merely the working of earlier conditions in later ones. In this book it is this perception of what is past that is called memory,not alone the reappearance (even though transformed) of what once existed,in a later form. Were we to use the word memory for the corresponding processes in the vegetable and animal kingdoms,we should be required to use a different word in speaking of man. In the

description given here the important thing is not the particular word used,but rather that in attempting to understand human beings this distinction should be recognized. Just as little do the apparently very intelligent actions of animals have any relation to what is _here_ called memory.

3 The term "Verstandesseele" is sometimes translated by "rational soul." From a certain point of view one might prefer the term "intellectual soul," because it expresses better the activity of the soul than does "rational soul." In the latter one thinks of the knowledge about a perception; in intellectuality,one thinks of the actual possibility of forming this knowledge through inward activity. In German the expression "emotional soul" only coincides as it should with the second member of the soul when the inward activity is kept in view.

4 No hard and fast line can be drawn between the changes which are accomplished in the astral body through the activity of the ego and those taking place in the etheric body. The one merges into the other. When a man learns something,and thereby gains a certain capacity for judgment,a change takes place in his astral body; but when this judgment changes his natural disposition,so that he habituates himself to _feel_ differently,in consequence of his learning,from what he did before,this means a change in his etheric body. Everything that becomes so much a man's own that he can always recall it,is based on the transformation of the etheric body. That which little by little becomes an abiding possession of the memory has its foundation in the transmission to the etheric body of the work of the astral body.

5 As a matter of fact,it is always very profitable for any one who is taking up the study of occult science to acquaint himself with the statements of those who regard this science as merely fanciful. Such statements cannot be so easily branded as due to partiality on the part of the observer. Let occultists learn as much as possible from those who regard their efforts as nonsense. They need not be disturbed if in this respect their love is not reciprocated. Occult observation assuredly does not require such things for the verification of its results,nor are these allusions intended as proofs but as illustrations.

6 In current theosophical literature,the condition of the ego from death to the end of purification is called "Kamaloca."

7 The assertion that a man's personal talents,if governed purely by the law of "heredity," must show themselves at the beginning of a line of descent,not at its end,might of course easily be misunderstood. It might be said,indeed,that they could not show themselves then,for they must first be developed. But this is no objection; for if we wish to prove that something has been inherited from an ancestor,we must show how that which was there formerly is repeated in a descendant. Now if it were demonstrated that something existed at the beginning of a genealogical line which reappeared in its further course,we might speak of heredity. We cannot do so when something appears at the end of it which was not there before. The reversal of the above proposition is only to show that the belief in heredity is impossible.

8 In different chapters of this book it has been shown how the world of humanity,and man himself,pass,in their progressive evolution, through conditions which have been named Saturn,Sun,Moon,Earth, Jupiter,Venus,and Vulcan. The relationship has also been indicated

in which human evolution stands with regard to the celestial bodies which exist besides the earth and which are called saturn,jupiter, mars,and so on. These latter planets are also passing through their evolution in the natural way. At the present period they have reached such a stage that their physical portions are seen as those bodies which physical astronomy calls saturn,jupiter,mars,and so forth. Now when the saturn of the present day is observed by occultism it is seen to be,in a certain sense,a reincarnation of the old Saturn. It has come into existence because of the presence of certain beings,who before the separation of the sun from the earth were unable,like the others,to leave with the sun. The reason of this was that they had gained so many qualities which are suitable for a saturn existence,that their place could not be where the qualities of the sun were specially unfolded. The present jupiter,however,arose in consequence of the presence of beings possessed of qualities which can only be matured on the future jupiter of the whole evolution. A dwelling place appeared for them on which they can already begin in antici pation of this later evolution.

In the same way mars is a planetary body on which dwell beings whose lunar evolution was such that further progress on the earth could bring them nothing. Mars is a reincarnation of the old Moon at a higher stage. The present mercury is the dwelling place of beings who are beyond the evolution of the earth; but this is just because they have developed certain qualities in a higher way than is possible on the earth itself. The present venus is a prophetic antici pation of the future Venus condition of a similar kind. It is consequently justifiable to give to the conditions preceding and following the Earth the names of their corresponding representatives in the universe.

9 Therefore it is perhaps scarcely necessary to remark that what has been described above could never actually happen. A contem porary man,as he is,could not have approached ancient Saturn as a spectator. The account was given merely for the sake of illustration.

10 In Christian spiritual science they bear the name of "Kyriotetes," that is,"Dominions."

11 In Christian esoteric science they are called "Thrones."

12 The Christian "Dynamis," or "Powers."

13 The Christian "Exusiai," or "Authorities."

14 The Christian "Archai," or "Princi palities."

15 The Christian "Archangeloi," or "Archangels."

16 The Christian "Seraphim."

17 The Christian "Angeloi," or "Angels."

18 The Christian "Cherubim."

19 The gas appears to clairvoyant consciousness through the effect of light which emanates from it. We might therefore speak also of light forms,which are apparent to spiritual vision.

20 In current theosophical literature they are called "rounds." Yet,if we bear in mind the more graphic description already given,we shall

guard against a too schematic concept of such matters.

21 In the next few pages,Sun and Moon are printed with capital letters when the _old_ evolutions are referred to,but are printed "sun" and "moon" when the Earth period is indicated.--_Translator_.

22 Further particulars on this subject will be found in my book, _Atlantis and Lemuria_,which deals with man's ancestors.

23 More detailed information about these Mysteries of antiquity is to be found in my book,"Christianity as Mystical Fact." More particulars will be given in the last chapter of the present work.

24 What is to be said further on this subject will be given in a later chapter dealing with supersensible knowledge.

25 All sagas concerning the twilight of the gods,and similar traditions,had their origin in this knowledge of the Mysteries in Europe.

26 It is a matter of no moment whatever whether the above thoughts are warranted or not by any of the views held by natural science. For the object is to develop such thoughts about the plant and man as may--irrespective of all theories--be gained by means of simple and direct contemplation. Such thoughts are of importance side by side with no less significant theoretical presentments of things in the external world; and here the thoughts are not adduced in order to prove a fact scientifically,but to construct a symbol that shall prove effective,irrespective of whatever objections may be raised by this or that person against its construction.

27 In my explanations of "How to attain Knowledge of the Higher Worlds," translated under the title of _The Way of Initiation_ and beginning at Chapter II,several other examples of methods of meditation are given,and especially efficacious will be found one which deals with the coming into being and fading away of a plant; also another may be particularly recommended,based on the dormant formative power dwelling in the seed of a plant,and others on the form and structure of crystals,and other substances. But the purpose in this book was only to show in one instance,the nature of meditation.

28 Special exercises going into greater detail on this subject may be found in my book entitled _The Way of Initiation_.

29 It must of course be clearly understood that such an appellation as "lotus flower" has no more bearing on the matter than has the expression "wing," if applied to the lobe of a lung.

30 In my books,entitled "_The Way of Initiation_" and "_Initiation and Its Results_," some of these methods of meditation and exercises for acting upon these different organs are set forth.

31 The appellation "two-petalled" or "sixteen-petalled," and so on,is used because the organs in question may be likened to flowers having a corresponding number of petals.

32 Intuition is in everyday life a much-abused word,which is made to stand for a vague and uncertain view of a matter; for some sort of "notion," which,while it may possibly "hit" the truth,can nevertheless give no immediate proof of it. It is needless to say that this kind of intuition is not meant here. Intuition,in this case,stands for knowledge of the highest and most luminous

clearness,of the justification of which the possessor is,in the fullest sense,conscious.

33 The suggestive points of view for the conduct of education resulting from a knowledge of these supersensible facts are presented in my little book_The Education of Children from the Standpoint of Spiritual Science_,in which will be found fuller details of what can here only be hinted at.

9 798869 109057

Printed by Libri Plureos GmbH in Hamburg,
Germany